Tiger Balm

Travels in Laos, Vietnam & Cambodia

Tiger Balm

Travels in Laos, Vietnam & Cambodia

Lucretia Stewart

Chatto & Windus
LONDON

Published in 1992 by
Chatto & Windus Ltd
20 Vauxhall Bridge Road
London SW1V 2SA

A CIP catalogue record for this book is
available from the British Library.

ISBN 0 7011 3892 0

Phototypeset by Intype, London
Printed in Great Britain by
Mackays of Chatham PLC, Chatham, Kent

In Memory of Janet Hobhouse
1948–1991

Acknowledgements

The events described in this book took place over the course of six months in 1990 but incorporate material from a brief earlier visit to Vietnam and Cambodia in 1989. I have changed the names of several people in order to protect their privacy.

I am grateful to a number of people who have been helpful to me during the writing of this book but especially to Hercules Bellville, Anne Billson, Jonathan Burnham, Antonia Gaunt, Terry McCarthy, James Pringle, Vivienne Schuster, Im Sophy, Tan Sotho, Jon Swain, Vicki Woods and Gavin Young.

I also owe a debt of gratitude to specialists in the field whose works were an invaluable research source. The following in particular provided both information and inspiration: Anthony Barnett, Elizabeth Becker, Melanie Beresford, Dennis Bloodworth, William Broyles Jnr., Wilfred G. Burchett, Joseph Buttinger, James Cameron, Phillip Caputo, Nayan Chanda, David Chandler, Georges Cœdès, Marguerite Duras, James Fenton, Frances Fitzgerald, Grant Evans, Martha Gellhorn, Graham Greene, D.G.E. Hall, Ellen Hammer, Michael Herr, Alan Houghton Broderick, Karl D. Jackson, Sidney Jones, Philip Jones Griffiths, Stanley Karnow, Ben Kiernan, Carole Kismaric, David Leitch, Norman Lewis, Tom Mangold, Someth May, Henri Mouhot, Eva Mysliwiec, John Pilger, François Ponchard, James Pringle, Kelvin Rowley, Sydney Schanberg, William Shawcross, Neil Sheehan, Susan Sontag, David Joel Steinberg, Perry Stieglitz, Martin Stuart-Fox, Jon Swain, Michael Vickery, Richard West, Gavin Young and Joseph J. Zasloff.

Contents

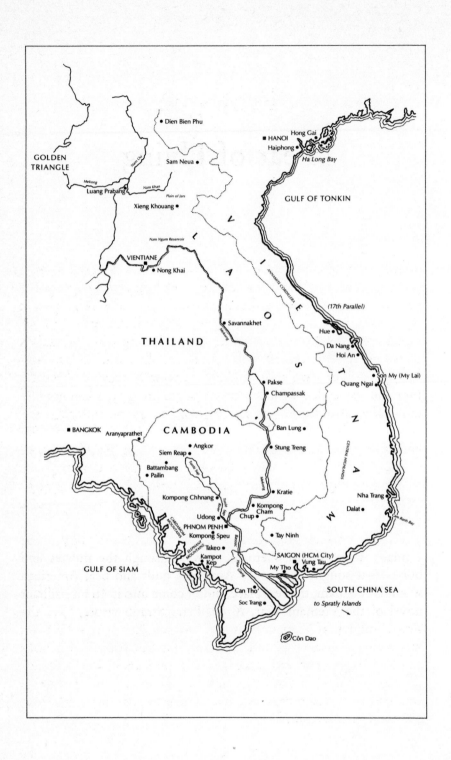

Prologue

Fear of Flying

When the first US Marines came ashore at Da Nang in 1965, I was twelve years old and at a convent boarding school in the south of England. My father, a diplomat, was then the number two at the British embassy in Washington and doubtless privy to the discussions that Britain would have been having with the United States on the subject of Vietnam. But, if he brought his work home with him – which is unlikely – I wasn't aware of it. By the time the war ended with the fall of Saigon in 1975, I had gone to university, abandoned my studies, tried to go on the stage and was presently living in Chelsea, teaching English to foreign businessmen. If, at any point in its miserable ten-year life, I was aware of the Vietnam War, I don't recollect it. My generation was one below the Vietnam generation, and Scotland, where I had gone to university, was even further, culturally speaking, from America than England.

My obliviousness goes some way towards explaining why, when I finally woke up to Vietnam, it was through the movies and books that sought to assuage American guilt and heal American wounds. Vietnam, the real place, didn't come into it. In his brilliant novel of the Vietnam War, *Koko*, Peter Straub wrote, ' . . . the actual country of Vietnam was now just another place – Vietnam was many thousands of miles distant, with an embattled history and an idiosyncratic and inaccessible culture. Its history and culture had briefly, disastrously intersected ours. But the actual country of Vietnam was not Vietnam; that was here, in those American names and faces.'

I

An alternative take on Vietnam was provided by the rose-coloured accounts of correspondents who had spent the happiest days of their lives in Saigon during the war and whose dearest dream was somehow to find themselves back there: living dangerously, sleeping with exquisite sloe-eyed oriental beauties, wearing fatigues, leaping into Jolly Green Giants (as the helicopters were called), having all the fun of war without having actually having to fight. In 1987 I flew back from Hong Kong with a correspondent who had reported from Saigon and Phnom Penh during the war. It was an overnight flight and we both slept. As we landed in England, dawn was breaking and he awoke, looking pensive and refreshed. 'I dreamt,' he said, 'that I was back in Vietnam.'

I became as seduced by the memory of those years as if I had been there and been one of the boys. In an article on Hollywood and Vietnam, William Broyles Jnr wrote: 'Vietnam isn't a real place anymore. It's a setting for stories now.' He's wrong, of course, but it is an easy enough mistake to make. Not having been to Vietnam and knowing nothing about it other than what I had read and heard (with the emphasis on 'heard'), I assumed, in a lazy way, that the Vietnam of their stories, Vietnam *then*, still existed. Paradoxically, however, I came at the same time to resent the war correspondents' hyperbole and wanted to discover a Vietnam untainted by macho fantasies. I wanted the best of both worlds. I wanted to step into the time machine and be there with the boys and I wanted to get away from those same boys and their time-warp visions of Vietnam.

I was born in Singapore, then still a Crown Colony, towards the end of 1952, and spent the first two years of my life there, surrounded by oriental faces, and flourishing like the hibiscus that grew in our garden. When I was seven, we went to China where my father had been appointed Chargé d'Affaires. We sailed from Southampton to Hong Kong and then took a train up to Peking. The journey took over a month, with four weeks spent at sea, and we lived in China for four years, from 1959 to the summer of 1962 during the lull before the storm of the Cultural Revolution.

In Peking, the winters were bitter and the summers torrid.

During the cold months, we skated on the Summer Palace lake and picnicked in the Western Hills and the Ming Tombs. In the heat, we went to the seaside at Bei Tei Ho for six weeks to escape the sultry claustrophobia of the city.

We lived in a big squarish brown stone house with an army of servants who were mainly known by numbers (Number One Boy, Number Two Boy and so on, even though, in some cases, the individuals concerned were old enough to be my grandparents). By then, I had a younger brother and sister and we all went to school at a Catholic convent which was burnt down by the Red Guards during the Cultural Revolution and the nuns forced to flee for their lives to Hong Kong. At night when I couldn't sleep, Soo Chin, my Chinese *amah* would sit on the end of my bed and talk to me in a mixture of Chinese and English. By the light from the passage, I could just make out her wrinkled features. She was a small, middle-aged woman always dressed in straight black trousers and a long white tunic, the uniform of all the indoor servants. She taught me to hug my pillow to help me get to sleep, to pretend that it was a friend or a pet. I still do so, though the memory of Soo Chin has long faded and I had to ask my mother what her name had been.

Long after we had left Peking, the editor of a literary magazine in New York commissioned a piece on my childhood in China but, when I sat down to write it, I found that I couldn't remember enough. There were isolated images or details like Soo Chin and the pillow, or the soft sweet taste of a persimmon from the trees in the Western Hills. I remembered startling a fox on top of the burial chamber of one of the Ming Tombs and playing on the marble statues of animals that made up the 'Spirit Way' which marked the approach to the valley of the Tombs. But the bigger picture remained elusive: there was nothing concrete, nothing to sink a writer's teeth into. It was too long ago and we had moved too often since. The legacy of that time was sensual, impressionistic and sentimental. I knew that we had been happy there and that after we returned to the West, nothing was ever as nice, as safe or as easy again. Our departure marked the end of childhood and the beginning of a grim and unfriendly world of boarding schools.

✳

Twenty-five years later, I went back to China. It was early December and freezing. The flight had taken twenty-four numbing hours. I climbed thirteen hundred steps up to the Great Wall and wandered round the Summer Palace where I used to play as a child. The vast lake was frozen over and tiny people in padded jackets, like figures in an oriental Bruegel landscape, skated across the ice. Try as I might, I couldn't remember any of it. Nothing seemed even vaguely familiar. It was exciting but completely alien.

Early one Sunday morning I drove out to the Ming Tombs. The day was bright and frosty, the sky a crisp clear blue and the fretwork silhouettes of the persimmon trees black against the skyline. The valley of the Tombs was deserted as I walked across the dun-coloured fields to Deling, the tomb of the penultimate Ming Emperor, Xizong, who ruled for seven years in the early part of the fifteenth century. Smaller and remoter than some of the other tombs, Deling had not yet fallen victim to renovation. It was very dilapidated with grass sprouting wildly through the roof of the stele tower and marble columns and broken carvings strewn around the ground. I walked through the corridor under the tower past a couple of women collecting twigs for firewood, to the burial chamber. There was a broad jagged crack running down one side. I squeezed inside and memory, triggered by the dank embrace of the burial chamber walls, came flooding back like water through a burst dam. It was here that I had seen the fox.

The next morning I flew down to Xi'an, home of the terracotta army, on a CAAC flight in a decrepit old Russian Ilyushin which took off hours late. The pretty Chinese stewardess handed out blankets in bright primary colours as icicles formed on the inside of the cabin windows. The army, awesome testimony both to the Emperor Quin Shi Huang's fear of loneliness and to his megalomania, was astonishing but left me unmoved. But in Canton, with its delicious humid heat and its profusion of flowers and scents and sounds, I found myself back in the landscape of my childhood, and content. As I lay that night in my room in the White Swan hotel and listened to the mournful hoot of the tugs on the Pearl River, I felt myself opening like a flower to the tropics and to the East. The past was there for me after all.

*

Up until this point, China – or more precisely, the East – had been, like childhood, a country whose frontiers appeared forever closed. The two were so linked in my mind and memory that it hadn't occurred to me that it was possible to go back. But once the barriers were down, I took to the East with a vengeance. The relationship with travel was more complicated: part fear, part ecstasy. I found it terrifying but liberating and the uneasy balance between these two powerful emotions made every trip a challenge, something I had to do both to prove myself and to prove to myself that I could do it. In *The Enigma of Arrival*, V.S. Naipaul perfectly catches the contradictory nature of the experience: 'Was there some fear of travel, in spite of my longing for the day and in spite of my genuine excitement? . . . Was it the fear of New York? Certainly. The city, my behaviour there at the moment of arrival, my inability to visualise the physical details of arrival, how and where I was going to spend the night – these were developing anxieties as we flew on and on.'

However much I travelled, it didn't seem ever to get any easier. I could never sleep the night before, my stomach churned and my fingertips tingled painfully as if from chilblains. Preparation, in the shape of large amounts of cash, hotel bookings or exhaustive guide books, helped a little – as if somehow they would guarantee an easy and enjoyable trip – but not enough, never enough. But I still had to go.

I was struck by how little I could find out about IndoChina – Laos, Vietnam, Cambodia – *now*. These countries had been the focus of such concentrated interest in the 1960s and 1970s and remained the source of so many dreams and fantasies but no-one seemed to go there any more. People spoke and wrote in clipped terrifying phrases: the Vietnam War; the Cambodian holocaust. Nobody ever mentioned Laos. It seemed the place to start. Back in England, I telephoned a journalist who had known IndoChina before 1975.

'James, have you ever been to Vientiane?'

'Mmm, years ago.'

'Well, what's it like?'

'I can't remember.'

'Why not?'

'That's the thing about Laos. No-one ever can.'

'I see. So the trick is to take lots of notes.'

'No. The trick is to realise that you won't understand a thing about it.'

There was no Lao embassy in London, only in Paris, so I went to Paris. Getting the visa became part of the adventure. I never managed to get through to the embassy on the telephone to learn the opening hours and eventually had to ask a friend who lived in Paris to go round there and find out for me. My plan was to go as the final leg of a trip that was to take in Malaysia and the Cambodian refugee camps on the Thai-Cambodian border.

I had to go to Paris to interview a journalist who had covered the Vietnam War and called in at the Embassy of the People's Democratic Republic of Laos on the way. Mr Southam shook his head decisively when I explained that I wanted an individual visa. '*Impossible, madame, seulement des groupes.*' How, I asked, would I meet Lao people and get to know and understand his beautiful country if I was travelling with French and American tourists? Mr Southam appeared to take the point and disappeared for twenty minutes to consult with colleagues. While I waited, I inspected the room, '*Paix, Indépendence, Unité, Socialisme*' the admirable motto of the Lao PDR was written in large letters above an unpromising display of black and white photographs of people engaged in ideologically correct activities: agriculture, folkloric dancing, processions with white elephants, and other aspects of Lao popular culture. There were also some wood-carvings of men with guns. Mr Southam returned with a bundle of mimeographed forms. I filled in three and handed over the same number of photographs. We parted exchanging expressions of mutual respect and he told me to telephone him in a couple of months.

Over the next eight weeks I had several nightmares in which I was refused a visa. I began to wonder whether I really wanted to go and why. In a description of travels in IndoChina in 1939, an Englishman called Alan Houghton Broderick wrote, after experiencing similar difficulties, 'And what did I want to see and do? There is nothing to see or to do in the Laos. Perhaps I just wanted

to experience a country where there was nothing to see or to do.'
Quite so. But early one morning after Mr Southam's deadline had
expired, I rang the Lao embassy and Mr Southam told me that I
had been granted a visa for a month's stay. All I had to do was
pick it up.

Back in Paris, Mr Southam seemed surprised at the emotion
with which I took possession of the visa. But he only said politely,
'*Je vous souhaite un bon voyage, Madame, mais je n'ai aucune
idée que vous allez faire en Laos parce que vous ne connaissez
personne*' – thereby setting in motion a whole new train of anxiety.

By the time I left for Vientiane, I was painfully nervous and my
anxiety was compounded by the sense that this trip was somehow
more serious, more purposeful than any before. Also I still had
no idea what to expect in Laos. The few people I spoke to who
had been there were less than helpful, either reminiscing happily
about opium dens and exquisitely submissive prostitutes or full of
patently apocryphal stories of 'love courts', white elephants and
Lao princes who, after being sent to Paris to further their education, would return home, having forgotten all their Lao and able
to speak only French. On a plane from Penang to Bangkok, I
came across an advertisement in an airline magazine: 'LAOS The
land pleasant and attractive in its own simple ways.' Even the
standard hype of the travel trade had been at a loss for words.

In Bangkok I spent half an hour with a suave young diplomat
at the British embassy who gave me details of the country's main
source of revenue (opium, forestry, sale of electricity to Thailand
and overflights). Ovaltine, he added, was the staple drink. The
Lao Government had sent a congratulatory telegram to the new
regime in Roumania and every evening all Vientiane was glued to
Thai television which could be picked up from the Thai border
town of Nong Khai just across the Mekong. Later that morning,
in one of the rabbit-warren streets near Silom Road, I had a
cappuccino with an Australian with a droopy moustache who had
claimed to have swum the Mekong eleven years before to rescue
his Lao girlfriend. 'Remember,' he said enigmatically, 'in Laos fear
is the great motivator.'

I

Vientiane

When you have heard,
you must listen;
When you have seen,
you must judge in your heart

Lao proverb

On the plane to Vientiane, a Lao Aviation flight in a narrow old
Antonov 24, I sat next to a fat Indian who introduced himself as
Ajit Singh and handed me his card which identified him as
senior marketing manager for a cement company in New Delhi.
He overflowed out of his tiny seat and smelt like a wet spaniel.
He behaved rather like a spaniel too, wagging his tail and begging
for attention. He wanted to have a serious conversation about the
meaning of life and demanded to know why I was travelling alone.

'Where is your husband? Why does he let you go off by yourself?'

'I haven't got a husband. I'm divorced,' I answered.

I should have known better than to answer his question – let
alone truthfully. Ajit, now behaving even more like a spaniel
but this time one who had scented a fat pheasant, launched into
a noisy stream of disapproval and analysis. I had forgotten, for an
unguarded moment, the total inability of any right-thinking Asian
or oriental to conceive of a happy life without a spouse or children.
A woman alone is regarded with a humiliating combination of
pity and curiosity. It seemed too early in the trip, the day and

our acquaintance for my life story so I opened my book. I was reading *Red Brotherhood At War – Vietnam, Cambodia and Laos since 1975* and had just come to a chapter entitled 'Laos: The Paradox of Extreme Backwardness' when my neighbour tried another conversational tack.

'Please, do you believe in palmistry?' he asked, making a sweaty grab for my hand.

'No.'

'I can tell your whole future from your palm. Let me have a look,' he insisted.

'I'd really rather not. Actually I'd rather not know,' I said wrenching my hand out of his damp clasp.

'But can I at least take you out to dinner while you are in Vientiane?'

People like Ajit are an occupational hazard for the solitary travel-ler. In any other circumstances, I would have been both tempted *and* able to run a mile, but, because I was travelling and alone, I felt obliged to indulge him, just in the unlikely event that something fascinating came of it. In the end we shared a taxi into Vientiane and Ajit kindly paid.

The taxi was an ancient car hand-painted a bright blue. We trundled the eight kilometres from Wattay airport into town through a landscape that contained few urban terms of reference. On either side of the road were emerald ricefields. There were few other cars: some motorcycles, the ubiquitous Honda, but the bicycle or *samlo* (a variation of the pedicab found throughout South East Asia) appeared to be the preferred mode of transport. We pulled up outside Vientiane's best – and, for all I knew, only – hotel, the Lane Xang, called after the old name for Laos (the full ancient name for Laos, Muong Lan Xang Hom Khao, translates as the Land of the Million Elephants and the White Parasol).

The Lane Xang, an undistinguished modern building with a long four-storey cement façade overlooking the Mekong, was hosting a joint Lao/US seminar to discuss what the KPL (Khao San Pathet Lao) daily newsletter described as *'la lutte anti-narcotique'* – drugs, specifically opium which was grown in the hills of northern

Laos and was, as I knew from my briefing in Bangkok, one of the country's main sources of revenue. Laos is the world's third-biggest opium producer and the United States, desperate to control its own drug problem, had agreed to offer aid to the country in return for the implementation of a crop-substitution programme.

The lobby was crowded with loud American customs inspectors and narcotics prevention officers, shoving each other around and yelling for beer. On the advice of the man at the embassy in Bangkok, I had sent a telex reserving a room but the desk clerk professed never to have received it. Eventually he managed to find me a room at the back of the hotel, looking out onto the garden and swimming pool. After I had unpacked, I went for a walk.

It was early evening, that golden hour between day and nightfall, and the air was full of the sound of birds and tinkling bells from the temples. After the traffic and smog of Bangkok, Vientiane – the 'Moon City' – seemed calm, remote, not part of the same universe. Clouds of butterflies as large as birds flitted from tree to tree and there were frogs croaking on the street corners. Children were playing in the dusty roads, flying kites made out of old plastic bags, and chasing kittens. A desultory game of football was in progress on the banks of the Mekong and outside the Vientiane tennis club small boys were taking turns with a single racket. There were chickens scratching in the roadside dirt and wandering in and out of buildings and large pigs were grubbing in the unkempt gardens of the once-elegant French colonial mansions. The heat of the day had eased and the setting sun cast a warm glow over the dilapidated mansions and destroyed pavements, concealing the full extent of the ravages of time and neglect. Along the Rue Setthathirat, where there were five *wats* in less than a mile, Buddhist monks in saffron robes were going about their business, saying their evening prayers.

The sight of the monks with their shaven heads, alms bowls and orange umbrellas, was pleasing and not simply because of the colour and texture that they and their rituals brought to Vientiane's somewhat drab landscape but also because of what their profusion and ubiquity revealed about the change in attitude of the country's Communist government, the Pathet Lao ('Nation of Laos'), which came to power in a bloodless coup in late 1975, towards the national religion. Laos, like Thailand and Burma, is profoundly Buddhist and attempts by Christian missionaries to convert the Lao met with an almost total lack of success. But when the Pathet Lao first took over, they were determined to subordinate the traditional Buddhist teachings to the political ideology of the LPDR. The old close relationship between the *Sangha* (community of monks) and the people was consistently undermined in order to reduce the possibility of popular support for any resistance that the *Sangha* might offer. Monks reluctant to include political material in their sermons were forced to attend re-education seminars and Pathet Lao criticism of Buddhist rituals and practices actively sought to debunk the Buddhist world-view, ridiculing the Buddhist cosmology of tiered heavens and hells, the existence of nature spirits (*phi*) and the notions of transference of merit. They attacked the non-materialism of Buddhism and stressed the importance of accumulating resources for social progress and the alleviation of want. The donations that the faithful were in the habit of giving to the *Sangha* in order to gain religious merit, should, they said, instead be directed to the state where they could be put to more obviously effective use.

But, since December 1979, when a more liberal policy was introduced, Buddhism has, in the dreary language of officialdom, come increasingly to be accepted as integral to the Lao national cultural identity and, in consequence, all but recovered its former strength. Unofficially, people were no longer frightened that they would be punished for practising a religion that had been part of their lives since it first came to Laos in the fourteenth century when King Fa Ngum imported Buddhist monks from Cambodia to Luang Prabang.

I walked back to the hotel as night was falling. The Mekong lay like a great sleeping snake alongside the Quai Fa Ngum and the lights of Nong Khai twinkled in the distance. Under cover of darkness, Vientiane was quiet and there were few people on the streets. I changed my shirt and went to have dinner at a little French restaurant opposite the Lao Aviation office.

It was called La Table de Souriya and owned by a Lao woman

who was married to a Frenchman. The menu seemed exotic for the tiny capital of what is supposed to be the tenth poorest country in the world, and included Russian caviar, venison in *sauce poivrade*, duck with grapes, a beef *entrecôte* with a mustard cream sauce and a splendid dish of *capitaine du Mekong* in a pink sauce with capers which I chose. There was soft music and the lights were dimmed. The waiters spoke French and among the other diners were a couple of beautiful tall slender black girls in blue jeans. They had high cheekbones and carried themselves like gazelles.

Early the next morning, I awoke to a soft swishing sound. It was just before six and the dawn had long since been and gone. Outside my window, two men were slowly and ineffectually sweeping up the leaves that fell all night and day from the frangipani trees. In the background, I could hear the jaunty tones of the municipality radio station broadcasting music and advertisements from loudspeakers on every street corner. I got dressed and walked through to the garden behind the hotel where cages containing wretched-looking animals surrounded the swimming pool. There were a couple of jittery little monkeys, two dormant racoons, a family of guinea pigs, some deer, two small furiously-pacing wolf-like animals, a forlorn bear and a crocodile sharing a cage with a heron. The cages were filthy; none of the animals except the crocodile had water and there was an air of neglect and despair about the whole area. I went back into the hotel and asked the desk clerk why the animals were there. '*Pour amuser les clients,*' came the answer.

After a breakfast of poached eggs and tea in the Lane Xang's gloomy dining room which was full of anxious-looking business-men, including my pudgy friend from New Delhi, and whose décor and menu evoked a boarding house on England's south coast, I went to telephone the Honorary British Consul. He was the Shell representative in Vientiane and had been recommended to me by the British embassy in Bangkok. I thought if anyone could help me overcome the problems that would almost certainly be posed by Laos's legandary bureaucracy, he would be the man. He suggested that I come to his office in the late afternoon for a cold beer and to discuss my needs and desires – which were to see as much of the country as I could, and not in a group.

Towards midday I walked across the road to an open-air restaurant that advertised Lao folk music in the evenings and possessed another sad animal garden. Its main exhibits were an enormous snake in a rabbit hutch and a one-armed gibbon whose cage was marked 'Dangerous' even though he never seemed to move, not even when the children who played in the garden, rattled the bars of his cage and shrieked at him. The waitress told me that he cried early in the morning.

I was looking queasily at the menu which included such dishes as Grilled Moose Bleeding, Baked Sealy Ant-Eater and Half Cooking Moose Salad, dishes eerily reminiscent of the Thai-style Uterus Salad and Lonely Beef that had been on offer at my hotel in Bangkok, when a figure whom I vaguely recognised as the *samlo* driver who had been trying to attract my attention as I came out of the hotel gates materialised at the table. His name was Leuth and he spoke excellent English. He was a slender, lithe, handsome man with perfect white teeth, a mole trailing long black hairs on the underside of his chin and a very long pointed fingernail on the little finger of his left hand (in the old days, men grew their fingernails to indicate that their owner did not do manual work – now just the little one was left long: part affectation, part tradition and rather sinister to the western eye). He wore tracksuit pants, a black-and-white striped tee-shirt, gym shoes and very dark glasses. These were so dark that, when he took them off and flashed his brilliant white teeth, the effect was quite startling and not unattractive.

In an instant, he was sitting down beside me, flicking through my guidebook, reading aloud from it in beautifully-accented French and advising me where to go and how to proceed. Another man joined us, a taxi driver, but Leuth was definitely in charge. There would, he assured me, be *absolutely* no problem in travelling by boat to Savannakhet. As it happened, he himself came from there and would accompany me. The boat left on Friday. Today was Wednesday. I should be ready to leave at dawn in a couple of days. When I enquired about the *laisser-passer* (the permission from the Ministry of the Interior without which no foreigner – or Lao – can legally move more than ten kilometres outside Vientiane), Leuth waved his hands dismissively and assured me that he could obtain it within a matter of hours. We talked on, about this and that, drinking foamy Lao beer which came in large bottles with a panther on the label. Leuth apologised for being a humble *samlo* driver but explained that, despite his good education (which was evident from his command of English and French alone), decent jobs were scarce in Vientiane. He told me that he was thirty-one but not married because it was 'too expensive'. He asked what I did and whether I was married. Some impulse – perhaps a desire to avoid another Rajan-style lecture, perhaps an instinctive distrust of Leuth (already he reminded me of a very shiny, very quick black snake) made me lie and say that I was. I invented a husband in the movie business who travelled a great deal. We had no children.

The Honorary Consul, a cheery chubby blond Englishman whose only concession to going native was a large ruby ring on one forefinger, was equally optimistic about my travel plans and set up a meeting for me at the Press Department of the Ministry of Foreign Affairs. The Laos, it was true, were not known for their enthusiasm for journalists but they were mustard keen on the foreign currency that increased tourism would bring and, if I promised not to ask any searching questions about re-education camps (in 1975 between 30,000 and 40,000 people had been rounded up and sent to such camps and a further 343,000 Laos fled the country) and other sensitive matters, he thought I should be fine. The men from the Ministry were equally positive. It was all at rather short notice but they would, they said, do their best to help me. I asked to visit Luang Prabang, the old royal capital in the north of Laos and Savannahket, Pakse and Champassak, site of Wat Phou, in the south. It was, however, unlikely that I would be able to go to the Plain of Jars, a vast expanse of land in Xieng Khouang province, dotted with monoliths, the famous 'jars', formerly tombs of a megalith monument people. It could only be reached by helicopter: the cost was prohibitive and anyhow the helicopter hardly ever worked. I should stand by at the Lane Xang and wait for their call. They would let me know in a day or two. I was not, at this stage, familiar with the Lao phrase which translates roughly as 'Maybe tomorrow or some day'.

Leuth meanwhile was anxious that I should set off for Savannakhet – or somewhere – with him. He couldn't understand why I was bothering with the Ministry. I tried to explain that it would be less than ideal if I was thrown in prison and then out of Laos (a likely fate if I was caught wandering around the country without a *laisser-passer*) but he wasn't interested. I had various bits of business to attend to in Vientiane and decided to retain Leuth's services by the day to avoid endless discussions about money. One morning we set off for the Cambodian embassy where I needed to apply for a visa to Phnom Penh.

Leuth was dressed in black from head to toe, like a cat burglar, and with his eyes still hidden by his dark glasses. As he pedalled through the broken-down streets of Vientiane in temperatures so humid that it was impossible to tell how hot it really was, he kept up a low buzz of speech, of which I could understand very little from my seat behind him, though I could make out the phrase 'My soul is so bitter' which kept recurring. Suddenly he said something that made me sit up and lean forward. He said, 'When I am in front of you, I feel like an animal in a zoo.'

He clearly didn't mean literally in front of me which, of course, is exactly where he was as he pedalled the *samlo*. I think he meant that I didn't see him as a person, a human being like me. His remark was startling and quite unexpected. I had been sitting in the cab, sleepy in the heat, not thinking of anything much except perhaps what I had to do at the Cambodian embassy or noticing yet again how the roots of the big trees by the roadside had forced their way up through the pavements, cracking them as if after an earthquake. But I said the only thing possible – that there was no reason for him to feel like that and of course I didn't think of him as an animal in the zoo. The truth was that I hadn't, until that moment, thought much about Leuth at all. When I thought about him, it was in connection with what I might do with him, or rather, in his company; it was in connection with plans for Savannakhet or some other part of Laos that I hoped to visit. But his remark, unsettling as it was, set off a train of thought.

I realised that, paradoxically, one of the pleasures of travel was the extent to which you could remain detached. It was possible to have casual, almost promiscuous, relationships in which it wasn't necessary to become very involved. In that sense, travel was a very selfish pleasure and I had sometimes wondered how the other people felt, the natives, the ones who couldn't get away. But Leuth was clearly voicing a rancour that went far deeper than anything I had come across before. Implicit in his comment was not only a criticism of me but also a disturbing degree of self-loathing. I had been told that the Laos often complain or at least deprecate their lot when talking to foreigners but, among other Laos I had come across (who tended to be people in humble positions – waiters, *samlo* drivers or stallholders in the market), I often got the sense that this was done almost for form's sake and that the very real hardships of their position were accepted without too much question or resentment. Not so with Leuth. Almost everything he said was expressive of a restless, profound dissatisfaction. As we bowled through Sisattanek, a semi-rural *quartier* of west Vientiane where there were a number of large houses in reasonable condition, I asked every so often to whom such-and-such a house belonged. Back came the inevitable answer in a tight angry voice, 'Rich man.' He was keen that I should move to another – cheaper – hotel, the Inter, where he said it would be easier for him to 'get at me' and, although I wasn't thrilled to be paying thirty-six dollars a night while I waited to hear from the Ministry of Foreign Affairs, I was beginning to find Leuth more than just a bit of a nuisance and accordingly grateful for the protection afforded by the Lane Xang's exclusivity. It soon became clear that the plan to spend a couple of nights in Vang Vieng with Leuth and his taxi driver friend would have to be abandoned.

Vang Vieng was some four hours' drive from Vientiane near Sayaboury and supposed to be rather beautiful but foreigners were not permitted to go there because of possible attacks by bandits or outbreaks of fighting (it was never clear between whom as the

official Lao line was to deny the existence of any right-wing
insurgents while the *Bangkok Post* delighted in presenting a
gloomy picture). I wasn't frightened of bandits or insurgents but
I was growing increasingly nervous of Leuth whose behaviour
was becoming more erratic by the day.

He had taken to telephoning me at odd hours of the day or
night, often quite late and sounding as if he had been drinking or
taking drugs. He would launch into long hysterical speeches which
were difficult to understand. One night he rang after eleven, just
minutes after I had returned so I thought he must have been
watching the hotel. He demanded to know where I had been and
with whom, adding fiercely that he needed to see me; it was very
important. I tried to calm him down, asking what was the matter
and finally why he was carrying on like this. I even dragged my
non-existent husband into the conversation but nothing had any
effect so I hung up.

If my nights were spent avoiding Leuth's calls, my days were
often spent with Darachit whom I had met late one afternoon in
a rather fancy food shop in the Rue Chao Anou which stocked
imported delicacies like Japanese sake and Tiptree's Strawberry
Preserve. I was gazing, with some astonishment, at an incongruous
display of English jams when Darachit politely introduced himself
in French and offered me his card. He was the *Troisième Secrétaire*
at the *Ambassade de la République Démocratique Populaire Lao*
in Moscow and, as I recalled the polished slightly ironic manner
of Mr Southam in Paris, I wondered briefly about the selection
process in the Lao diplomatic corps.

Darachit was a small earnest man – not good-looking like Leuth
– with a few, perhaps twenty, stiff black hairs on his chin and the
same on his upper lip. It looked as if they had been trimmed
rather brutally with a pair of blunt scissors so, rather than creating
the impression that he was unshaven, it looked as if they were
deliberately kept at this unusual length. Lao designer stubble perhaps. Because the hairs were so sparse, the effect was odd and not
entirely successful. He was wearing a white shirt with a thin grey
stripe, a pair of grey flannel trousers, pale grey socks and black

lace-up shoes. I never saw him in any other clothes. He wore spectacles and had a small leatherette pouch attached to the belt of his trousers. After we had been talking for a few moments, he asked with exquisite formality, '*Est-ce qu'on peut vous connaître?*' (literally 'might one know you?') so I said, yes, of course, and gave him my card suggesting he come to the hotel the next day around noon.

Darachit arrived a little late for our rendezvous and found me quietly distraught. Early that morning I had telephoned the Ministry of Foreign Affairs where Mr Bounneme had reiterated his intention to 'do his best to help me'. I had planned to spend the morning lying by the swimming pool and was peacefully sunbathing when Ajit lowered his considerable bulk onto the dilapidated lounger next to mine and began abusing the Laos and complaining about the impossibility of doing business in Vientiane. As the days went by and I waited to hear from Mr Bounneme, I was beginning to feel similarly frustrated but I hated the idea of being at one with Ajit on any subject and, in a fit of temper, took offence. It was Ajit's boasting more than anything else that got to me. He had started by telling me that he used to earn £5000 a month in 'the UK' and that anything less than that was 'worthless because, every time you go out for a slap-up dinner, you have to pay at least £250'. Having failed to draw me on the subject of my private life, he now wanted to talk about money.

'How much money do you make a month?' he asked.

'Well, it depends.'

'And how much do you get paid for an article?'

'It depends on the length and the subject matter.'

'Who has paid for you to come to this place?'

'I paid for myself.'

'What!? You are not having expenses? My God, you mean to say you paid to come here yourself? Why on earth?'

At that, I got up from my chair in a rage, wrapped by sarong tightly round my waist and stormed into the hotel, saying, 'I do wish you would mind your own business. I don't like to discuss my personal affairs with strangers,' leaving Ajit struggling to get up from the chair, his mouth opening and shutting like a goldfish's.

Inside the clerk behind the front desk handed me a letter from the Ministry of Foreign Affairs. Despite Mr Bounneme's earlier assurances, he would not, after all, be able to help me. His letter began: 'I would like regretfully to inform you that we are not able to organise the programme for you due to some reasons . . .' He went on to say, 'We do not want you to waste your time without hope, thus you are suggested to join a tour of the Tourist company . . . ' and ended, 'May I wish you success and happiness while you are travelling in Lao PDR.' This was a frightful blow and I had little confidence that Lao Tourism would be able to help me, even if I could afford to pay the inflated prices charged to tourists.

When Darachit arrived, I was sitting on one of the uncomfortable carved wooden chairs in the foyer of the Lane Xang remembering gloomily the advice given to the French naturalist and explorer Henri Mouhot when he visited Laos in 1860. A Chinese man told him: 'the only plan to get rid of all the difficulties which the Laotian officials will be sure to throw in your way is to have a good stick, the longer the better. Try it on the back of any mandarin who makes the least resistance and will not do what you wish. Put all delicacy aside. Laos is not like a country of the whites.' A Norwegian aid worker at one of the refugee camps on the Thai-Cambodian border, who had spent ten years in Laos, had told me that the key to understanding Lao bureaucracy lay in the years between 1893 and 1953 when the country was under French control. He said that, after years of foreign domination, the Laos were finally in a position to wield a little power over westerners and that they seized every opportunity to do so, refusing requests or placing obstacles in the path of a foreigner whenever possible. Given the realities of the country's economic situation (pretty desperate), this was difficult to credit but, if you interpreted each exercise of bureaucratic control, each flex of the official muscle as an expression of the Lao desire to be finally in charge of their own destiny, then it made a sort of sense. Even so, it was difficult to believe that Mr Bounneme and his colleagues were being obstructive just for the fun of it but it was clear that I wasn't going to make any headway at the Ministry, particularly as when I telephoned, I was told that Mr Bounneme's mother had died suddenly and he had gone to her funeral.

Darachit wanted, quite simply, to become my friend and when he saw how upset I was and heard why, he was eager to help. We went to have lunch and drank beer in the restaurant overlooking the Mekong. On a long table in the middle of the restaurant were a hundred or so jam jars, each one containing a little fish for sale. Over grilled river fish, a bony poor relation of the magnificent *capitaine du Mekong*, and sticky rice, I explained my predicament. His view was that, as a writer, I would stand a better chance of getting assistance in the shape of a *laisser-passer* from the Ministry of Culture where he had a friend, so when we had finished eating we set off.

The Ministry of Culture was housed in a tall shabby building in the Place Nam Phou whose focal point was a large fountain that clearly hadn't worked for a number of years. There were a couple of inches of stagnant water in the basin into which passers-by had thrown plastic bags, banana peel and other bits of rubbish. The Ministry itself sported a large electric silhouette of the hammer and sickle but, in the absence of any light bulbs, it seemed unlikely to have seen much recent use.

We climbed sweatily up to the second floor where Darachit's friend or acquaintance had his office and, while I sat in a corner, they discussed my situation. After some twenty minutes they came over to me and I put my case. But despite frequent invocation of the magic phrase 'I will do my best to help you', it soon became obvious that his best wasn't going to be good enough and we were sent on our way with a recommendation to try the Ministry of Commerce. Darachit was all for going straight there but I thought that we might as well pay a visit to Lao Tourism which was just over the road. There they, too, after prolonged explanation and negotiation, promised to 'do their best to help' me, adding that they saw no reason why I shouldn't stay in Luang Prabang and Pakse for as long as I wished. Much cheered, we parted in a spirit of mutual congratulation and Darachit took me off to visit his wife and children.

Though Darachit was presumably glad to have a proper job, his salary in Moscow was pretty low and the cost of living there plus the airfares meant his family were not able to join him. He got a month's holiday a year when he came back to Vientiane to see them. It didn't take long to work out that his son, Darasengphet (the name included a prefix from his name and a suffix from his wife Kamphet's), must have been conceived just before he was posted to Moscow and that Kamphet must have been pregnant on his last trip home. This visit would have been the first time that he had seen the baby.

His three-year-old daughter, Darachayphet, (the name chosen or manufactured in the same way as his son's) was out but Kamphet, the baby, and her younger brother who lived with them, were at home. As we walked up the stairs of a tenement building in one of the nameless shabby streets that ran between the Mekong and Rue Setthathirat, Darachit apologised, saying more than once, '*Ce n'est pas très agréable.*'

They lived in two rooms off a long corridor. In the first, Kamphet with her hair in curlers, was tending to a stolid-looking child of about eight months who wore neither nappies nor knickers. Kamphet was a slender graceful woman in her late twenties or early thirties with a large black mole on her upper lip. The room contained almost no furniture, just a couple of chairs, two single mattresses along one wall and a vast stereo tapedeck and speakers and a television set. Kamphet poured me a glass of tepid water and Darachit and I took a chair each and chatted whilst he played with the baby who, he said, did not know him. By western standards, the visit wasn't a great success. Conversation didn't exactly flow but it didn't seem to matter and after ten minutes, Darachit took me to see their other room which was divided into two parts.

In the front part, there were two large beds which took up

almost the entire space. The other part, which gave onto the corridor and had no window, was entirely filled by a big loom on which Kamphet was weaving an elaborate and beautiful *sin*.

Almost every woman in Laos wears a *sin* which is a more formal and austere garment than the batik sarongs common in much of Thailand and Malaysia. Unlike a sarong, it is not simply a length of cloth but has been shaped and sewn to hang like a tailored skirt. It consists almost invariably of a mid-calf length piece of material in a dark solid colour with a band of design in brighter colours woven round the bottom. The *sin* is sewn to form a tube and folds from right to left to form a neat skirt with a single big pleat on the left and fastens with a hook or button and the whole thing is then clinched around the waist with a silver belt. On top, Lao women wear ladylike blouses, and on their feet, mules or sandals of some kind. At the airport there were trim little female soldiers fetchingly kitted out in khaki-coloured *sins* and matching shirts. Just as it is very rare to see a Lao woman clad in jeans or a tee-shirt, so it is almost unheard of to find one looking untidy or anything less than immaculate. It is as if they had just paid a visit to a beauty parlour, and the contrast between their exquisite appearance and the squalid buildings from which they emerge each morning, is a source of continual surprise.

On this visit, however, I was clearly seeing Kamphet's private face because, when we next met, she was smartly got up in a black-and-white polka-dot blouse with a ruffled neckline and a *sin* which she had woven herself with a design of green and orange antlered deer round the bottom. Her daughter was wearing a frilly pink party dress with pink plastic sandals to match. It was a Sunday and we were going for the afternoon to a *boun bang fay* at a village called Nong Heo some twenty miles from Vientiane on the road beyond Thaddeua where you board the ferry for Nong Khai. I had been growing desperate with frustration and a desire to see something of Laos other than the grimy streets of Vientiane and the interiors of the various unhelpful ministries. A laconic Frenchman who had been in Laos since 1954, had advised me somewhat irritably, when I probed him for information, to 'observe the Lao in the street; go to a *boun*'. So when I heard that there was a *boun* in the area, despite the restriction on foreign visitors travelling more than ten kilometres outside Vientiane without a *laisser-passer*, I bullied Darachit to find out where it was and invited him and his family to accompany me.

A *boun* is both a festival and a fête and, in the absence of much other entertainment, the Laotian calendar, an almost incomprehensible combination of lunar and solar in which the year itself is reckoned by solar phases and the months are divided according to lunar phases, abounds with them. The biggest of these are probably *Boun Pi Mai* in April which celebrates the New Year; *Boun Ok Vassa* in mid-October which marks the end of Buddhist Lent, and *Boun Nam*, the water festival. In November, the whole of Vientiane springs into unaccustomed life with the festival of That Luang which begins two days before the full moon and centres round the large sixteenth-century stupa, the 'great shrine', of the same name which dominates the eastern side of the city and is supposed to contain a relic of the Buddha. The *bouns* are also a means of raising money for the *wats*, or pagodas and, in the case of the one we were going to, the money would go towards the completion of the building of the *wat*.

Boun Bang Fay is the 'rocket' festival which takes place before the sowing of the rice. It is both a Buddhist and secular festival, designed to encourage fertility, a good harvest and rain. The idea is fairly straightforward. All the villages and also a number of individuals in each village make rockets which are fired off. The further the rocket goes, the better the harvest and prizes are awarded.

Darachit and I found a taxi by the morning market and, after some friendly haggling, a price was agreed on – the equivalent of about twelve dollars for the afternoon. The car was an extremely battered old brown Corona with no windows on either side and a strip of nylon fur along the back window ledge. There was some kind of religious good luck charm hanging from the driving mirror festooned with the saffron-coloured wool. The car didn't appear to have any suspension and jerked and juddered as it went along but it went.

We collected Kamphet and the children and set off for the *boun* which was supposed to start at two. It was impossible ever to know what Kamphet was thinking. She never addressed me, probably because she could speak neither English nor French and my Lao was limited to about five words, and, unlike Darachit who aways had an apprehensive scared-rabbit air to him, she was serene and withdrawn. Her daughter was also completely silent and Darachit complained that he never knew what *she* was thinking.

Nong Heo was about three-quarters of an hour away. We drove past a cigarette factory on the outskirts of Vientiane and the usual motley collection of water buffalo, stray dogs, chickens, naked infants and sleeping men. When we reached Nong Heo, it was easy enough to tell where the *boun* was. There were crowds pouring through the gateway to the *wat*, youths on motorcycles and everyone else on foot and the sound of loud electronic music with a strong bass beat. Inside the atmosphere was festive. There were people selling balloons on strings and I bought Darachayphet a pink one to match her dress. There were stalls for soft drinks, cans of beer, toys, grilled chicken skewered on pieces of split bamboo, sticks of hollowed-out bamboo filled with sticky rice coloured and flavoured, I think, with tamarind jam, meatballs and any number of other bits and pieces. There was a large dance floor with a band and huge speakers to the right as we entered the grounds of the *wat*. This was where the younger people were clustered together. In Laos, you sit down at the end of every dance, even if it means that you just turn straight round and go back to the dance floor. No-one stays on the floor between numbers. But when the band was playing, the floor was packed, often with weaving drunks dancing on their own.

There were gallons of *lao-lao* around. *Lao-lao* is a cloudy white spirit, the lethal home-brewed rice liquor of Laos which tastes like a cross between sake and turpentine. The Laos love to drink and so, as the afternoon wore on, the men got more and more drunk.

Further into the temple complex was a group of elderly men and women. The men were playing the sort of traditional stringed instruments that I'd seen in the open-air restaurant across from the Lane Xang and the women were dancing the *lam vong*, a slow weaving dance in which the hands move up and down and from side to side in a leisurely flowing movement like a sort of oriental 'patty cake' but without ever touching. These dancers with their graceful upright carriage, their dreamy distant expressions and their party *sins* (the women were wearing *sins* made of brightly-coloured silk woven in squares and broad stripes and usually worn by men) were infinitely more appealing than the younger dancers and the electronic band but, as Darachit was fond of saying and without apparent regret, '*Les traditions ne sont plus respectées.*'

Next to the old dancers was one of the rockets made by the village. These were all constructed on the same basic principle. The rocket proper with its fuse would be attached to a very long bamboo pole which might measure as much as twelve or eighteen feet. The special rockets, like the one representing the village of Nong Heo, the ceremonial rockets as it were, were decorated with strands of orange wool, the same colour as the monks' robes, and bits of tinsel, and resting on a specially constructed stand surrounded by offerings of food and fruit. The largest one was truly enormous with a rocket measuring about three and a half feet and a bamboo pole about twenty feet long.

The launch pad was out in the rice fields some distance from the *wat* and the dancers and food stalls. A tall bamboo climbing frame had been erected and fixed to a clump of trees in the middle of the paddies and small boys and grown men were swarming up the frame with their rockets, attaching them and firing them off. Depending on the distance each rocket travelled, and some of them went really quite far, practically back to Vientiane, there would be shouts of jubilation or cries of despair, the judges would come to a decision and a man with a microphone back near the *wat* would announce the verdict.

As I walked out towards the rice fields to have a closer look, I passed a crowd of men and women pressing tightly round a young woman who was being supported by two other women. She appeared to be in some kind of trance or as if she had just come out of a faint. When I caught up with Darachit, I asked him what was going on. 'Her husband and her lover are going to fight over her,' he answered. But when I went back later, everyone had disappeared.

The paddies were incredibly muddy. You had to walk along a narrow strip of high ground and it required considerable skill to avoid slipping and falling into the mud. As I was carrying two

Nikon cameras and properly conscious of the figure that I would cut if I fell flat on my face, I was extremely careful. Several Lao youths who had been happily rolling in the mud like water buffalo, shouted at me as I walked past. 'What are they saying?' I asked. 'They would like you to fall over and lie down in the mud too,' said Darachit.

The mud was a nasty greyish brown and, as the afternoon wore on and the sun grew hotter and hotter and the men became more and more unsteady on their feet, there were more bodies caked from head to toe in a greyish paste, looking strange and prehistoric. One boy, who had been struggling to carry his rocket to the launching frame, had a bottle attached to a piece of string round his neck which he kept hitting with a stick, and every yard or so, he would trip over his rocket and fall on his back in the dirt and lie there, banging on his bottle.

The air was filled with dreary, monotone sounds from an assortment of instruments. There was a drum which beat solidly and dully as each rocket approached the base and a series of irritating tinkling little bells. The sun bore down and I began to feel unpleasantly hot and slightly menaced by the level of drunkenness around me. I was the only foreigner there. I seemed to be the only woman out in the paddies, and, as such, an object of some attention, not all of it friendly.

The very big rocket was due to be launched at five o'clock. By now, most of the men had been drinking steadily for three hours and could barely stand, let alone carry their rockets. I was hot and not a little bored but Darachit insisted that we stay to see the big one go up. Kamphet and the children had stayed in the shade of the pagoda and were waiting there. Eventually it was time. The big rocket was carried by the elderly dancers from its shrine out into the fields where it was baptised with *lao-lao* by a distinguished-looking old man. Then slowly, so slowly that I was almost screaming with frustration and a desire for them to hurry up and get on with it, the big rocket was carried to the foot of the bamboo frame. Then precautions had to be taken to ensure that the rocket head, which was made of metal, did not land on the cigarette factory. The drum beats intensified as the rocket was laboriously hauled into place. Darachit went to fetch his son so that the baby could watch the rocket disappear over the horizon.

Then, just as it seemed as if finally everything was ready, the sun disappeared behind a vast grey cloud and the low rumble of thunder filled the air. A long fuse, like the tail of a giant rat, hung down to the ground. With much ceremony, a burning torch was held to the fuse and the flame crept up towards the rocket.

The fuse fizzled out and had to be re-lit. This time the flame reached the rocket which started to gather itself up like a crouching beast preparing to spring. Suddenly it collapsed sideways into the trees and crashed to the ground. I assumed that everyone would be filled with gloom and despondency, given that the rocket's failure could well be interpreted as a bad omen, portending a rotten harvest for the village, but Darachit said that there were more rockets to come from Nong Heo and there was no need to despair yet. All around us, mud men were rising from the ground like characters out of a horror film and small rockets were continuing to blast off into the countryside, making sharp angry spluttering noises. The sun was sinking fast and all the rockets had to be fired before dark so that the judges could see how far they had gone. Rain was imminent and the baby, who didn't care for the explosions, began to cry. I realised that Darachit's insistence that we stay till the bitter end arose more out of courtesy to me than any desire of his own and said that I thought we should leave. The heart had gone out of the day and I was suddenly very tired.

We found Kamphet and the little girl and climbed into the old Corona. As we drove back towards Vientiane, it started to pour with rain which blew in through the empty window frames. Kamphet unbuttoned her blouse and put her howling son to her breast. When we got into town, she and the children disappeared up the stairs of their tenement block without a word.

Leuth had not entirely dropped out of sight though I had grown very expert at avoiding him. I took to leaving the hotel by the back door and cutting through the garden but sometimes he would still appear suddenly and silently behind me when I was out walking. One morning he caught me on my way back from visiting

the Museum of the Revolution. On my third attempt, I had managed to find the museum open. It was housed in a beautiful old
pale pink palace on the Rue Samsenthai. The custodian behaved
as if I had somehow outwitted her by catching the place in a rare
moment of accessibility and confiscated my camera to fiddle with
while I inspected the museum. Inside there was a motley collection
of soil samples, rusty weapons, field telephones, Lao handicrafts
and musical instruments. There were black-and-white photographs documenting the heroic struggle of the Lao people, and
pictures of Lenin and Lao heroes. There was also a medical display
which included some sets of false teeth and various repulsive
objects in jam jars which I took to be intestinal parasites preserved
in formaldehyde.

Afterwards I was dawdling along the banks of the Mekong when,
all of a sudden, there was Leuth, like the proverbial thief in the
night. He greeted me and asked for my address. I reminded him
that it was on my card but he refused to believe me until he had
got it out of his wallet and checked. He needed it, he said, so that
he could write to me, adding – giggling wildly behind his hand –
that my husband would be very jealous. I had more or less forgotten about my husband but drew myself up and said rather pomp-
ously, 'My husband and I trust each other absolutely.' Leuth
leered knowingly and cycled off, saying, 'When we are very close,
I will tell you my dream.'
    About a week later, I bumped into Leuth on the Rue Setthathi-
rat. I had been with Darachit to visit some of the *wats* and we
were wandering back to the Lane Xang when Leuth appeared at
my right shoulder. He and Darachit exchanged a few guarded
sentences in Lao and Leuth rode on. Darachit told me that Leuth
had been at college with him in Leningrad but had been sent home
'*parce qu'il était un peu fou*'.
    Later that day, at about half-past seven, the telephone rang –
just as I was preparing to go out for dinner. It was Leuth but, in
contrast to his usual frenzied jealous behaviour, he sounded quite
calm. He asked what I was doing. I lied and said that I hadn't yet
decided. His response was unexpected. He said resignedly, almost

sadly, 'Something has changed between us but don't worry. No problem.' Even though he had been making my life a bit of a misery, I found the conversation oddly distressing. That Leuth was genuinely hurt and confused by *my* behaviour was clear; that he was unaware of the effect of *his* conduct and manner was equally apparent. I knew that nothing I could say or do would provide an adequate explanation.

Some impulse of guilt or conscience took me out looking for him. The Mekong was like black glass, gleaming with the reflection of the flames of the tiny fires on which the riverside stallholders simmered their pots of noodles. In the sky, a large cloud, shaped like a crouching tiger hid the full moon and the air was full of the sound of crickets, twanging like a Jew's harp. I went into the open-air restaurant where I had first met Leuth and then walked along the river bank. There was no sign of him anywhere.

One evening I went alone to the cinema in the Rue Chao Anou. Despite Darachit's best efforts and Leuth's unwelcome attentions, life in Vientiane was beginning to pall and I had almost exhausted the city's limited attractions. I had tried to go to the National Theatre but was told that I had just missed a troupe of dancers from India and that there wouldn't be another show for six months. Loud music was coming from a large shabby building which had always been closed before and crowds of young Laos were queueing to go in. I thought that it might be a dance hall and stopped to buy a ticket. The cinema was showing a Thai film dubbed into Lao and set in a kind of Far Eastern Wild West. It opened with a shot of a young woman riding very fast through cornfields and cut to a shot of hooves drumming on the ground. The woman was rounding up her cattle. In the next scene, a large customised jeep filled with men with guns was driving across the same fields. One of the men shot one of the cattle which they skinned and roasted over an open fire in their camp. The gang leader, who bore an uncomfortable resemblance to Leuth, was easily recognisable by his dark glasses and his possession of a girlfriend in tight black trousers and a top that displayed her navel. When he wasn't tearing open cans of Heineken and pouring the beer down his throat from a height, he was urging his men on to further acts of beastliness. He and the girl smoked continuously. A battle developed between the forces of good in the shape of the pretty ranchowner and the forces of evil in the form of the beer-swilling chain-smoking fornicating gang leader. Finally, after a sequence of exhausting chase scenes, the movie ended with the triumph of good and a climax that would not have disgraced *The Texas Chainsaw Massacre*.

Throughout the film, the audience which included nursing mothers and tiny children, sat in complete silence, apparently unmoved either by the excessive violence or the vulgar picture of popular western-influenced culture that it portrayed. Lao tolerance of, or rather stoicism in the face of, violence must be fairly deeply ingrained. From the middle of the sixteenth to the middle of the seventeenth century, war raged with Burma and a long troubled relationship with Siam (the name was changed to Thailand in 1939 after an outbreak of right-wing nationalist sentiment) came to a bloody head in 1828 when Siamese troops burnt the city of Vientiane to the ground in response to an unexpected declaration of war by the Lao king of the time, Chao Anou. (Anou eventually died in 1835 after four years in captivity in Bangkok where he was displayed in an iron cage and perished of the ill-treatment he received.) Of the eighty *wats* in the city, only Wat Sisaket was left standing. According to W.A.R. Wood, author of a history of Siam, the Siamese on this occasion rivalled the Burmese in 'frightfulness'.

Twentieth-century Laos has been no less *mouvementé*. The relative torpor of the French colonial era was followed by a period of factional in-fighting between right-wing forces – the Royal Laos Governments (RLG) backed by the United States – and the Pathet Lao, supported by Hanoi and the Communist bloc. In 1964 the Americans began secretly bombing Pathet Lao areas and, once the Vietnam War got into full swing, the bombing intensified. During the war, over two million tons of bombs were dropped on Laos, one third higher than the total tonnage dropped on Germany by American aircraft throughout the Second World War, and an average of a hundred and seventy-seven bombs a day – or one plane-load every eight minutes – twenty-four hours a day for nine years. It is hard to imagine what Laos could ever have done to deserve this. A large number of these bombs still lie unexploded along the old Ho Chi Minh Trail, ready to blow limbs off peasants working in the rice fields. In the Plain of Jars, which was also carpet-bombed, between five and ten people are killed or maimed each month by what the Laos call *bombis* – bomblets containing about two hundred and fifty steel pellets.

Since 1975 there have been constant skirmishes with Thai troops and 'insurgents' along the border between the two countries, including a notable exchange of fire in 1983 which damaged the Lane Xang hotel while an international Mekong Committee meeting was in progress. Between December 1987 and February 1988, Thailand and Laos fought a bloody border war over disputed territory in which a hundred Laos and five hundred Thais died and which encouraged Kukrit Pramoj, a former Thai prime minister, to urge the Thais to burn down Vientiane again.

One rainy afternoon I went to see Michel Drouot, the francophone assistant director-general of the national radio and television station. The Honorary Consul had thought that he might prove useful. The potholes in the roads and pavements had turned into huge puddles and, by the time I got to his office, my shoes were soaked through. I had intended to keep one pair to ruin, as it were, and one to preserve but, like so many such schemes, I never seemed to manage to put it into practice. One alternative was to wear rubber 'flip-flops' but I felt that I would look even more of a mess and I was already fed-up with the contrast that I presented, with my frizzy sweat-sodden hair and flushed face, to the slender immaculate Lao women.

Drouot, who also went under his Lao name, Somsanouk Mixay, was an elegant man, languid and good-looking like many Laos, but his manner was initially guarded. He was clearly anticipating very specific questions and my fumbling attempts to get some kind of insight into Laos seemed to make him uneasy. National radio is, of course, government-run and government-controlled and, as such, Drouot, for all his western sophistication, was a government employee. I often found it difficult in Laos to remember that I was in a Communist country ('an apparent comic-opera world of royal courts, sacred elepants, ancient temples and orange-robed monks' was how one writer described Laos before the Pathet Lao takeover and that was still often the flavour of the place). Its poverty and backwardness could not be immediately attributed to the country's Communist policies, as Thailand, for all its glossy consumerism, often illustrated with sometimes even more distressing hardships, many as a direct result of Bangkok's role as the pan-sexual brothel of South East Asia. In Laos, most of the time, the iron fist of communism tended to remain concealed in the velvet glove of oriental sensibility and only revealed itself in the most unexpected ways. For instance, in both Thailand and Cambodia, the *wai* (Thai) or *sampeah* (Khmer), the graceful gesture in which both palms are placed together and the head inclined as a gesture of respect, is widely practised. I noticed that it didn't seem to be much in evidence in Laos and asked why. '*Mais, madame, vous savez, nous sommes un pays socialiste,*' was the reply.

The relationship between Laos and Vietnam was a close one and had been strengthened by Thailand's response to the Communist victory in the region. Both countries are Laos's most immediate neighbours. If Thailand was the beautiful gregarious elder sister, Vietnam could be seen as the protective older brother (depending on whom you're talking to). In November 1975, Thailand closed its borders with Laos and in doing so accelerated the Pathet Lao takeover. Thailand, previously Laos's main trading partner, then enforced an economic blockade on a list of over 200 'strategic' items, including medical supplies, construction materials, canned food and bicycles (the last was designated a strategic item on account of its use during the Vietnam War). Since 1975 Thailand has twice again closed its borders with Laos, each time causing predictable hardships.

There are over 1700 kilometres of border between Laos and Thailand, much of it marked by the beautiful Mekong river. The Mekong is the seventh longest river in the world and, given that Laos has no seaport, no railway and few serviceable roads, it is also the country's lifeline, its aorta. Everything heavy must be transported by river. The Mekong's watery division between the two countries begins at Laos's frontier with China where the remote province of Louang Nam Tha joins southern Yunnan; from there the river flows down to the infamous Golden Triangle where Laos, Thailand and Burma meet briefly in a haze of opium fumes, then it strays away from the border into Laos and to Luang Prabang, rejoining the border at Vientiane and staying with it almost to the southernmost tip of Laos just before Pakse.

Without access to Thailand, essential goods such as building materials had to be trucked across the Annamite mountains from the Vietnamese port of Da Nang, a difficult journey of many hundreds of miles and one that takes considerably longer than the twenty-minute ferry ride across the Mekong. This has had far-reaching consequences, the effects of which are still being felt today.

One night in the mosquito-trap restaurant on the banks of the Mekong, I met an Australian engineer who was in Laos to conduct a feasibility study for a road and rail bridge across the Mekong (costing US $31 million and to be paid for by the Australians). Between great swallows of Lao beer, he complained about the quality of the cement sent from Vietnam. 'It's not like wine, you know. After three years, it goes off. It's too old,' he said. Most of the recent buildings in Vientiane had been erected with the help of this 'corked' cement which went some way towards explaining their crumbling appearance.

In the face of Thai hostility to the new political order in Laos, the Laos had no choice but to turn to the Vietnamese. To a certain extent, they would have done so anyhow. After an alliance which came into being in the 1930s with the founding of the IndoChinese Communist Party, the two countries were now formally allied under the umbrella of Communist government (which, for the time being anyhow, looked set to replace the old White Parasol) and thus intent on fraternal relations of the cosiest nature. The Vietnamese, anxious to consolidate their victory against the United States, sought also to reinforce Communism in the region, and in 1976, a joint communiqué signed by Kaysone and Le Duan, the

Lao and Vietnamese party secretaries of the time, declared that a 'special relationship' existed between the two countries.

The relationship however is, and always will be an uneven one. Vietnam is a larger country with a much bigger population (67.4 million to Laos's 3.8 million); Hanoi has more power and influence than Vientiane. But the friendship and protection of Vietnam had at least made it possible for the Laos to stand up to the Thais.

Time and money were running out and Lao Tourism had still not come up with a *laisser-passer*. Every afternoon I would walk up to their offices on the Rue Setthathirat and be told, with unfailing courtesy, to come back the next afternoon. The uncertainty was driving me crazy. Finally I gave them and myself a deadline – Queen Elizabeth II's official birthday which the Honorary Consul was proposing to celebrate in fitting manner with prawns flown in from Bangkok. This seemed appropriate since one indication that Vientiane was beginning to get to me was that I was dreaming furiously every night; often about the British Royal Family, about home, about cocktail parties in London, ridiculous dreams of social embarrassment. One night I dreamt that Placido Domingo asked me to sing Gilda from *Rigoletto* opposite him.

'But, Placido,' I said, hissing the 'c' thickly through my teeth like you're supposed to, 'I can't sing in tune.'

'Don't worry, my dear. You will be wonderful,' he answered.

And I was. But still no nearer to getting my *laisser-passer*.

As a contingency measure, I visited the offices of Lao Air Booking, a small travel agency, and explained my problems to the beautiful young lady behind the desk. She called for her boss and I told him that I would do *anything* – do you understand? anything at all for a *laisser-passer*. He said that he would see what he could do and mentioned a small fortune.

'Yes, yes,' I cried, 'anything!'

'Come back tomorrow.'

While I waited, I thought that I might as well go to see the white elephant. No visitor to either Thailand or Laos can fail to be aware of the immense religious and propitious significance attached to white elephants. This particular one, nicknamed Dollar by the expatriate community, had come to my attention through the pages of a pictorial quarterly called *Laos* which was one of the only two English-language publications in Vientiane (the other was roneoed edited transcripts the BBC World Service produced and distributed daily by the government news service, KPL). The relevant story read rather like a description of the announcement to the shepherds by the Angel Gabriel of the birth of Christ:

'However, a dream of the Lao people to see a white mascot-elephant has become true in the new regime, and hence they believe that Laos will be prosperous. This white elephant was rounded up on Dec. 30, 1984, at Khoksaphayakeo region bordering Attopeu and Champassak provinces, by Mr Bounteum and Mr Bounmy, inhabitants of Phapho village, Champassak province. In 1988, the elephant was brought to Vientiane and a procession was organised in conformity with the traditional rites.'

According to the local guidebook, the elephant was in Vientiane zoo so I asked for directions.

'The elephant is not there. Mr Kaysone has taken it.'

'Well, where's he taken it to?'

'To his house.'

'What for?'

'To feed it.'

'Where's his house? Can I look at it there?'

'He has many houses.'

There the conversation ended.

Soon after this, I met a man who told me with undisguised relish of the King of Thailand's attempt to buy the elephant for 'many millions of *baht*' and of his government's refusal to part with the beast.

The Laos were, however, less successful in hanging on to the famous so-called 'Emerald' Buddha or Phra Keo, which was brought by King Setthathirat from Chiang Mai in the sixteenth century. He constructed a special shrine for it, Wat Phra Keo, from which it was taken when the Siamese attacked Vientiane in

1778. The statue now occupies pride of place in the Grand Palace in Bangkok and represents yet another thorn in the Lao flesh in the long saga of Lao-Thai relations. Houghton Broderick had no great regard for the statue, describing it in the following unflattering terms:

'It is fashioned in green jasper and is undoubtedly of Laotian workmanship, for the image, as you behold it in the Siamese capital, has a most Laotian face, vehement, cunning and, it may be, lecherous.'

It was not just the impossibility of making any plans that was irritating. Vientiane itself was without doubt the sleepiest place I had ever been and I was finding it increasingly difficult to stay awake. The whole city, indeed, I suspected, the whole country, the Rip Van Winkle of South East Asia, came to a complete standstill between noon and two and nothing was permitted to disturb the sacred siesta hour. All over Vientiane men were fast asleep and in positions of such Houdini-esque contortion that it looked as if they, like Sleeping Beauty's guards, had been quite suddenly overcome by slumber. Every time I walked past the Ministry of Foreign Affairs, there was the same parked car, its driver snoring softly, his bare feet stretched out into the road. And at the end of the Quai Fa Ngum was a little wooden sentry box whose occupant was also always asleep, his head on his arms, his legs wrapped round his waist. James Cameron, who visited Laos briefly in the late 1950s, wrote, 'Morale was high, and when Laotian morale is high it relaxes into torpor.' Morale must have been sky-high as I waited in Vientiane for a *laisser-passer*. Nothing, I was told, had changed in the city for twenty-five years. Vientiane was petrified, frozen in time and gone to terminal rack and ruin. A favourite excuse put forward by the authorities to explain various delays and evasions was that they were worried about my security. In fact, the greatest danger in all Laos probably came from the pavements of Vientiane.

Lao Tourism finally confessed to failure and later that afternoon, Mr Phanh Keophilaphanh at Lao Air Booking told me that he too had been unable to secure a *laisser-passer* for either love or money.

Somehow this didn't come as much of a surprise. The Honorary Consul tried to console me with similar hard-luck stories: he told me about the BBC correspondent who had languished for twelve days in Vientiane waiting unsuccessfully for a *laisser-passer*, about the flat refusal of any visa at all to National Geographic and so on. The Lao authorities had, it seemed, flung open the doors of the Kingdom of a Million Elephants only to find that hundreds of hippies had poured across the Mekong looking for somewhere unspoilt to spoil. A group of them nearly drowned when a storm blew up at the Nam Ngum dam and their boat capsized, leaving them in the water for four hours, and a guesthouse behind the market full of dope-smokers caught fire and burnt down. The Laos were having second thoughts about individual travellers. Groups were what they wanted, groups of docile elderly men and women with fistfuls of lovely green American dollars.

It was my last day. Darachit miserably agreed to organise a boat trip a couple of hours up the Mekong to visit a 'grotte des Bouddhas'. We took a motorised *samlo* out to a tiny village on the outskirts of Vientiane where a handful of fine-looking boatmen with white teeth and tattoos on their rippling muscles were smoking cigarettes. One man had a tattoo of a huge tiger across his pectorals. Darachit claimed that this would protect him if someone tried to shoot him: a bullet, he said, couldn't penetrate as long as the tiger was there.

We chugged up the Mekong in a long low boat. The water was its usual confusing colour: at times, the shade of pale milky chocolate; at others, like heavily-diluted tomato soup; sometimes, even at noon, the same rosy pinks and baby blues as the dawn sky. If you put your hand in the water, it came out coated in a thin red dust. There were always boys swimming in the river but I wouldn't have chosen to. The sewage and garbage of Vientiane had to end up somewhere. I sat up at the front of the boat, staring ahead at the vast expanse of the river, leading all the way to China. I was in a strange mood which the river heightened. Laos had, in many ways, been so disappointing, so frustrating and now on the water, the same water that I had hoped so much to see in the north and in the south of the country, I felt almost tearful. And yet it was impossible not to be exhilarated by its beauty.

The same could not be said of the Buddhas which were hideous, garishly-painted, smirking and fat as pigs. There were hundreds of them, in all sizes from six inches to over six foot and all poses, all with silver fingernails and elongated earlobes. They filled every nook and cranny of a large cave overlooking the river. I had taken off my shoes so as not to get them wet and the thick red mud of the Mekong oozed through my toes. A black centipede a foot long was making its way up the hill. Darachit and I panted behind. Darachit was wearing his usual outfit of grey trousers, white shirt, grey socks and black shoes, the latter increasingly bespattered with terracotta clay from the riverbank. I worried that these were either his good clothes or possibly his only clothes but didn't feel that it would be polite to ask. At the top of the hill was a vast cement Buddha squatting under a corrugated iron roof. It was difficult to think of anything complimentary to say and Darachit looked dejected.

On the way back to Vientiane, we stopped at a little island in the middle of the river. There, in the jungle, half-hidden by foliage, was a small dignified *wat* of weathered stone, a moving contrast to the Buddhas upstream. To one side of the entrance stood a headless statue of a goddess or female of some kind. She stood straight and simple, her robe unadorned; one arm was missing, the other hung by her side; an eastern Venus de Milo. According to Darachit, the island was called Done Sing Sou which meant 'the island where men fight each other for the love of a woman' and the little *wat* bore the same name. I asked him to write it down for me and he added a comment of his own in his tiny cramped handwriting: '*il paraît très mystérieux*'. As we left the island we picked up a hitchhiker, a young man in shorts who was carrying a gun. He wanted a ride across to the mainland. I asked Darachit what the gun was for: the island had seemed too small to be much good as a hunting ground. It turned out to be for guarding it against marauding Thais.

Back in Vientiane, I said goodbye to Darachit and gave him a present of a Parker pen.

'Will you come back to Laos?' he asked.

'Yes, of course.'

'But I will be in Moscow when you do,' he said with a gloomy smile.

At dusk I went to pay a final visit to the animals by the swimming pool. I had grown very fond of a female macaque in one of the cages and liked to feed her peanuts which I bought in tiny cellophane bags from a stall on the Rue Setthathirat. Half the time she wasn't particularly interested in the nuts but would reach through the bars and take my arm and start very gently to groom me, picking through the fine hairs, trying to remove the odd freckle. It was always touching but this evening the poignancy of her situation reduced me to tears. There was a new bear too, lying on his side in a dark smelly cage. His eyes were cloudy and his nose looked bleached and cracked, instead of a healthy shiny black. Suddenly I was glad to be leaving if only because I knew that I could do nothing for the animals and the spectacle of their pathetic little lives had become intolerable.

One lunchtime I had met a French photographer in the oldest restaurant in Vientiane, Arawan, which lay at the far end of the Rue Samsenthai and was run by a Corsican. He too was waiting for a *laisser-passer* and that evening he came to take me out to dinner. We went to a drab government-owned Chinese restaurant in the little grid of streets between the Rues Chao Anou and Nokeo Koumane that was the Chinese quarter. The tables were divided from each other by screens like the ones that are put round a hospital bed when the patient is being subjected to a particularly intimate examination. We ate Mongolian hotpot, a kind of oriental *fondue* in which you cook meat and vegetables and even an egg or two in a fiercely boiling soup heated by hot coals. After dinner he suggested we go dancing at the discotheque in his hotel. Vientiane, in the bad old days of the Vietnam War, had quite a reputation. A Swedish forestry expert who was on his way to investigate the effects of slash-and-burn in Luang Prabang, told me that in 1973, it had been 'one big brothel' and twelve years before in 1961 a British journalist described a nightclub as advertising 'Fifteen fresh girls from Bangkok'. Now what nightlife there was, was almost painfully sedate. The music which was usually live was a cautious mix of traditional Lao melodies, Thai pop and safe American love songs like those popularised by The Carpenters. The boys and girls did a version of the *lam vong* and anyone could join in, with or without a partner. An enormously fat American girl in shorts and a sack of a tee-shirt who would have been sitting in a corner by herself back home was happily cavorting to *One Way Ticket To the Blues*. We danced and drank beer till the disco showed signs of closing around midnight and then Alain walked me back to the Lane Xang. There was, as always, almost no-one about. Outside the gates of the hotel Alain gave me his address (which I lost almost immediately) saying how sad he was that I was leaving and begged me to write to him in French. His mournful advances were welcome only up to a point and, when he tried to kiss me, I responded with a display of Lao-like decorum.

Inside the hotel, the drug enforcement officers were making a racket in the bar. One of them, a tall dark man with blue eyes called Michael, grabbed me by the arm and dragged me in to join them. Almost all the men there had fought in Vietnam and we fell into a discussion about the rights and wrongs of that war. It wasn't much of a discussion because, within seconds, it became clear that they had been drinking steadily for some time and that anyhow, as far as they were all concerned, America had been perfectly correct to do everything it had done in Vietnam. It was not the time or place to get into a fight. The conversation shifted to easier topics.

'Will you have dinner with me in Bangkok?' asked Michael.

'Maybe.'

'Boy, I can't wait to get back to Patpong [Bangkok's notorious red-light district],' said one of the others, a short man with the sharp ginger features of a ferret.

'Nor can I!' said Michael.

'I thought you wanted to have dinner with me,' I said.

'That's right. I do and then I won't *need* to go to Patpong!'

Early the next morning I went out to look for Leuth. I wanted to give him a book. He had always asked me for books and I still felt guilty about him. I had only seen him once since the final telephone call and then out of the corner of my eye, on the edge of a group of *samlo* drivers vying for my custom. I caught sight of his lively malicious face and experienced a small shiver of fear. We didn't speak.

To my surprise, I found him now lolling in the cab of his *samlo* under a tree outside the gates of the hotel. He got out and sauntered towards me. I held out a copy of *Despair* – it was the only book I had left – Nabokov's cruel funny novel about a man who meets a tramp whom he believes to be his double.

He looked at it and then said, 'What's it about?'

'Look, Leuth, it's impossible to explain. You'll just have to read it and see.'

He continued to look dissatisfied. I said coaxingly, 'It's by a very brilliant, very famous Russian writer.'

'It's in Russian?'

'No, Nabokov was unusual in that he is one of the few writers who was able to write in a language other than his mother tongue. This book was originally written in Russian but then Nabokov translated it himself into English and added to it after he had left Russia and gone to America.'

'He emigrated?' Leuth's face lit up. 'I, too, would like to emigrate but you need a lot of money to do this.'

'I have no money, Leuth, and cannot help you emigrate.'

'No-one will help me. I know.'

2

A Sidetrip to Hanoi

I hadn't really planned to go to Vietnam on this trip but, lodged in the back of my mind, was a remark made by a friend, William Shawcross, who had written a couple of books on Cambodia and had known Vietnam during the war. He had said, 'If you get bored in Vientiane, you can always take a sidetrip to Hanoi.' Well, I had got rather bored in Vientiane and had decided to take his advice. I had less than a week before I was due to return to England and one of my few successes in Vientiane had been to persuade the Vietnamese embassy there to issue me with a visa at very short notice. I left a tranquil sunny Vientiane in the morning and arrived at Hanoi's Noi Bai airport in a slow grey drizzle on the afternoon of the same day. If I had thought I was unprepared for Laos, it was as nothing compared to the condition in which I reached Hanoi. Mlle Ouane Xaymana in Lao Air Booking had let me photocopy a couple of pages from a guidebook so I had at least the name of a hotel. One paragraph struck me as interesting, if not exactly relevant to my needs: *'La prostitution occasionelle ou organisée a refait surface jusqu'à Hanoi. Les sourires trop appuyés de certaines dames dans les dancings sont rarement désintéressés. Si les autorités ferment les yeux sur les fréquentations des résidents étrangers, il est plus prudent pour le touriste de s'en tenir aux plaisirs de la conversation.'*

There were a couple of French businessmen on the plane, which left three hours late without a word of either explanation or apology. They asked me how long I had been in Vientiane. When

I told them, one said: 'But you must be going to write a book. Journalists normally never stay more than twenty-four hours.'

There were rows of youthful soldiers hanging round the airport and the passport checkers and customs inspectors were, like those in Vientiane, in uniform, but the atmosphere was quite different. There were many more people around and a perceptible tension filled the air. I negotiated passport control and customs successfully and went outside in search of a taxi. There weren't any. In fact, there aren't any in Hanoi but, of course, I didn't know that. There was also no sign of the promised Vietnamese Tourism desk.

A young man with a fresh rosy face and an olive-green military-style jacket and jeans ran over and grabbed my suitcases. I followed him through the rain into the carpark and prepared to get into an old saloon car of indeterminate manufacture. He gestured instead towards a battered army jeep with a cracked windscreen where a thin boy with a pencil moustache sat behind the wheel. Before climbing in, I made a half-hearted attempt to discuss a price.

We set off in the pouring rain. I had been told to sit in the back and, as a result, could see almost nothing. The back of the jeep was shrouded in canvas without windows or slits and both halves of the front windscreen were so cracked it looked like a spider's web. The road was terrible, full of bumps and holes. The jeep had no suspension and I shivered and shook in the back.

After we had been driving for about twenty minutes, we stopped in a stretch of almost deserted countryside. The rain was lashing down. There were a couple of rusting oil drums by the side of the road and some miserable-looking figures huddling under a shelter made of sheets of thin plastic. The man who had seized my cases got out and, after a moment or two, came back and asked, by gestures, for money for petrol. I reached into my bag and pulled out five dollars. He indicated that was nothing like enough. I added another five dollars. His face clouded over and the driver produced a piece of paper on which he wrote '$30'. I wrote '$15'. They started shouting furiously and the fact that I clearly could not understand a word made no difference. The face of the first man was distorted by rage. It bore an expression of deep loathing and disgust as though I had committed some hideous

43

crime. He kept shaking his head, flaring his nostrils and curling his upper lip as if dismissing with incredulous revulsion what I was saying. I tried to be calm. I made soothing noises. I suggested that we go back to the airport and find out what the price should be. I didn't get angry. I didn't *feel* angry. I felt scared. Eventually I felt so scared that I handed over thirty dollars. The storm immediately abated and, under cover of darkness in the back of the jeep, I transferred my wad of dollars from my handbag to the inside pocket of my jacket. It was the first time I had felt the need to take any such precautions while travelling in South East Asia.

The first man climbed into the back of the jeep and sat next to me. I was still shaken by the speed and intensity of his anger and pretty frightened too. I had no idea where Hanoi was and how far we had to go. I didn't even know that we were going to Hanoi. I had been lulled by the warmth and courtesy of the Laos and had forgotten that the rest of the world wasn't like Vientiane. We set off again and the man next to me reached over and patted me on the knee. He wanted to draw my attention to a scratch on his hand which, he indicated, he had acquired while getting the petrol. The clear implication was that I was somehow to blame. He offered me a cigarette. I refused. He insisted. I refused again. I was determined in some small way not to make friends with him. He had frightened me and though I didn't want him to know that, I wasn't prepared to pretend that the scene by the roadside hadn't happened. He kept reaching across to touch my hand and showing me the cut on his hand. We stopped to pick up an old woman and a young man and I immediately felt better because I thought that with the old woman there I would be safer. They all talked together in fast jangling tones. At one point, I heard the words 'dollars' followed by much laughter. That made me feel worse again.

The drive seemed interminable. It went on and on over appalling roads. I was damp and beginning to feel cold and shivery, probably more from fear than anything else. I tried to peer through a gap in the canvas sideflaps but could see almost nothing, just the grey blur of a desolate unhappy landscape and some exhausted men and women slipping and sliding in the mud as they struggled under the weight of a pole at each end of which hung a basket full of bricks. We drove on over a couple of bridges. The old woman got out; then the young man, leaping into the oncoming traffic at a roundabout. I was left alone with the two men, still no clearer as to our whereabouts. The one next to me continued to stroke my hand and I smiled back, anxious to avoid another terrifying display of temper.

When we had been travelling for over an hour, the driver said: 'Hanoi,' and smiled. I had the name of a hotel, the Thong Nhat (Hotel of the Reunification) which had been the old Metropole where journalists usually stay and asked to go there. Another half-hour went by before the jeep juddered to a halt outside a large building whose windows were shuttered. I threw one of my bags to the ground and prepared to follow it. The driver got out of the jeep and replaced the bag on the front seat. Quite suddenly and without any warning, the man next to me went into his rage-and-disgust mode. It was extraordinary to behold. One minute he was patting my hand, the next he was gibbering like a lunatic. Having seen the performance before, I was not frightened by it. My fear had been replaced by anger. I was angry with myself for having been frightened and now I was angry with him for trying to frighten me. They wanted more money, a further ten dollars. I refused and indicated that we should go into the hotel to discuss the matter there. He made gestures to indicate drinking, then suitcase-carrying and finally pointed to the little scratch on his hand as if to say that he should be compensated for this injury. I stayed calm and firm. I opened the door of the jeep. They slammed the door shut. They produced a large piece of paper covered with calculations and waved it at me as proof that they were entitled to more money. Finally, I threw my camera bag out onto the pavement and started tugging at the rest of my luggage. At this point they gave up and the mask of fury was replaced by an amiable expression. My luggage was released and my captors drove off, waving cheerfully as if we had parted on the best of terms.

I staggered through the doors of the Thong Nhat into a large vaulted foyer, lit by one dim electric bulb. By now it was late afternoon and the light, such as it was through the rain, was beginning to fade. There was no-one about. After a few minutes

45

a boy appeared through a door behind the front counter and asked what I wanted.

'Do you have a room?'

'No, we haven't.'

'Please, you really must have a room somewhere.' The prospect of having nowhere to sleep in Hanoi was making me nearly hysterical.

'No, we have no rooms. You see, the hotel is closed for renovation.'

Rather in the manner of an exhausted Georgette Heyer heroine at the end of her tether, I sank down onto one of my suitcases and covered my face with my hands. The desk clerk came out from behind his desk and regarded me with interest and some sympathy.

'If you like, I can telephone the Hoa Binh hotel to see if there are any rooms there.'

The Hoa Binh (the Peace Hotel) had a room for one night only and I was advised to take it. We loaded me and my bags into a *cyclo* and I was wheeled to the hotel which was a couple of streets away. It was dark by now and Hanoi seemed even larger, immeasurably more urban than Vientiane. The streets were poorly lit though there were little pockets of yellow light around the stalls selling cigarettes or noodles. Despite the rain there were people squatting on the pavements and strolling in the roads, all clad in the same drab olive. I was reminded of the photographer Philip Jones Griffiths' description of the city: 'Hanoi, capital of basic living.'

The Hoa Binh must have been built in the 1930s. It lacked the shabby magnificence of the Thong Nhat but was not without charm. A graceful curving staircase led up off the foyer and a glass bead curtain with one of those angular art deco designs threaded into it hung across the entrance to the dining room. I was shown to one of the cheapest rooms in the place whose windows opened onto an unlit internal corridor. It contained two beds with blankets and mosquito nets concealed in flat presses behind the beds and a small bathroom smelling of warm damp. I arranged my possessions and went out into the night.

The experience in the jeep had shaken me. I only realised how much when I saw how I was reacting to all the other olive-green jeeps in Hanoi; I was keeping a nervous look-out for the spider's web windscreen and, instead of wandering through the streets in a relaxed and curious frame of mind, I was jumpy, on guard, ready to duck and run.

It was still raining and the city looked impossibly dreary. The large state-run department stores had little in them and all of it of poor quality: piles of unfashionable sweaters in horrible colours – salmon pink, lime-green and magenta – and massive nylon brassières with padded pointed foam cups which surely no Vietnamese woman could ever wear. There was something menacing too about the groups of youths in khaki lounging on the street corners: many of them had razor-blades hooked over their forefingers and were gently stroking their cheeks with them. I was too depressed to try and make a go of the evening and bought a bottle of Stolichnaya vodka for eleven dollars and returned to the hotel with the intention of drinking all of it or at least as much as I could manage before falling asleep. I was re-reading *Madame Bovary* and could look forward to a maudlin couple of hours.

Back at the Hoa Binh life was not much better. There was water cascading down the walls of the corridors and the stairwell, and around nine, the whole hotel began shaking with the sound of a loud mechanical roaring like the racket made by a power drill or electric sander. I went out into the corridor to find out what was happening but there was nothing to be seen. The noise grew closer and louder and people poured out of their rooms and started shouting. After twenty minutes or so of appalling noise two men appeared down the stairs, one of them carrying something that looked like a chainsaw. A dumpy little Englishman with spectacles and frizzy sandy hair who had emerged from a room near mine told me that they were spraying for insects. The fumigators disappeared down one of the hotel's interminable damp corridors and, after another half-hour, the din stopped.

Despite having drunk half the bottle of vodka diluted with hot water from the Thermos on the bedside table, it was difficult to get to sleep. I remembered Fowler, the English journalist in Graham Greene's *The Quiet American*, saying, ' . . . you can rot comfortably in the damp in Hanoi', but the sheets were almost wet and

I couldn't stop worrying about where I was going to spend the next few nights. When I finally managed to fall into an uneasy slumber, I was plagued by dreams. I dreamt that the poet James Fenton said to me: 'You see, I told you you wouldn't understand anything about Laos,' and that I bumped into the editor of *Tatler* magazine in the street. She looked at me in amazement and said: 'What do you mean you don't know a soul in Hanoi? I'm going to dinner at the British embassy tonight. Don't tell me you haven't been asked!'

By morning, the rain had stopped and the receptionist, a severe young woman with frosted talons and beautiful waist-length black hair, unbent sufficiently to tell me that I could keep my room till Sunday when I was due to leave. Over breakfast of bread and sweet black coffee, the waitresses in the art deco dining room taught me the Vietnamese for 'please' and 'thank you' and, armed with these phrases, I took a *cyclo* to Dong Xuan market.

In contrast to the drab shops of the previous evening, there was no shortage of goods on the market stalls. There were tee-shirts with pictures of Ho Chi Minh on them, frilly nylon dresses, rubber sandals, and jeans and more jeans. Denim had arrived in Hanoi with a vengeance. There were piles of cheap enamel plates and dishes with brightly-coloured flowers painted on them, heaps of baskets stacked together, huge Thermos flasks for hot water and precarious leaning towers of little green glasses for tea. There were tiny bright blue tricycles with the word 'Peugeot' painted on the seat, and flimsy cane furniture. There were little shops where you could have your photograph taken or your portrait drawn or buy a charcoal drawing of Clark Gable as Rhett Butler. There were stalls selling snakes and birds and small furry animals. Towards the end of the market there was a row of small dark antique shops selling ivory figurines, some very old and expensive though probably cheap for what they were. I was tempted by a little carving of a pekinese in ancient yellowed ivory for thirty-five dollars but said I'd come back some other time.

There was mud everywhere and people with tired resigned faces carrying cripplingly heavy loads hanging from wooden yokes balanced across their shoulders. You could tell when a load was particularly heavy because the carrier would trot along with a fast tripping little step, almost a run, as if slowing down would make it impossible for him to keep going. Despite the mud and the grime, it was possible to see how beautiful the buildings had once been. They reminded me of Macao: an architecture which effortlessly combined the Mediterranean with the oriental. They were coloured in faded pinks and blues and yellows. The people, by contrast, were almost all clad in olive, denim or black and not much given to smiling. There were a few blowzy Russian women pawing through the piles of clothing with eager hands. It made me wonder just how bad things must be in the Soviet Union.

I emerged from the labyrinth of little streets that make up the market to find myself facing a small lake with an exquisite little three-tier pagoda in the middle. This was Hoan Kiem Ho or the Lake of the Restored Sword. The story behind the name is a Vietnamese variation on the Arthurian legend of Excalibur. In 1418 Vietnam was once again under attack from its powerful Chinese neighbour. Le Loi, a wealthy landowner from Thanh Hoa province (who was later to become emperor of Annam – literally the 'pacified south', as northern Vietnam had been named by the Chinese – and the great hero of Vietnamese history), looked to the heavens for assistance. The tortoise of Hoan Kiem lake answered his prayers by presenting him with a magic sword that flashed lightning from its blade. Sword in hand, Le Loi saw off the invaders. Once the Chinese were gone, the tortoise swam to the surface of the lake, the sword promptly leapt from Le Loi's scabbard and vanished to the bottom of the lake.

I was standing admiring the view – the sun was squinting through the cloud and the lake was like a delicate misty water-colour – and thinking that perhaps Hanoi was not such a bad place after all when I felt two hands grab me hard from behind, one across my breasts, the other firmly clamped into my crotch. I caught a whiff of hot sour breath and experienced a moment of pure terror. I started violently and let out a shriek. In one swift panic-stricken movement, I flung the hands off me and whirled around. The man who now stood facing me looked like something from my worst nightmares, a character from a horror novel by

Stephen King. His clothes were torn and filthy beyond belief. His face had the heavy beaten-up look of a wino's with patchy mottled skin and his hair was matted and caked with dirt. He was laughing excitedly and rubbing his hands against his thighs. There were a number of sober elderly Vietnamese dressed in black sitting on the benches by the lakeshore. They looked with flat expressionless faces at me and at the madman. Nobody said anything or moved.

I turned away, my heart still pounding furiously, and walked briskly round the lake in the direction of a curved red wooden bridge. There were professional photographers every five yards or so with examples of their work displayed on easels: portraits of simpering young women with one hand coyly tucked under a cheek or trailing through a lock of hair or holding a single rose. There were couples at a chaste arm's length from each other on the benches under the willows and flamboyant trees, enjoying the lake and wondering where to pose for their photograph. It was a peaceful, almost idyllic, scene and I was beginning to wonder if I had imagined the lunatic.

By the time I reached the little bridge, my heartbeat had slowed to its normal pace and I stopped to look at some of the photographs. Suddenly I felt someone come up very close behind me and I turned quickly. There he was, sniggering, and panting like a dog. I ran towards the bridge, bought a ticket for 200 *dong* and hurried across, not daring to look over my shoulder.

The bridge led to a pretty little pagoda which doubled as an art gallery and café. Some small children were playing outside by an ornamental pond but as soon as they saw me, they demanded money and cigarettes. When I declined to give them either, they turned rather nasty. Hanoi was not proving much fun.

I went into the pagoda. It had a subdued, refined atmosphere: sticks of incense were burning at one end of the room and green tea was being drunk from little china cups. I wandered round, looking at the paintings. They were mainly scenes of everyday life in Vietnam: people working in the rice fields, wearing those 'mollusc' hats that shield the wearer from the sun, children astride water buffalo, processions of bicycles, houses with curved tiled roofs. There were pictures of beautiful women wearing *ao dais*, the long floating tunic and loose trousers that were the traditional costume of an earlier, easier age before the rigours of war and socialism decreed other garments more suitable for the new Vietnam. Some of the paintings were very good but what was more surprising was how romantic they were. Nowhere was there the grinding poverty that I had observed on the streets of Hanoi nor the devastated countryside nor the khaki and olive fatigues and the black pyjamas that most of the men and women wore. This was a Vietnam unwracked by war and indigence. These were perhaps dreams of Vietnam. And, despite the very local content of the subject matter, there was little of the oriental in the mood or style of the paintings. You could tell that they hadn't been painted by Europeans but they were somehow stylistically divorced from their origins.

A couple of young women came over to tell me the prices of the pictures. They seemed ridiculously cheap to me but most Vietnamese earn less than $180 a year and would be unlikely to have anything left over to spend on works of art, even at these prices. I was so grateful to have escaped from my persecutor that I bought two paintings: one on silk of two almond-eyed girls seated almost back to back, their graceful hands in the air and their faces blank against a background of peonies; and a little watercolour of a cat and kitten, a bold witty sketch with nothing of the kitsch or cute, a picture that Klee or Miro would have enjoyed. The pictures were packed up in a large flimsy makeshift envelope of brown paper and I set off back across the bridge with my unwieldy package dangling from my hand.

As I approached the little towers that guarded the bridge, I saw the madman skulking in the shadows. My nerve failed me completely and I fled like a bat out of hell across the grass to the road, hailed the first *cyclo* I saw, jumped into it and demanded to be returned to the safe haven of the Hoa Binh.

There I telephoned my only contact in Hanoi, a man called Adam Ford who was attached to the Swedish embassy and whose name had been given to me by the Swedish forestry expert in Laos. After three attempts, I managed to get through and, down a line so fogged by static that I might have been talking to Ulan Bator rather than somewhere in the same city, asked Dr Ford whether he had a few minutes to spare later that afternoon. He sounded busy and a little irritable but told me to come at three, adding that I should get a car to bring me: it was too far to go by *cyclo*.

Dr Ford was an extremely tall Englishman who spoke fluent Vietnamese and had a doctorate in Vietnamese studies. In a way, he was right to suspect me of wasting his time because my only reason for calling him was to have someone to complain to. He wasn't surprised by my account of my ride from the airport and, before I had a chance to describe the argument in the middle of nowhere, said: 'And then they demanded money with menaces from you?' as if it were an everyday occurrence. The incident by the lake was more unusual but he added briskly, 'Nothing like that has ever happened to me. Of course, that may be because I am a man, six foot four and speak perfect Vietnamese.' He said that he liked Hanoi and the North Vietnamese but agreed that the city could be intimidating. The people were desperately poor and suffered from massive over-crowding. Life was extremely tough. We talked in a desultory fashion about this and that but he was pressed for time and soon suggested that a possible solution to my unease in Hanoi might be found in a student from his English class who could show me around and practise the language at the same time.

I left Hanoi two days later but for the rest of my stay, I had Thuy, the pretty eighteen-year-old daughter of a journalist, by my side. We visited the mausoleum of Ho Chi Minh where the body of the great leader lies like a waxwork statue, with all the blood drained out of it, giving his skin a ghostly sheen like mother-of-pearl. We went to the zoo and to the Museum of Fine Arts where there was an enormous painting of a huge US marine towering over a tiny kneeling Vietnamese woman dressed in black. Nobody bothered me. As a farewell present I gave Thuy my copy of *Madame Bovary* and a biro with a view of the Houses of Parliament from the Thames and a boat that slid up and down when you shook it. In return she offered me a Vietnam version of *True Love Confessions* magazine but I told her to keep it.

In the evenings I sat cross-legged on my bed, drinking vodka and playing patience or reading *Sophie's Choice*, William Styron's depressing novel about concentration camps, often by torchlight.

The Hoa Binh had added to its repertoire by introducing random powercuts. One night I was awakened around four by the sound of something very heavy being bumped down the stairs and then dragged past my door along the corridor to the accompaniment of whispers and giggles. I didn't want to investigate. I went back to sleep and dreamt for the second time on the trip that my best friend's husband had died.

I got up early on Sunday morning and was taken to the airport in a minibus arranged by Air Vietnam. It cost ten dollars though the driver tried to persuade me to part with more when we got there. I presented my passport and prepared to leave. The uniformed boy behind the desk scowled and demanded to know why I hadn't registered with the authorities. I told him truthfully that I hadn't realised I was supposed to. He sent me off to talk to a man in another part of the airport and, for an awful moment, I thought that I wasn't going to be allowed to leave Vietnam. I imagined breaking down into floods of tears and begging the ugly little official on my knees to let me go. It wasn't necessary. I was fined fifteen dollars.

When I collected my luggage in Bangkok, I discovered that my rucksack had been rifled and that two packs of playing cards, an inflatable pillow and a *krama* which I had bought in the refugee camps on the Thai-Cambodian border had been stolen.

3

Saigon

I arrived at Tan Son Nhat airport in a thunderstorm. Madonna's *Like A Virgin* was playing in the customs hall and on the other side of the barrier were Mr Dang and Mr Nguyen. We got into a twenty-year-old blue Mazda and drove the eight kilometres from the airport to the city. The car windows didn't work and the rain splashed in onto my face. At the Caravelle hotel (renamed Doc Lap, meaning Independence, after 1975, but now generally known again by its old name), I was given a room at the back of the hotel looking out onto the air-conditioning plant and across to the windows of the hotel laundry. If I squinted to the right, I could just see the broad sweep of Boulevard Le Loi. The air-conditioning plant vibrated with a loud steady continuous hum.

Upstairs in the restaurant, we discussed, to the lugubrious accompaniment of a violin and piano duet, how I would like to spend my time in Vietnam. Mr Dang turned out to be from the Ho Chi Minh City branch of the Ministry of Information and Mr Nguyen was an assistant film producer who supplemented his income by acting as a translator for foreign journalists and television crews. He knew and profoundly admired the Australian journalist John Pilger.

Mr Dang was a fit-looking man in middle-age with a splendid set of very white teeth and I later discovered that he was a Kung Fu fanatic and given to asking women to punch him in the stomach to prove how strong he was. He was also an actor who had appeared in many films. He produced a newspaper cutting which described him as the Vietnamese Charles Bronson. Actually he looked much more like Klaus Maria Brandeur and, as I got to know him better, I noticed that he displayed the same careless arrogance and chauvinism with which the actor had endowed Blor Blixen in the film *Out of Africa*. I once asked him whether he had ever heard of Brandeur. He said he hadn't. He spoke no English but years of working with foreigners had left him perfectly capable of understanding almost everything I said and, for some odd reason, though I never managed to learn more than a few words of Vietnamese, I could usually guess what he was saying. Perhaps it had something to do with him being an actor. Nguyen (for some reason, I called him just by his name but Mr Dang was always *Mr* Dang) had a soft sad face with a straggly moustache and blackened teeth.

Despite repeated requests from both the Vietnamese embassy in London and the Ministry of Foreign Affairs in Hanoi, I had found it almost impossible to finalise what they called my programme. It was very difficult to get hold of recent practical information about Vietnam and, as a result, I had almost no idea about distances, flight or train times and costs. Journalists in Bangkok had warned me that Vietnam could be very expensive and that only cash in the form of US dollars was any use. I hadn't expected to be met at the airport since my last communication from the Press Department of the Ministry of Foreign Affairs had been a telegram sent to the Lone Pine hotel in Penang which read 'IMPOSSIBLE TO SEE YOU ON JUNE 27TH ON THE NAME OF MME THE LAN BEST REGARDS'. Even so, I had made a sort of list which included such well-known names as Dalat, Da Nang, Hue and Dien Bien Phu. The prospect of another visit to Hanoi was less appealing and I wanted to spend most of my time in the South.

We roughed out an itinerary which included, at Mr Dang's suggestion, a few days in the Mekong Delta, and then had an inconclusive conversation about money. It all looked set to cost a fortune and Mr Dang's blithe assurance that I could owe the Ministry of Information in Hanoi seemed likely only to pave the way to unlimited expenditure.

The money question was to dog me throughout my time in Vietnam. I was always conscious of the enormous gulf between my lot and theirs which rendered any discussion of money absurd and embarrassing. The nightly cost of my room at the Caravelle was more than the combined monthly salaries of Nguyen and his wife, Minh Phuong, who taught the piano at the Saigon Conservatoire. How could I begin to quibble with people who couldn't afford medical bills, who didn't have electricity, running water, lavatories? And yet I couldn't afford to splash money around: there weren't unlimited funds back in England.

That evening I went to the restaurant next door to the hotel. It was still drizzling and the Lam Son had a forlorn damp air with its faded green ironwork and green bamboo blinds pulled down against the rain. The big high-ceilinged room was almost empty, except for a table of noisy young drunks, and a piano tinkling sadly in the corner. A little man with white hair rushed over and asked me whether I wanted to dine '*à la française ou à la vietnamienne*'. I ordered *cha gio*, or *pâté impérial*, which turned out to be a large plate of delicious tiny spring rolls, and a Saigon beer. I was overwhelmed and a little exhausted by the novelty of it all and I ate slowly. The patron, Mr Thuan, returned to his seat at a table with three men, all drinking Black & White whisky. When I had finished my dinner, they asked me to join them. One of them, a man with a moustache and an expression of fierce concentration, said that he was a Customs Inspector at Tan Son Nhat airport.

'What mean "careless whisper"?' he asked.

'In what context?'

'What mean "We are the world"? What mean "my heart overflows"? What mean "Heaven can wait"?'

These phrases rang distant bells. They and others he wanted to know the meaning of were the titles or lyrics of songs by Wham, the Carpenters, the Bee Gees or Abba. He wanted to know about Karen Carpenter and why she had died so young. I said that she had been suffering from anorexia.

'What mean "anorexia"?' he asked.

'A disease in which the sufferer refuses to eat,' I said.

He looked puzzled. 'Why she doesn't want to eat?' he asked.

'Because she wants to be thin, she thinks she is too fat.'

As I struggled to explain and make sense of the bizarre western perception of self that would lead a person effectively to starve herself to death, I had a sense of *déjà vu* and remembered an incident in H.R.F. Keating's *Go West, Inspector Ghote* in which the Bombay detective has to go to California on a case. Soon after arriving, he sees a jogger on the Los Angeles freeway. He turns to his companion, a fat caricature of a Californian private detective, and asks what the man is.

' "Jogger," he said.

' "Please, what is a jogger?"

' "Jeez, Gan boy, where d'you come from? A jogger's a guy who needs to cut down on the flab. So he gets out there and buys himself a pair of running-shoes and some shorts from one of the stores especially for joggers and then he hits the road and pounds that extra flesh into the ground."

' "I see," Ghote said.

'He thought of asking whether it would not be better not to eat so much in the first place.'

We sat up late drinking whisky and a wine made from goats' testicles, or so they said, and puzzling over the English language. The Customs Inspector was Mr Thuan's son-in-law, married to one of his nine daughters. Mr Thuan, whose ninety-year-old father lived in France, had been in the restaurant business in Saigon since 1950. He said *'Entre les Français, les Japonais, les Américains et les Russes, les Français étaient les meilleurs parce qu'ils comprenaient les Vietnamiens. Les Américains ne comprenaient rien et les Russes sont gentils mais trop pauvres.'*

Mr Thuan introduced me to his friend, a teacher who used to work for the Americans. He whispered in my ear about the secret police whom, he said, you could recognise by their trousers – khaki with a thin stripe of red piping up the leg.

'Look,' he said, 'look at the men at that table over there. They're members of the secret police.'

I looked across at the table of young drunks. They all looked about sixteen and were indeed wearing khaki trousers with a red stripe. The teacher told me of a secret newspaper called *Résistance*. I asked to see a copy but he said it was too dangerous even to have in your possession. You read it and passed it on. If you were caught with it, the secret police would get you.

The Customs Inspector was a patriot, passionate in his love for his country – 'Everybody equal, everybody free in my country' – and his disapproval of western decadence. Madonna, he said, wrinkling his nose in disgust, was 'no good; very sexy, ugh', and I got the feeling that he didn't think I was much better. 'Divorce very bad, nothing like that ever happens in Vietnam.' Just to tease him I pointed out that Communism was collapsing all over Eastern Europe. He banged his fist on the table and changed the subject to Salman Rushdie. He made a pun on the word 'Rushdie' – Rush Die – saying 'Him want to die' and that Rushdie was being deliberately provocative. I tried to argue with him but he saw everything in black and white and wasn't receptive to the complexities of the Rushdie situation. But he saw nothing incongruous in his commitment to the party hardliners and his enthusiasm for the most sentimental of western pop singers and asked me to bring him a copy of *Love Story* and the theme music from Franco Zeffirelli's *Romeo & Juliet* next time I came to Saigon.

So much of Saigon is a question of contrasts. There is, for a start, the contrast between Saigon and Ho Chi Minh City. It is as if there are two cities with two distinct personalities. Saigon is a city of memory and the imagination, hinted at in the broad sweep of the boulevards, the rolling curves of the river and, above all, by the buildings: the *fin-de-siècle* absurdity of the Hôtel de Ville; the Opera House now reduced to showing videos; the newly painted gray-green-and-white façade of the nineteenth-century Continental Hotel, open again after being closed for years; even the hideous Saigon Floating Hotel, a great tub of a place all chrome and smoked glass, which had been towed all the way from Australia's Great Barrier Reef to wallow in the waters of the Saigon river opposite the statue of Tran Hung Dao, the thirteenth-century Vietnamese hero who withstood Mongol advances and is now worshipped as a god; even this monstrosity plays its part in creating a vision of Saigon. These buildings suggest not just the past: Saigon during the days of the French and the ghosts in the Rue Catinat over which Mr Phanh Keophilaphanh of Lao Air Booking would sigh nostalgically; Saigon during the war, teeming with soldiers, journalists and beautiful bar-girls in *ao dais*; but also a future Saigon, a nascent Bangkok or Manila. Meanwhile Ho Chi Minh City is a city on paper, a place created by the party ideologues and politicians, intent on imposing their will on the South Vietnamese. Everyone calls the city 'Saigon' in implicit rejection of the Hanoi government but, in the language of official-dom, it suddenly becomes Ho Chi Minh City. Even so, the board-ing passes issued by Air Vietnam read 'Saigon'.

But the images of neither city tell the full story. Phi, a *cyclo* driver who hung around outside the Caravelle looking for fares, offered to show me what he called the real Saigon. Phi's father was Chief of Police in Da Nang before 1975 and has been in prison since then. This puts Phi into the large group of South Vietnamese whose chances of getting on in the world in which they live are slim.

Phi took me to a slum called Dong Thien situated in a wasteland somewhere between Saigon and Cholon, the Chinese sector of Ho Chi Minh City. We waded through scenes of unimaginable squalor and poverty. Here, in an area less than a mile square, over 3,000 people were crammed together in fragile thatch-and-bamboo huts. They were, Phi said, mostly refugees from the so-called New Economic Zones which had been established by the Communists after 1975 in the highland regions and in areas which had fallen out of use through war-time destruction, in an attempt to alleviate the massive unemployment and overcrowding that occurred after the American withdrawal. But the New Economic Zones had left the people disorientated and dissatisfied and gradually a number of them had crept back to Saigon with no option other than to settle in filthy and depressing conditions like these. Dong Thien was the worst place I had ever been. By comparison, the refugee camps on the Thai-Cambodia border seemed oases of civilisation, cleanliness and order. I have never wanted to get out of anywhere so badly as I wanted to leave Dong Thien and yet I couldn't run away.

There were people tugging at my sleeve on every side. Phi was indefatigably cheerful in the face of all this human misery, his face like a bright sparrow's as he pointed to yet another starving baby, yet another mutilated man – evidence that all was not well in Ho Chi Minh City. Children with runny noses and who were covered in open sores crowded round. I felt like a reluctant Pied Piper. There was the corpse of an old woman lying, curled like a foetus, in the rain. A woman asked me to take her newborn baby, saying that she couldn't afford the rice to feed it – or herself.

In a hut in the middle of the slum were three good-looking teenagers, smoking cigarettes and blowing smoke rings. They were unusually tall for Vietnamese – but then they weren't really Vietnamese, they were Amerasians, the children of American servicemen. One had green eyes and another, a girl, dark skin and a mane of frizzy hair. Their bodies revealed the good food and strong genes of their fathers and they looked healthy, unlike everyone else. In a society where everyone had straight black hair and black eyes, the Amerasians were disconcertingly different. They were also, in the phrase of one writer, 'wearing history on their faces'. These ones told me that they were going to the United States to find their fathers in a couple of months – or maybe a year.

A man who spoke good English and used to interpret for the Americans asked me if I would write about Dong Thien, if I could help them. But the next day, Mr Dang and Nguyen said that they had never heard of the place.

I asked to visit the Amerasian Centre. At the height of the war, there were nearly half a million American servicemen stationed in Vietnam and they made their mark in more ways than one. Since 1980 approximately twelve and a half thousand Amerasians have gone to America (the Orderly Departure Programme was set up in 1982 and the Amerasian Homecoming Act passed in 1987) and in January 1990, an Amerasian centre was formally established to process applications. The Centre received eighty dollars a head for each successful applicant. No-one knew exactly how many Amerasian children were born but it is thought to have been between thirty and forty thousand.

The Centre was a dusty modern building some distance from downtown Saigon. It cost $800,000 to build, $500,000 of which was contributed by the United States Foreign Ministry. Stupidly I was expecting to see children but, of course, all bona-fide Amerasians were conceived before the American withdrawal in 1972 and are now young adults, most of them aged between twenty and twenty-four. Those who are over twenty-six require 'closer scrutiny'. I was told by an amused official of one man aged thirty-four who gave a French name when asked what his father was called. He was sent away.

There is an average of 800–1,000 Amerasians in the Centre at any one time. They were lounging around with the sort of watchful indolence you expect to find on street corners and there was, or so I thought, an atmosphere of suppressed anticipation. These were people waiting for a future.

Once the successful applicant had been processed, the Amerasian would wait for a flight to the Philippines where he or she would spend five to six months preparing for life in America. Over 8,000 Amerasians had already gone to the Philippines in the six months since the Centre had been open. In an upstairs room, Dr Robert McKelvey, a child psychiatrist and former marine who was stationed in Da Nang during the war, was conducting a series of tests and interviews designed to demonstrate that Amerasians have special problems and therefore special needs. Amerasians in Vietnam, he said, were often discriminated against and discouraged from attending school. To be an orphan or fatherless is difficult enough in any society but Vietnamese family relationships are, roughly speaking, comparable to Sicilian ones – without the fierce code of vengeance. The father is all-important and ancestor worship is widely practised, co-existing harmoniously with other religions like Buddhism or Catholicism. Frances Fitzgerald wrote, 'As the whole society was modelled on the family, so every relationship . . . was analogous to the primary one between father and son. The nature of that primary bond was at the heart of the Vietnamese *terra incognita* . . . In the Confucian world filial piety was the key to all wisdom and virtue.' Though the traditional Confucian world order, and with it the family structure, have been undermined and fragmented by the war and earlier by the French determination to exploit both the land and its people, enough remains of the Vietnamese concept of family and its importance to leave the Amerasian, without a father and with his features proclaiming his unhappy parentage, a kind of leper, a fish out of water.

Dr McKelvey was surrounded by people who were laboriously completing forms with questions like 'What do you expect to happen to you when you reach the United States?' The answer would often be 'My father will take care of me'. The reality is that most of them do not know who their fathers are and less than five per cent of those who have already reached America have succeeded in making contact with their father. A crippled girl dragged herself across the room to ask him for help with her form and I wondered how welcome she would be when she finally made it to Chicago or San Francisco.

Outside I stopped to talk to a half-black girl of twenty who showed me a photograph and a letter from her mother, torn and crumpled from many readings. Her mother and full-blooded Vietnamese younger brother and sister had gone to America twelve years before and she had received regular letters until 1988. Suddenly the letters stopped. The girl said, 'We have heard there has been a big earthquake in California and I think maybe my mother was killed.' I pointed out that the envelope was postmarked Seattle, Washington, and that it was impossible for the Californian earthquake to have touched her mother. She asked, 'Then why haven't I heard from her?'

One Sunday we went to Vung Tau. Mr Dang drove like Toad of Toad Hall, hooting, swerving, braking and overtaking blindly all the way. Despite the appalling condition of the roads and the constant procession of people, bicycles, water buffalo and pigs, we covered the hundred and twenty-five kilometres in an hour and a half. Mr Dang had insisted that we leave at seven so, when we got there by 9.30, I could not imagine what we were going to do for the rest of the day.

Vung Tau, which the French called 'Cap Saint Jacques', is a small pretty town built on a peninsula to the south-east of the bottom right-hand corner of Vietnam. It looks out to the South China Sea and across to the Spratly Islands to which, along with the Paracel Islands further north up the coast, both Vietnam and China lay hotly-contested claim. It was popular as a seaside resort with the French who also used the nearby islands of Con Dao, or Poulo Condore, as a huge and brutal penal colony where Vietnamese nationalists were kept imprisoned. Con Dau continued to be used for political prisoners during the American-backed regime of President Ngo Dinh Diem in the 1950s and early 1960s and today there is a little museum in Vung Tau full of photographs of the emaciated and exhausted victims.

In a drawer in my room at the hotel, I had found a picture postcard of a crowded beach. It showed rows of people sunbathing in deckchairs under coloured umbrellas and a violet sea crammed with swimmers. It was a picture of one of the beaches in Vung Tau. The guide book said that people went in droves from Saigon to the coast at weekends but this Sunday, the place was almost empty.

I was dazed from the drive. Mr Dang's style of chauffeurship was neither relaxing nor conducive to sightseeing. The countryside had sped by, a blur of vivid colour: the brilliant green of the rice fields; the gold of the mounds of harvested paddy drying by the roadside; the pale blue of the watery oases of the shrimp farms; the elephant grey of the water buffalo in the cool green of a rubber plantation. There were occasional hideous modern pagodas and occasional charming dusty Chinese temples sprouting dragons' heads. Nguyen was reading a novel by Sidney Sheldon called *Master of the Game*, a fat paperback carefully protected by a brown paper jacket. Between its pages impossibly rich people flew around the world in Lear jets. They commuted between South Africa and New York and went to Paris, Rome and Monte Carlo for breakfast. They talked about diamond mines and billion-dollar deals and wore designer clothes and ate extravagant meals. Improbable though it seems, Sheldon has a following in Vietnam. In *Brothers in Arms*, William Broyles writes of his guide saying how much he likes Sidney Sheldon because ' . . . he is very good on the excesses of capitalism'.

I think Nguyen just longed for the excesses of capitalism. He loved the glamour of Sheldon's characters and their lives. He had seen the movie of *The Other Side of Midnight* and his eyes would grow misty as he relived the intricacies of the plot. I told him that I had once had lunch with Sheldon and that the writer had said that he never described anything that he hadn't personally experienced – except presumably the deviant sex and murder that feature in most of his novels. Every mouthful of Iranian caviar, *foie gras* or hand-reared baby this or that; every sip of vintage Bollinger or Château Lafite 1953; every caress of silk or cashmere or sable, he claimed personally to have sampled just to give his writing the right note of authenticity. Nguyen slowly turned the pages of *Master of the Game* with even greater reverence.

While Mr Dang waited below, Nguyen and I climbed a small steep hill covered with Buddhas. Vietnamese Buddhists practise Mahayana Buddhism (the Greater Vehicle), while in Laos and Cambodia, Theravada, or Hinayana, Buddhism (the Lesser Vehicle) is the religion of choice. Mahayana, the 'northern school' of Buddhism, spread historically from India to Nepal, Tibet, Mongolia, China, Korea, Japan and northern Vietnam. Theravada, the 'southern school' or 'southern family', spread from India to Sri Lanka, Burma, Thailand, Cambodia and Laos and strictly follows the words of Gautama Buddha. The Mahayana insists on broader interpretations and is more eclectic: Theravada venerates only the Buddha himself as the founder of the religion and considers Mahayana, with its worship of *bodhisattva* (men, lay or ecclesiastical, who had become Buddhas-to-be but who compassionately helped others to reach Nirvana before entering it themselves) to be idolatrous. Theravadins practise religious devotion to save themselves; Mahayanists to save themselves and others. Mahayana tends to allow laymen and women a greater role in its religious community than does Theravada, which insists on strict separation between monks and lay people. Theravada monks in Laos and Cambodia wear saffron robes and accept alms for their food, while Mahayana monks in Vietnam wear brown robes and do not accept alms. Mahayana Buddhism traditionally plays a far less important part in Vietnamese society than Theravada Buddhism does in Lao or Cambodian society. This is partly because the values of Confucian familism and filial piety (which required the procreation of sons to continue the family and its ancestor worship) made monasticism less popular in Vietnam than in the neighbouring countries. The Theravadins regard their religion as the purest form of Buddhism.

I couldn't properly comprehend all the differences between the two strands of Buddhism but it didn't take long for me to warm to Theravada. For a start, the art and architecture associated with Mahayana Buddhism – at least in its Vietnamese incarnation – were generally crude and unappealing. Perhaps many of the older and more beautiful pagodas were destroyed during the war but many of the Vietnamese temples looked as if they should carry a stamp saying 'Made in Taiwan'.

In Vung Tau there are 114 temples and pagodas but the jewel in the city's religious crown was clearly Niet Ban Tinh Xa meaning 'Nirvana'. The hill was liberally scattered with statues of all shapes and sizes: gleaming white Buddhas squatting serenely in pink marble lotus blossoms and gazing tolerantly down at huge white plaster elephants uncomfortably prostrate, their tree-trunk legs splayed in all directions; displays of twelve-foot goddesses, monkeys, even a couple of horses complete with bridle and saddle. The approach, in somewhat grotesque contrast, was festooned with beggars, many were limbless war veterans and others were ancient women cradling tiny babies. As we got out of the car, Mr Dang spoke sharply to Nguyen who, in turn, told me firmly that I was not to give any of them any money.

At the top of the hill was a hexagonal stone column with inscriptions carved in Vietnamese, English and Chinese on each side. One side read:

> The glory of him who is energetic
> Mindful pure in deed. Considerate
> Self-controlled right-living
> And heedful steadily increases

Another inscription read:

> Calm is his mind, calm is his speech
> Calm is his action, who rightly knowing
> Is wholly freed perfectly peaceful and
> Equi poised

When we descended from the hill of Nirvana, having re-run the flesh-and-blood gauntlet of human misery on the steps, we found Mr Dang sitting in a small café surrounded by girls to whom he was showing photographs of himself in his various film roles. The girls were cooing like turtle doves and giggling behind their hands. Mr Dang never went anywhere without these pictures and also never missed an opportunity to get them out of his briefcase and pass them round. Mr Dang enjoyed three things in life: food, women and attention, and an ideal outing was one which combined all three pleasures. He never accompanied Nguyen and me into a temple, a villa or a museum, but when we emerged stupefied with culture and heat he was always to be found installed in a comfortable low chair with two or three women in attendance, showing them his snaps and signing autographs.

We drove on to the Villa Blanche, up a winding drive through a cool tunnel of overhanging trees. The Villa was a beautiful big white two-storey building fringed with bougainvillaea and frangipani. It had masses of windows, the better to see the spectacular view, but these were all shuttered now to give the house a curious blank air. There was a frieze of art nouveau tiles running round the top of the building and on the terrace, beyond which gaped an endless vista of sky and sea blues, a little girl pirouetted with an umbrella. The umbrella was a rich royal blue and it blended agreeably with the other blues.

The Villa Blanche was built in the 1920s and used as a summer house by the last emperor of the Nguyen dynasty, Bao Dai, and later by Nguyen Van Thieu whose presidency of South Vietnam oversaw the republic's death throes. We took off our shoes and went inside. Downstairs, spread over what had once been state apartments, was an exhibition documenting the development of the Vietnamese/Soviet petroleum plant which was now Vung Tau's principal *raison d'être* and had made the town rich. There were endless photographs of small smiling Vietnamese shaking hands with stocky smiling Soviets, exchanging promises of mutual co-operation and eternal friendship, and a model of the plant itself complete with miniature drilling rigs, rafts, buoys and cranes.

We had lunch in a fly-blown restaurant at the seaside, over-looked by an enormous statue of the Virgin Mary, her arms outstretched to the water. We ate fried squid with lime and salt, and a soup made of aubergine and eel. Afterwards, while Mr Dang and Nguyen snoozed, replete, in deckchairs facing the sea, I walked along the beach, looking at the fishing boats. There were a few plump Russians under big umbrellas and some teenage boys whizzing up and down the coast on water scooters. A slender Vietnamese woman in a black bathing suit was lying alone in the shallows of the waves and a small boy was hunting for shrimp or sand crabs in a rock pool. The sea looked clean enough and stretched all the way to Borneo. Mr Dang woke up and professed to be disappointed that I was not intending to swim. He said that he wanted to see me in my bathing suit.

We returned to Saigon much as we had left it. As we entered the city and crossed the bridge over the Saigon river by the museum commemorating the life and times of Ho Chi Minh, it began to pour. The rain blew in through the open windows and the traffic on the bridge grew worse than ever. Mr Dang was hooting and braking as always, weaving in and out of traffic, often driving directly at oncoming traffic, often overtaking three or four things at a time so that he would be overtaking a car overtaking a motorbike overtaking a bicycle overtaking a pedestrian. Suddenly he braked hard and I looked ahead out of the window. In the middle of the bridge, a young man lay in the road, a dark-red pool of blood about two feet long seeping from his head. His Honda lay on its side next to him. Nguyen said: 'He's dead' and then, 'Forget it.'

That evening I went to mass in Saigon Cathedral. Notre-Dame de Saigon, a large romanesque red-brick edifice with twin bell-towers, lies at one end of Dong Khoi Street. Dong Khoi, formerly the famous Rue Catinat, then Tu Do (Freedom) Street, was re-named after *dong khoi*, the synchronised uprisings that were launched at the end of 1959 by the Communists against Diem and the Americans in the Mekong Delta and the hill country of central Vietnam. Once regarded as the most beautiful street in the city, if not in all Indo-China, it runs through the heart of central Saigon, from the cathedral down to the banks of the river. It is lined with little restaurants, tailors displaying embroidered silk blouses on dummies with improbably pointed breasts, and antique shops mostly selling lovely old Swiss watches dating from the 1940s and 1950s: Rolex, Jaeger-le-Coultre, Omega, Patek Phillippe – all, according to the not entirely truthful claims of the shopkeepers, in perfect working order. Some of the shops have odd pieces of Lalique glass or art nouveau cutlery with fantastic traceries etched into the handles, all hinting at a past infinitely more easeful and luxurious than the present. Others sell bits of sculpture looted from ruined temples and almost certainly not supposed to leave the country. In one, just around the corner from the Caravelle Hotel, I found a little gilded wooden Buddha, reclining on his side, one hand tucked beneath his head, an expression of serene indifference on his faded featurers. It was a fragment of a larger carving, broken off, perhaps, from a pagoda door and probably Khmer; it seemed too delicate, too relaxed, to be Vietnamese.

Outside the cathedral, hundreds of bicycles were parked. There were inert bodies in the doorways, often looking like nothing more than bundles of old rags. Inside, the church was packed with the faithful, rising and falling to the mumbled instructions of Nguyen Van Binh, the Bishop of Saigon, a tall man in crimson vestments with a dove embroidered on the back, and flanked by a bevy of robed acolytes. There were candles, incense, a choir, confessionals and little altars at the foot of each of the twelve Stations of the Cross. Communicants, returning to their seats, would stop off at one of these to kiss the bleeding feet of the crucified Christ.

Christianity was formally introduced to Vietnam by the Jesuits in the early seventeenth century. In the second half of the sixteenth century, French monks, Dominicans and Augustinians, from Macao and Manila, had paid brief visits but it wasn't until the Jesuit fathers established a mission just south of Da Nang at Faifo (now called Hoi An) that Catholicism took root in Vietnam. The French Jesuit, Alexandre de Rhodes, likened Vietnamese – a tonal language– to the sound of 'twittering birds' and devised *quoc ngu*, the romanisation of the Vietnamese written language, which had previously been written in Chinese characters. This new written language was used in the printing of prayerbooks, doctrines and catechisms, which facilitated the spread of Christianity thanks to those missionaries who had succeeded in mastering *quoc ngu.*

Unlike in Laos and Cambodia, the Catholic Church met with great success in seventeenth-century Vietnam where it left a deeper imprint than on any other Asian country apart from the Philippines which Spain governed for four hundred years. Both in the North and the South, hundreds of thousands of Vietnamese of all levels of society, embraced Christianity. Local merchants were eager to ingratiate themselves with Western traders and the peasants took to the new faith, seeing in it freedom from the traditional Confucian system and its oppressive mandarins. Entire districts converted. Centuries later, in 1946, many of these fought against both the French colonial forces and the Communist-led Vietminh nationalists. And in 1954, following the French defeat at Dien Bien Phu and the establishment of a Communist government in North Vietnam, whole Catholic villages fled south, attracted by the apparently more congenial regime of Ngo Dinh Diem – whose ancestors, like their own, had been converted to Christianity centuries before.

After the French defeat and the Geneva Accords of the same year, in which Vietnam was partitioned into a Communist North and a non-Communist South (supposedly only for two years after which free general elections were to be held: thanks to Diem and his American backers, these never took place), an armistice was signed by both sides. This included a provision for the movement of civilians between the re-groupment zones south and north of the 17th parallel within a three-hundred day-period. During this time, approximately one million people followed the French south. Many were Catholic peasants. By 1988, the number of Vietnamese Catholics was estimated at five million or six per cent of the population.

One morning we drove to Cholon, stopping en route to look at the Church of St Francis Xavier where, in November 1963, Diem and his brother Nhu, took refuge before being assassinated. We were going to look at Chua Ba, an old Chinese temple. 'The oldest in the city', said Nguyen. Barren women or those who have borne only daughters come here to pray for better luck. Inside there was a faint musty smell and the atmosphere was heavy with smoke from the joss-sticks stuck into bowls of sand and the large conical spirals of incense hanging from the ceilings. Small strips of scarlet paper, inscribed in black Chinese characters with the names of the dead, hung limply in the humid air and a pair of hundred-year-old tortoises staggered around on the floor. Outside in the street a woman was selling little wicker cages full of tiny birds for people to set free for good luck and to acquire spiritual merit. I bought a cageful, ten birds for 5,000 *dong* (less than one dollar) and set about releasing them, an experience both pleasurable and painful. Pleasurable because of the excitement of playing God and seeing them fly off; painful because I knew they would just be recaptured and imprisoned again.

The first time I had come across this custom was in 1987. I was in Chiang Mai with a journalist friend and a man selling tiny birds in individual cages shaped like purses and made of fine strips of bamboo came into the café where we were sitting. I borrowed 500 *baht* and bought every bird he had. The café owner offered to grill them for me. We went outside to where there were some trees and I started to undo the first cage. At first, all the little birds were very quiet. Then, when one had been freed and the others guessed what was in store, they started chirruping furiously.

Back in Bangkok later that evening, in the Lipstick Bar in Patpong surrounded by pretty young bar-girls all chattering to each other in tinkly voices, I started crying. My journalist friend was supposed to be researching a story on an attempt by some of the girls to form a union and we had gone to meet the woman who was mobilising them. I was upset by the sight of the girls; some of whom looked no older than twelve, enveloped by fat German businessmen with huge beer bellies and arms like tentacles. As we walked away from the bar, away from the flashing lights and disco music of Patpong, I said to him: 'You see, they remind me of those little birds. I'd like to set them free, like the birds.'

The range and diversity of religions in Vietnam certainly added to the interest of the place but unfortunately I wasn't allowed to visit Tay Ninh, site of the headquarters of the most colourful and bizarre of the four main faiths practised in the country. This was Cao Daism, invented in 1919 by a civil servant in what used to be known as Cochin China. (In the nineteenth century the French divided Vietnam into three parts: Tonkin in the north and Annam in the centre were protectorates; Cochin China in the south was a colony.) Today Cao Daism commands a following of two million throughout South Vietnam. Both Graham Greene and Norman Lewis wrote hilarious accounts of expeditions to the Cao Dai headquarters at Tay Ninh, featuring a Pope, female cardinals, a cathedral which combined the worst elements of Disneyland and the Hammer House of Horrors and more. The Cao Dai symbol is the Masonic eye of God, all-seeing, all-powerful; they worship all the world's religious leaders from Buddha to Jesus Christ and their calendar of saints includes such unlikely figures as Victor Hugo, Joan of Arc, de la Rochefoucauld, the Jade Emperor and Sun Yat-Sen. Mr Thuan's Customs Inspector son-in-law had made various enigmatic references to Victor Hugo and I wouldn't have put it past him to swallow all this nonsense but his interest turned out, predictably, to be to do with the musical, *Les Misérables*.

Tay Ninh is up near the Cambodian border and a couple of months before my arrival an American journalist, Michael Morrow, had been arrested, detained and then expelled, allegedly for stealing Vietnamese secret documents and smuggling them across the border into Cambodia. Mr Dang shook his head and said we would have to give Tay Ninh a miss.

The last of the four main religions in Vietnam, the Hoa Hao, is far less exotic than the Cao Dai. Named after a village in the Mekong Delta, the Hoa Hao emerged in 1939 as a brand of reform Buddhism invented by Huynh Phu So, a faith healer reputedly endowed with prophetic gifts. The simplicity of the sect proved irresistible to thousands of poor peasants who today still comprise its main following, estimated at one and a half million, in the western Mekong Delta.

I had two introductions in Saigon: both tentative and both to women. One was to Dr Hoa, the other to Madame Dai. Dr Duong Quynh Hoa was the director of the paediatric centre in Saigon. Her father had taught at a French *lycée* in Saigon and she herself studied medicine in Paris where she joined the French Communist Party. In 1954, back in Saigon, she became part of the resistance against Diem and was afterwards appointed Deputy Minister of Health in the Provisional Revolutionary Government, hiding in the jungles. Madame Dai was a lawyer trained in Paris after World War Two and a dissident member of Thieu's National Assembly. During the war, she provided asylum for members of the resistance. After 1975, she turned her former law library into a restaurant which she called La Bibliothèque. Both women were elderly but full of vigour and disdain.

Dr Hoa discoursed briskly on health problems in Vietnam. She ran through the usual depressing litany of Third World diseases and disaster: malnutrition, diarrhoea, tuberculosis, syphilis. The quality of care was mediocre, people ate too much rice and noodles: they lacked protein and fats. In the south, the situation was worse in the towns; in the north, in the countryside.

'But Vietnam,' she continued, 'cannot formulate a logical development policy as long as it feels menaced by the threat of the Khmer Rouge and China. Only when a solution has been found to the Cambodian problem will Vietnam be able to stop having a war economy.'

I called on Madame Dai late one afternoon. She was upstairs having a siesta but descended briefly, in a lilac silk kimono, to suggest that I return later that evening when the restaurant was open.

By then I had Kim Fork in tow. Fork was a Chinese Malaysian businessman who telephoned me in my room at the Caravelle one morning after I returned, battered and dripping with sweat from a couple of hours in the maelstrom of Cho Ben Thanh market, my ears ringing with a Vietnamese version of the country and western hit, *Rhinestone Cowboy*, and my nostrils filled with the rich rotten reek of durian.

Durian is a very large, oval fruit with a thick woody rind,

looking a little like a pineapple, and a soft custard-like flesh. It has such a strong smell that it is not permitted on planes in the East but it is regarded as a great delicacy. I was once invited to a durian party in Penang to sample the new season's crop and spent the rest of the evening trying both to get the taste out of my mouth and to work out what that taste was. I eventually came up with rotten Irish stew. 'Durian smell like hell, taste like heaven,' a Thai friend used to say. I have never learnt to like durian despite Anthony Burgess's apparent insistence that it was the test of a true orientalist.

'Stewart?' said a voice straight out of Wodehouse or Noël Coward.

'Ye-es,' I answered.

'Stewart, it's Fork here. Kim Fork. They told me at the front desk that you're an English writer and I wondered if we could get together for a drink. It would be so marvellous to have some civilised conversation. We could stroll across to the Continental. It's the only decent place in town, don't you agree?'

I was very keen to see inside the Continental but hadn't yet plucked up the courage to go alone. We agreed to meet downstairs in the lobby at five o'clock.

Kim Fork turned out to be the tall good-looking man whom I had seen in the coffee shop of the hotel, deep in a conversation being conducted through an interpreter. I had caught odd phrases and sometimes whole sentences: 'one million US dollars'; 'live seafood restaurant'; 'computerised speaking lift'; 'the sticking point is price' and 'no-one in slippers will be allowed in'. They were, I think, discussing building a new hotel and, by the sound of it, one aimed exclusively at affluent foreign guests. This and other such deals are all part of the fall-out from the government's *doi moi* or 'Renovation' policy which, in 1986, legalised capitalism and encouraged private enterprise in order to try to rescue the country's collapsing economy.

We walked across Lam Son Square, skirting the beggars and *cyclo* drivers, and through the double plate-glass doors of the Continental. The Continental, by name and reputation at least, ranks with the great old romantic hotels of Asia: Raffles in Singapore, the E. & O. in Georgetown, the Strand in Rangoon and the Oriental in Bangkok. Most of these have had the charm refurbished out of them: the Strand alone sits grubbily in Rangoon, a testament to past and better days, though it too will be given a face-lift if and when Burma emerges from its current political chaos. And now the Continental, immortalised by Somerset Maugham and Graham Greene, and still the nostalgic focus of a thousand foreign correspondents' daydreams, has gone under the developers' knife and lacks any soul at all.

We drank imported beer and then Scotch, and Kim Fork complained about the Vietnamese and the difficulties of doing business in Vietnam. He was, he said, appalled and astonished by the state of the country as a whole and the lack of good restaurants in Saigon in particular. He showed me photographs of himself playing polo at the Selangor Polo Club with Dr Mahathir, the tyrannical right-wing Malaysian Prime Minister. His English was perfect and his accent uncanny but he kept calling me 'Stewart' which I didn't much like. I asked him why and was told that he had looked at the hotel register where I had written 'Stewart, Lucretia' and assumed that Stewart was my first name.

It was time for dinner. We left the Continental and walked slowly up Dong Khoi. It was early evening and not yet dark, that lovely time of day when the light softens and everything looks rosy and beautiful. I thought of Marguerite Duras' exquisite little novel, *L'Amant*, set in Saigon in the 1930s, in which she writes, 'It's a city of pleasure that reaches its peak at night. And night is beginning now, with the setting sun.' There were swallows swooping and gliding overhead in the violet sky and the tamarind trees cast long shadows over the worn shopfronts. We passed the bookshop selling Russian and Vietnamese books and teach-yourself courses in spoken English. At the back of the shop were old volumes in French and English: copies of *Bonjour Tristesse* in the *Livre de Poche* edition; a story called *L'Aventure du Clan de Sept* by Enid Blyton; Henri Parmentier's guide to Angkor, and potted histories of Vietnam written while the war was still going on. The old man who ran this section usually had to be summoned to serve from where he lay dozing in a hammock strung between two pillars, but he would let me borrow mystery stories left behind by the Americans. I asked to keep Ross Macdonald's *The Instant Enemy* in a hardback first edition (1966) that had come from the United States Special Forces library in Soc Trang and gave him some shiny new paperbacks from Bangkok in return.

The street was full of bicycles and little motorbikes, often carrying entire families. *Cyclos* were not allowed in Dong Khoi. Some of the women were wearing wonderful outfits: loose flowered pyjamas, like those designed by Pucci in the 1960s, 'mollusc' hats fastened under the chin with pieces of net so they looked like Edwardian veiled driving hats, and elbow-length gloves. I had asked Nguyen about these gloves and he said, 'They don't want their hands to be black.' At first I thought he meant dirty but then understood that it was a suntan and the resulting dark skin, which denotes social inferiority, that they were anxious to avoid.

Madame Dai was out but a man with a long face like a charming donkey showed us to a table. He said that he had worked for the *New York Times* during the war and used to be known as the Vietnamese Dith Pran (Dith Pran was journalist Sydney Schanberg's Cambodian assistant about whom the film, *The Killing Fields*, was made). He said that I reminded him of Frances Fitzgerald and that he had spent many evenings with her and Kevin Buckley, the *Newsweek* correspondent at the time. I was reading her book, *Fire In The Lake*, and was flattered.

While we waited for Madame Dai, we talked in a room full of old law books. He was a sad man and I felt that his life now was neither easy nor happy and that he was nostalgic for the past.

'Do you know Gloria Emerson?' he asked.

'Not personally. By name and reputation, yes.'

'She was very tough. She wanted to keep up with the men. I worked for her. Very strong lady.'

I asked him about his life now.

'There is an old Vietnamese saying: "When the water buffalo and the cow are fighting, the casualties are flies and mosquitoes". So, as flies and mosquitoes, we try to keep away.'

Dinner at Madame Dai's was the most expensive meal I had in all Vietnam – crayfish with mayonnaise, Russian salad and cold white Burgundy – but worth every penny and, anyhow, Kim Fork insisted on paying. In a dark corner of the restaurant, sitting very close together, was an odd couple. He was a bulky Russian with a gold chain and medallion round his neck; she was Vietnamese and had clearly made an effort for the occasion. Her face was extravagantly painted, almost like a Noh actor, chalk-white with purple wings of eyeshadow, blusher like a slap across both cheeks and crimson lipstick. Her outfit matched: wobbly stilettos and an off-the-shoulder dress with a low ruched neckline and a skirt in layers like an emerald-green lamé artichoke. I wished that she had been wearing an *ao dai*, discreetly buttoned at the neck and infinitely more alluring.

Madame Dai made her entrance when we were halfway through the crayfish and came to sit next to me. She was a small plump woman in her late sixties, impressive and slightly terrifying: a confident feminist, highly intelligent, educated and articulate. She had worked all her life, was married to a man whom she freely admitted she didn't have much time for, and had not seen her two children – who were in America – for twenty-two years. There was an instant rapport between us and we fell into a long conversation that ranged far and wide. We talked about love and marriage and the differences between the sexes and what men want and what women want. We talked in French and Kim Fork sat by in silence. I had a soft spot for Nguyen and was amused by Mr Dang but it was wonderful to have a proper conversation.

Having observed Mr Dang, who was married with five children, in action, I was curious about the combination of prudishness and licentiousness that seemed characteristic of much of Vietnamese life. On the one hand, videos showing the Lambada were banned because they might inflame young people ('That might be okay in your country, but not in Vietnam,' Nguyen had observed, with a prim look); on the other, it was apparently perfectly all right for Mr Dang to be forever on the look-out for what Nguyen would euphemistically term a 'girlfriend'. Every waitress was fair game.

'All men are unfaithful, all men have mistresses,' declared Madame Dai, 'but Vietnamese women are very jealous, like tigresses. Still the position of women in Vietnam has improved now that polygamy has been outlawed and since women were given equal rights in 1960. Ho Chi Minh rejected the Confucian principle of the three submissions [the 'three bonds' – *tam cuong* – which, roughly speaking, enjoined wives to obey their husbands, to become chaste and enduring widows when their husbands died, and to cherish the children of their husbands' concubines as if they were their own]. Of course, many men still have a *petite amie*. You can never change men. It's not even worth trying.'

4

Dancing With Mr Dang

Mr Dang came originally from the Mekong Delta and he was happy to be going back there. In fact, as it turned out, that was why we were going. Mr Dang had a motor to deliver to his brother, Mr Lam, who lived in Hau Giang province somewhere in amongst the maze of waterways that criss-cross the lower part of the delta. We left early, while it was still vaguely cool and after I had changed a wad of dollars for an armful of *dong* at the money changer's on Le Loi. The black-market rate was rising fast, now at over 6,000 *dong* to the dollar. Saigon was already up and on the move, and the roads were jammed. We stopped briefly at a pavement kiosk to stock up with cigarettes. Mr Dang and Nguyen bought cartons of State Express 555. At 3,700 *dong* a packet, they were the most expensive of the imported cigarettes and an important status symbol. Both men chain-smoked from six in the morning onwards and it was a source of some friction between us. I said to Nguyen, 'You know, you'd be much richer if you gave up and anyhow you'll die if you go on smoking so much.'

He answered, 'If I stop, I will die.'

'Oh, really, why?'

'I will die of sadness.'

I asked Nguyen to ask Mr Dang to drive slowly so that I could see the countryside as we went along. Also, I said, Mr Dang's driving made me feel sick. Nguyen looked puzzled and said, 'But Mr Dang is a very good driver, very fast, and we save time like this.'

I said, 'But there's no need to save time. I'm not in a hurry'.

So Mr Dang tried to slow down and our progress was further hindered by a couple of ferry crossings. At Phnom Penh, the capital of Cambodia, the Mekong divides and in the nine provinces of the delta there are over a hundred ferry crossings over the different branches of the river. We crossed first at My Tho, and then again across the river Hau Giang, the right fork of the Mekong, called the Bassac in Cambodia, which flows through Phnom Penh to Can Tho, capital of the southern delta and of Hau Giang province where we were to spend the night. During the war Can Tho was full of American servicemen attached to a huge airbase, the biggest to be built in Vietnam by the Americans.

Once we were on board the ferries, Mr Dang got out of the car and laboriously tugged the windows shut by hand so that I should not be bothered by beggars and hawkers. I said I didn't mind but he was adamant and so we all three sat and sweltered inside the airless car. The ferries were jammed with all manner of humanity: children selling cigarettes and Wrigley's chewing gum; women carrying palm-leaf trays on their heads piled high with twigs bearing clusters of little sweet lychees and parcels of cooked rice wrapped in leaves; and beggars – beggars everywhere, old and young, crawling on their stumps, raising a wretched hand. I found it almost impossible to continue a conversation while I was being importuned but Mr Dang and Nguyen just ignored them.

The Mekong Delta, the 'rice bowl' of Vietnam, was once a part of Cambodia, known as Kampuchea Krom, and annexed by the Vietnamese centuries ago in a war against the old Khmer Empire. Between 1976 and 1978 Pol Pot's attempts to regain what he saw as his country's rightful possessions led, in part, to the Vietnamese invasion of Cambodia. During the Vietnam War, much of the delta was under the unacknowledged control of the National Liberation Front, and its proximity to the Cambodian border which the Americans believed to be a safe haven for Vietcong guerrillas, led to extensive bombing raids and the use of chemical defoliants over the whole area. Today, the extreme fecundity of the land has ensured its recovery and it looked as lush and verdant as ever. The landscape was so rich that it dazzled the eyes. All around us the delta lay, like a vast fertility symbol: an intricate mosaic of paddy fields and silvery irrigation channels; rivers, canals and streams with fishing nets poised like gigantic predatory daddy longlegs over the water; boats of all shapes and sizes from ferries to tiny dug-outs paddled by children who stared at me in open-mouthed amazement. The Cyclops motif on the façades of the Cao Dai pagodas cast its numinous blank gaze over the land. The seasonal ritual of the planting and harvesting of the rice was like a constant theme running through the life of the country, through the life of the region, of the continent. A Canadian geologist in Hanoi had quoted an old saying to me:

> The Cambodians plant the rice
> The Vietnamese harvest the rice
> The Laos watch the rice grow

The Vietnamese, like colonies of ants, were lovingly engaged in the ancient rituals of creation, the bones of their ancestors buried in the soil they were so busy tilling. The peasants spend most of their lives in the rice fields and, when they die, they are buried there. They believe that their souls will pass through the soil into the rice and thus be inherited by their descendants when the rice is eaten. Rice is their staple diet but it has a significance greater than that of food. Just as bread has a religious significance for Catholics so rice has a comparable symbolism for the Vietnamese. The word for 'rice' is the same as the word for 'food'.

We arrived in Can Tho just before one. Mr Dang and Nguyen disappeared upstairs to their room for a nap and I lay down on my bed under the ceiling fan. It revolved slowly with a click on every turn, scarcely stirring the damp air. Outside Can Tho was blissfully quiet after the din of Saigon.

I fell asleep and was startled into wakefulness by a knocking on the bedroom door. I had been dreaming that I was at work in our dingy old offices in Cambridge. In the dream, the magazine had a new managing director. She called me into her office to fire me. I said, 'Isn't that up to the editor? After all, he hired me.' 'No,' she answered crisply, 'he's got no real power any more. I make the decisions around here now.'

I woke with the unpleasant taste of premonition in my mouth and it took me a minute or two to realise where I was and what was happening. Outside my door was the hotel receptionist. She indicated that I should come downstairs, there was someone waiting to see me. In the bar was a short tubby man wearing a grubby tee-shirt and trousers that hung precariously below his fat belly. He wrote his name and organisation in my notebook. He was Mr Pham Quang Loc, the representative of the Foreign Relation in the People's Committee of Hau Giang Province (*sic*) and had come to welcome me and discuss my programme. He seemed jolly enough, putting his bare feet on the table and wriggling his dirty toes, ordering can after can of beer, saying how much he liked Morris West and Shakespeare. We seemed to be getting on fine and when I told him that I would like to go by boat to Soc Trang rather than visit a pineapple or frozen food factory, he assured me that there would be no problem. It would mean getting up at four in the morning but why not – imagine the spectacle of the dawn and the sun rising over the Mekong Delta. By the time Mr Dang and Nguyen came down, everything was virtually settled.

Mr Dang and Nguyen exchanged looks as I told them what we had arranged and then Mr Dang unleashed a flood of Vietnamese. Mr Loc picked his nose while Nguyen translated. Mr Dang was apparently of the opinion that the boat trip wasn't such a good idea, that it would be much better to go by car, much faster. I said that I didn't want to go fast. What I wanted was to see the countryside and the people going about their daily business and, as it was obvious that the life of the delta was intimately concerned with water and the river, I wanted the opportunity to observe it at close quarters.

The reason for Mr Dang's reluctance became clear a minute later when Mr Loc announced that the cost of the river trip would be $100. I looked at him in absolute amazement. This princely sum was, after all, the equivalent of three months' salary to some of the better-off Vietnamese and therefore a fortune to any boatman. Furthermore, desperate as I was to take a boat through the Mekong Delta, I just couldn't afford that much.

'It can't cost $100,' I said, 'I just don't believe it.'

'That's the price,' said Mr Loc.

'But how is it possible?'

'The cost of gasoline is very high and then there is the fee for the driver.'

'I know all that, but come on, $100? I'm sure if I could speak Vietnamese and went down to the waterfront here in Can Tho, I could find a boatman who woud gladly do it for much less – for, say, twenty dollars or thirty dollars.'

'That is your opinion. If you want, go to the waterfront and look for a boat, but, as you admit, you can't speak Vietnamese and I, Mr Loc, who am in the Foreign Relation in the People's Commitee of Hau Giang Province, tell you the price is $100. You are nobody. You are one British woman. You are a minority person and when I tell you something, that is how it is.'

'Fine', I said through gritted teeth, 'fine, let's just forget the whole idea. I couldn't care less.'

By this time I was in a towering rage and so was Mr Loc. The heat, the boredom of the endless discussions about money, the effort of having to be polite and patient the whole time, the sense that he was trying to rip me off, my bad dream, Mr Dang's driving – it all suddenly became too much for me and I knew that if I didn't get out of there, I would say something terrible. I stood up and walked out of the hotel. Behind me, I could hear the rapid rise and fall of Mr Loc's voice, still talking and, for some reason, still in English. He was repeating over and over, like an incantation, the phrases 'one British woman' and 'minority person'. Mr Dang's deeper tones broke in soothingly as I moved out of earshot.

By dusk, Mr Dang had come up with a solution that permitted both parties to save face. We would drive to Phung Hiep, a small town an hour or so south of Can Tho and hire a boat there to take us to My Tu, a couple of hours' journey by boat. In My Tu, we would find a dug-out to go to visit Mr Dang's brother and family for lunch. We would return to My Tu in the same boat and continue our journey to Soc Trang by car. The cost of the boats would be in the region of ten dollars and I would have plenty of time to get a feel of life on and around the river. I was delighted and Mr Dang took the opportunity to suggest very politely that in future I didn't make plans or arrangements without first consulting him. Most things were, he said, possible but there was always a best way to tackle a problem and I was not the best person to do it. Furthermore Mr Loc, however ghastly he appeared, was clearly a person of some importance, otherwise he wouldn't be dealing with foreigners, and it wouldn't do to antagonise him.

The alarm went off at 4.30 while it was still dark and I fumbled my way into my clothes and threw my things together. Despite a comfortable bed and an unusually soft pillow, I had barely slept. Downstairs Mr Dang was peering into a showcase in the hotel foyer. It contained a few tubes of toothpaste, a couple of bars of soap and some bottles of scent or cologne. He made the sleepy receptionist open it up and reached inside for the scent. It was called 'Paris' and smelt sweet, strong and cheap. Mr Dang asked me what I thought. I said, 'Very nice' and he bought a bottle and started applying it liberally, sniffing happily.

We went to collect Mr Loc, who emerged scratching and grunting from his room, his eyes gummy with sleep, and then drove on down to the port to see the dawn. It was still pitch-black but as I watched, the sky started to warm up like a fire that has caught and begun to blaze. The river too turned the colour of a blood-orange and it became almost impossible to tell where the water ended and the sky began. Out of the darkness, shapes began to appear and resolve themselves into recognisable objects. Houseboats with low curving roofs lay moored in silence and their inhabitants now began to stir, coughing and spitting as they commenced the familiar early morning rituals of fire-lighting and washing, crouching over the side of the boat to scoop up water from the river. There were other boats, long narrow ones, ferrying people from one side of the river to another. Orderly queues of women carrying bundles balanced on their hips disembarked and disappeared into the awakening city. The water was like stained glass. In the distance, away by the skyline, fishing boats were either returning or departing, and as the sun crept up over the horizon, turning the sky from orange to pink, the shapeless bundles on the ground around us gradually came to life and transformed themselves into *cyclo* drivers, curled up under the cabs of their *cyclos*. Steaming blocks of ice the size of tombstones were being tied onto the backs of bicycles and wheeled away. Suddenly, just as the last traces of the night were being smoothed from the sky, music, popular and strident, poured from loudspeakers and a huge silver-coloured statue of Ho Chi Minh appeared at the other end of the square, his gleaming face and torso catching the rays of the rising sun and dominating the quay.

Mr Dang had left his home and family thirty years before. As an eleven-year-old boy he had joined the South Vietnamese revolutionary forces – the National Liberation Front – and at the age of sixteen he went north to Hanoi. Soon after he had left home, his father died and then his mother was killed by an American helicopter. After her death the family left My Tu and went to Bien Hoa near Saigon. When Mr Dang first returned from Hanoi after 1975, he could not find his family. In 1977 the family moved back to My Tu.

Mr Lam, Mr Dang's older brother, was a beautiful man in his early sixties. His face was fresh and open, the face of a man who had led a decent life and had nothing to hide. He lived with his five daughters and their husbands and ten grandchildren in a square stone house draped with bougainvillaea and built on land which had belonged to his parents. It was accessible only by water. The heart of the delta was like Venice: you either went by boat or you walked. We got lost finding the house, taking a wrong turning down one of the myriad brown canals and we ran out of petrol because the top hadn't been properly secured on the spare can, but it was an entrancing journey. We waved and shouted greetings at fishermen squatting with their rods at the end of little jettys; at women scrubbing clothes in the rivers and canals; at barges lying low in the water, weighed down with timber; and at long boats carrying sacks of rice and salt, firewood, cane for export to Malaysia, unsteady piles of china, ducks lashed together into huge squawking bundles and piglets squeaking in wire baskets.

Eventually we arrived. We moored our dug-out and climbed ashore. At first the children were shy, screaming with laughter and rushing away every time I looked at them but after a little while, they got used to me – that is, I was still a source of great fascination but no longer frightening. Mr Dang went immediately to light some sticks of incense at the shrine of his ancestors and I looked around. The house seemed to have a main room for eating, sleeping and general living, and then some smaller rooms, including a kitchen. There was no electricity and daylight filtered through the doors and windows. The living room was cool and dark with a high ceiling made of intricately woven coconut matting and strips of bamboo.

We sat down to lunch. I was the only woman at the table. Mr Lam's wife and daughters were busy in the kitchen and the grandchildren were shovelling rice into their mouths out on the terrace. Mr Dang was, as usual, behaving like Escoffier. He had been in the kitchen preparing a very special soup and now he insisted that I should try it. It was a soup of rice and chicken stock, tasting faintly lemony like the Greek soup *avgolemone*. I had been complaining of stomach pains and Mr Dang had determined that this soup, bland, soothing and nourishing, was just the thing. I tasted it. It was good. Then came the difficult part. All the choicest morsels of the chicken were passed to me as the honoured guest. Mr Dang reached into a huge bowl and selected, with his chopsticks, first the liver, then the heart, then something pungent and dark red which Nguyen described as 'pressed blood'. These I swallowed manfully but I baulked at the greatest delicacy of all – the bird's fertilised ova, rich glossy butter-cup yellow globules. I didn't know what to do but I knew I couldn't eat them so, when no-one seemed to be watching, I slipped them under the table to one of the dogs. Mr Loc ate everything in sight, loudly sucking the meat from the bones of the chicken and spitting them out onto the table.

We lingered over lunch, finishing with hard-boiled duck eggs. I remembered Norman Lewis writing of semi-hatched eggs with small openings cut in their sides to allow the potential purchaser to select the degree of incubation and thought also of the duck eggs that I had seen for sale in Cau Ong Lanh market in Saigon with a partly-formed chick emerging from the shell. I dreaded taking a bite and encountering something solid and gristly instead of soft orange yolk and so declined, pleading repletion. Mr Dang tut-tutted and slipped three duck eggs into my bag while I wasn't looking. These I later found smashed against my camera and notebook and filling the bag with bits of shell and crumbling yolk. The men were drinking some kind of fiery liquor and I was offered the odd glass but, on the whole, women were neither expected nor encouraged to drink. Pigs and dogs and scrawny bald chickens ran in and out of the house and under the table, brushing against my legs.

After we had finished and the plates been cleared away, the men lay down to sleep. I went outside and walked towards the fields. Mr Lam was involved in some kind of land dispute which he and Mr Dang had been discussing over lunch. During the war, he had rented out a ten-hectare field to a neighbour who was now refusing to give it back to him, despite the new laws governing property that had been passed since 1975. The main problem, however, was that the neighbour had a brother who worked at the court so Mr Lam and Mr Dang doubted they stood much chance of seeing justice done.

I walked along a narrow walkway between the paddy fields. The sky had a steely luminous cast to it as though presaging a thunderstorm and it was very still and quiet. A pair of egrets flapped their delicate wings and rose languidly into the air. In the distance, a small figure straddled a water buffalo and the image seemed to encapsulate both the place and the moment. I felt moved almost to the point of tears and at the same time triumphant. I loved the idea that I was alone in the heart of the Mekong Delta and I was pleased and amazed to be there.

Back at the house, the smallest grandchild was crying in his mother's arms. As I changed the film in my camera, I gave him the little plastic canister to play with. He stopped crying and the other children clustered round and looked with envious eyes at the box. I opened my camera bag and started taking used and unused films out of their boxes and distributing the plastic cases. One little girl, the prettiest, was offered the choice between one with a blue lid and one with an orange lid. She chose the latter and then changed her mind. I told her that it was too late and she went off sulking, saying that if she couldn't have the blue, she didn't want either. I was amused and touched by this display of spirit from a child whose only other toy appeared to be an old helmet from the war and gave her the one she wanted. Mr Dang awoke from his nap and disappeared off into the fields behind the house with a gun that he had brought all the way from Saigon. A few minutes later, we heard a couple of shots and he reappeared carrying a couple of egrets, their snowy plumage stained with fresh blood. A tiny boy, no more than four years old, took the birds away and started to pluck them, tearing carelessly at the feathers and dropping them on the ground.

As I watched the children, I thought of Michael Herr writing in *Dispatches*, 'I think that Vietnam was what we had instead of happy childhoods.' He meant, I imagine, that for some western soldiers and journalists the experience of the Vietnam War was a kind of coming-of-age, a late adolescent happy childhood. He meant that they enjoyed themselves. 'A few extreme cases felt that the experience there had been a glorious one, while most of us felt that it had been merely wonderful.' I thought of Mr Dang leaving home aged eleven to join the revolutionary forces and of Nguyen who was seven when the war began and whose father was a major in the Army of the Republic of [South] Vietnam. After 1975, Nguyen's father was sent to a re-education camp. Nguyen told me that, once, as he arrived to visit his father, his father saw him and waved. He was punished for waving to his son by two hours in solitary confinement.

Before we left, I lined up all the children and took their photograph. Then I got in behind them and made Nguyen take a picture of us all together. They had insisted on running to change into their best clothes and in the photograph they look fresh and clean. I am standing, twice their size, tanned and sweaty, my hair flying round my head. I have seen many such photographs, the foreigner towering above the small delicate natives, appearing more alien than ever. At the time, I felt pretty foreign but nothing like as foreign as I really was.

We chugged slowly back to My Tu. Mr Loc was snoring gently after his lunch. In the morning he had been infuriatingly garrulous, his conversation an odd mixture of statistics – the number of ducks, chickens, pigs, pineapples and shrimp produced by each district – and cocktail party chatter.

'Do you know Mr Tim Page?' he had asked, referring to the photographer who had covered the Vietnam War and who had returned many times since. 'He is a very good friend to Vietnam. He is my very good friend.' I was still sulking about the $100 and his remarks about women and minority people and stared out at the river, pretending not to hear.

As we approached the landing stage, children ran along the bank shouting and waving and by the time we docked, crowds of people had converged. They all wanted to see and touch the foreigner. An old woman pinched the soft flesh of my upper arm. Nguyen said she wanted to feel how fat I was. Physically I was intriguing to people in the East. One night in Saigon a man standing next to me in a queue had suddenly reached over to stroke and then smell my hair; another time – a couple of years before in Ayutthaya, Thailand's ancient capital – a group of giggling schoolgirls had approached me just after seven in the morning asking to practise their English.

'Go ahead, ask what you like,' I said.

'Please, how much do you weigh?'

There must have been over three hundred people, pressing against each other. I fought my way through the crowd and got into the car. Immediately it was covered with flesh, so much so that I couldn't see out at all. Every inch of glass was filled with a face. It wasn't a particularly comfortable feeling. We started up. Bodies scattered as Mr Dang shouted and the car began to move forward. We went to meet the local vice-chairman of the party and the vice-director of the district. We drank bitter green tea and exchanged courtesies. They said that I was the first western woman ever to visit the delta and, on hearing that I was a writer, presented me with a history of the revolutionary movement in My Tu in fifteen volumes – in Vietnamese, of course.

The road to Soc Trang was riddled with pot-holes and thick with mud from the monsoon rain, and more than once we had to turn back and take another road which was little better. The sky had darkened and the storm clouds threw an intense eerie light over the land, making the green of the rice fields more brilliant than ever. Across the plains of paddy the coconut palms were whipped and bent almost double by the wind. We drove through little villages full of pigs and chickens, and wide open spaces where small boys were urging the water buffalo home after a day in the fields. Bicyclists draped in sheets of transparent cellophane crouched over their handlebars, their bodies hunched against the wind and the rain, their bicycle wheels slipping in the rich red mud of the delta. Mr Dang's old car ploughed on. At one point in the middle of nowhere there appeared, like a vision or a mirage, a beautiful big old Khmer pagoda, its roofs adorned with writhing *nagas* – the stylised polycephalic cobra of Hindu mythology – and supported by gilded caryatids, their arms stretching up to the heavens. I wanted to stop to have a proper look at it but it was getting late and the threatened storm was up and running so we kept going. Mr Loc sang and whistled all the way.

We reached Soc Trang at sunset. The foyer of the Phong Lan – 'winged orchid' – hotel was illuminated by tiny petrol lamps but electricity from a generator was promised for later, and I had my torch. I was given a big room on the first floor that looked as if it hadn't been cleaned for months. It had a double and a single bed and gave onto a balcony that ran the whole way round the building. I poured a bucket of cold water over myself and, wrapped in a sarong, stepped out onto the balcony to have a look at the town. Soc Trang had a kind of gritty, grimy look to it, rather like a mining town. The sun was sinking into the river and the air was filled with a deafening cacophony of wailing transistor radios, revving motorbikes, car horns, truck engines and people shouting at their children and animals. Mr Dang, Mr Loc and Nguyen had the room next door and I peered through their window. They were all lying down, seemingly exhausted. I went back inside and attempted to bring some order to my room. I removed the sheet – dark green nylon with red roses – from the mattress of the double bed and shook it out over the balcony. I hung the pale blue mosquito net from the rusty nails on the bedposts and constructed a pillow from my underclothes and dirty laundry. I spread my sarong out to dry and dressed in clean clothes. I even put on some lipstick. Mr Dang had told me that it would be a great honour for some friends of his to entertain me to dinner and that they had laid on a singer.

The restaurant was over on the other side of town and we had a private room upstairs. Miss Tao, the singer, was the only other woman there – apart from the waitresses who kept filling our glasses with beer and chucking the cans under the table so that every time you moved your feet, there was a tinny clatter. In one corner of the room there was a whole crate of Heineken on the floor. The Vietnamese drink their beer with jagged chunks of ice but I did not want to get sick from the water and asked for it to be cooled in a bucket of ice instead. We ate crab in our fingers and then Miss Tao stood up to sing, accompanying herself on the guitar. Nguyen, urged on by Mr Yung, our host, whispered a translation:

> The sadness fills my heart
> But you don't know about that
> It is raining
> Outside the window
> My singing is nothing
> Do you know how my heart is now?

She had a high sweet voice and, as I listened to her, my eyes filled with tears, as did the eyes of Mr Yung. Nguyen told me that she was singing a song by Trinh Cong Son, the Hue-born composer whose anti-war songs were banned by the Thieu Government, earning him the title of the Bob Dylan of South Vietnam. Then Mr Yung stood up to sing. He sang in a deep powerful bass of the love that the South Vietnamese feel for their country. He sang of the wind from the south whispering through the rice fields and the coconut palms. Then, with a hideous inevitability, it was my turn. I had, of course, read books by writers like Gavin Young and Redmond O'Hanlon in which the traveller, the guest, is required literally to sing for his supper but I hadn't really believed that it ever happened.

As a child, I had been told that I was tone-deaf and though this was later contradicted by my piano teacher, it had left me extremely self-conscious about singing. And there was another problem. I knew the complete words of only two songs, both English folksongs. One was 'There is a Tavern in the Town' and the other, which I had last sung in public fifteen years before at a drama school audition, was 'The Foggy Foggy Dew' which I had learnt as a child from a recording by the tenor, Peter Pears. The song is about a weaver who saves a fair maiden from the foggy foggy dew of the title and in doing so, somehow gets her pregnant. Here are the first two verses:

> Oh, I am a bachelor
> I live by myself
> And I work at the weaver's trade
> And the only, only thing
> That I ever did wrong
> Was to woo a fair young maid.
>
> I wooed her in the winter time
> And in the summer too
> And the only only thing
> That I ever did wrong was to save her
> From the foggy foggy dew

Given the sentimental tears coursing down the faces of my host and fellow guests, I thought that 'The Foggy Foggy Dew' would be more in keeping with the mood of the evening. I sang as best I could but I was terribly nervous and my voice came out in a thin high quaver. When I had finished, Nguyen translated Mr Yung's comment on my performance, 'He thanks you for the effort you have made,' he said. Nobody suggested I sing again and Mr Loc leapt to his feet and begun half-singing, half-declaiming what appeared to be a work of his own composition, a kind of stream-of-consciousness blank verse.

> What is Hau Giang Province
> A small detail
> But solidarity

Tiger Balm

Woman English always very welcome
We must to know to understand to you
We are family
Population
Especially we are Indochinois

Mr Loc was flying. Over half the crate of beer had been drunk and he was shouting in English and French. 'You must,' he said, 'to be respective to me because I represent the People's Committee of Hau Giang Province. You must to listen to me because I know everything and everyone. *Allons enfants de la patrie/Le jour de gloire est arrivé . . .* ' His good friend, Tim Page, reared his head once more. He yelled at Nguyen because I had asked Nguyen to translate something and he said that he, Mr Loc, needed no translator. Our urbane Chinese host looked uneasy and Mr Dang got up and began to dance with Mr Loc. Mr Dang did Kung Fu dancing, pointing his fingers and hissing like a snake, and Mr Loc waggled his fat behind like a Turkish belly dancer, claiming to be demonstrating Khmer dances. I was laughing so much I thought I was going to be sick. Then Mr Dang pulled me to my feet and we danced a sort of samba, or maybe a tango, while Miss Tao sang of love and patriotism. When we had finished, Mr Dang kissed me. It was rather nice and set me thinking about sex and oriental men and western women and western men and oriental women.

It is well-known, almost to the point of being a standing joke, that oriental women, tiny, submissive and versed in the arts of love, are irresistible to western men. Oriental women are truly feminine and have smaller and therefore tighter vaginas (or so the marketing manager for Tampax told a girlfriend of mine: tampons for the Far Eastern market had to be made in smaller sizes). They are beautiful, graceful and rarely speak much English or German which means that men don't have to worry about conversation and can concentrate on the important stuff. The plane-loads of German businessmen who fly into Bangkok's Don Muang airport on 'sex' tours bear daily witness to the efficacy of such propaganda. 'The girl of your dreams for the price of a packet of cigarettes,' is how one man described it. And it is not just men who believe that in the arms of an oriental woman, perfect bliss will be attained. I once caught sight of myself in a mirror while waiting to catch the Star Ferry from Kowloon across to Hong Kong Island. I was scarlet in the face and seemed to be double the height and width of all the delicate Chinese women around me. Who could blame anyone for preferring these fragile creatures?

But for a western woman, one of the particular pleasures of travelling in the Far East is the near-certainty that you won't be molested. You don't desire the men – they are too strange, too alien. This is how the French heroine in *L'Amant* described her Chinese lover from Cholon. 'The skin's sumptuously soft. The body. The body's thin, lacking in strength, in muscle ... he's hairless, nothing masculine about him but his sex . . . Touches the softness of his sex, his skin, caresses his golden-ness, the strange novelty.'

So, believing instinctively, and despite years of experience to the contrary, that desire is reciprocal, you feel safe. They can't or won't desire you. On the one hand, every male fantasy is a small-boned, exquisite oriental woman-child and, on the other, no oriental man would ever wish to lay a finger on a western woman. The truth is that there is no real evidence to suggest that oriental men don't find western women, particularly blonde ones, desirable. King Mongkut of Siam, for instance, seemed to cherish a *tendresse* for the English governess, Anna Leonownes, and it may only have been the innate good manners and reticence of the oriental that has prevented such desires from being made crudely obvious in the way that they would have been in the West. It is also worth giving serious consideration to the theory that after years of watching their own women being appropriated and exploited by western men, they might just feel like evening up the score.

Later that night when I was settled in bed, I heard the sound of raised voices from the room next door. Mr Loc was still shouting in English and then Mr Dang's guttural tones, short and sharp, like a smack, broke in. I shifted uneasily on my mattress and the bottom end of the bed collapsed with a loud crash, leaving me lying at an angle of forty degrees. Suddenly there was silence next door. I lay there hopefully for a minute or so until I realised that I would never get to sleep in that position. I got up, reassembled the bed, then rearranged myself gingerly on it. My skin began to crawl and in amongst the pattern of roses and green leaves I saw little black insects. My doctor in London had told me that fleas in Vietnam carried bubonic plague and it was almost the only thing that I was seriously frightened of catching. I looked up at the blue nylon mosquito net. It seemed clear. The insects were obviously all on the inside. I swallowed a Valium with a mouthful of whisky and told myself it didn't matter. I was brave, intrepid. I could sleep anywhere. Next door the shouting had faded to a low mumble. I switched off my torch which I had been using to freeze the fleas rather in the manner of a rabbit caught in a car's headlights and composed myself for sleep. It was useless. I got out of bed and went over to the single bed on the other side of the room. I dragged the mattress onto the floor, went out onto the balcony and appropriated a couple of what seemed to be slightly damp white sheets from a drying rack and put them on the mattress. I lay down, covered myself with my dressing gown and fell into an uneasy sleep.

I woke soon after four. The noise from the street was unbelievable. Soc Trang was coming awake and its inhabitants would clearly have felt at home in a discothèque. I got up – feeling like hell – and replaced the sheets on the drying rack, realising as I did so that they were the table cloths from the hotel dining room. Soc Trang was misty in the early dawn, the damp from the humid night not yet burnt away.

We ate *beignets* and drank sweet black coffee from a stall in the street. Mr Dang and Nguyen also gulped down a couple of bowls of *pho*, the Vietnamese noodle soup that everyone eats for breakfast. It consists of a thin clear broth flavoured with ginger and *nuoc mam* (fermented fish sauce) with white rice noodles, bean sprouts, coriander, parsley, shallots and chicken, beef or pork. Nguyen would heap spoonfuls of tiny fierce red chillis into his *pho*, leading Mr Dang to speculate anxiously about the condition of his stomach lining.

The day turned out to be one of ceaseless activity. First there was a meeting with the vice-chairman of the district of Soc Trang, a fat amiable lady waving a sandalwood fan, who wanted to know why football hooliganism was such a problem in England. I said that it was because young people in Britain didn't have enough to do; unlike the children of the delta, they weren't kept busy working in the rice fields. The vice-chairman was accompanied by an entourage of minor dignitaries including the local cultural director and Mr Linh, the author of five novels about the war, whom I had already met in Can Tho. Ten people in all were delegated to accompany me and we all climbed into a mini-bus to visit first a large dreary Chinese temple, the An Nghia pagoda, built seventy-five years before and then a pleasantly dilapidated Khmer temple erected at the turn of the century on the site of a sixteenth-century wooden building. The trees in the surrounding grounds were infested with bats who had been there for 300 years and who hung in thick black clusters from the branches high above us, like sinister fruit. The monks lit a couple of fires at the foot of the trees and as the smoke rose upwards, the bats fled their sanctuaries and the sky turned black as they shrieked and spread their wings. Inside the monks' living quarters, an old monk seated in the lotus position and wearing horn-rimmed spectacles, stared at me. It was only when I came close to him that I saw it was a statue, life-like in every detail.

But the highlight of the morning was a display of Khmer dancing and theatre. This was an energetic blend of the traditional and the contemporary with electric guitars played rather in the style made famous in the 1960s by The Who's guitarist, Pete Townsend: that is, with the guitarist flat on his back or on his knees. The chief *chanteuse* wore a long red velvet dress and long white lace gloves. She sang a duet with a young man and Nguyen passed me tiny slips of paper on which he had written a translation. The song was about a mother's teachings to her son. Nguyen's note read 'The son is very sorry about what bad things he did (because of forgetting his mother's words)'. There were dances illustrating scenes from the Ramayana, the great Hindu epic, with men in monkey masks portraying Hanuman, the monkey king, who rescues Sita, the beautiful wife of Rama. It was all very jolly and at the end Nguyen handed me a note instructing me to shake hands with all the performers and make a speech. The entire show was recorded on video, as was my speech. Once again I was the first western woman ever to have visited the district and my visit was a major event in the life of Soc Trang. Everyone was delighted at the opportunity to have a day out and a good look at the foreign visitor.

We said goodbye to the vice-chairman and the cultural director and trooped back to the hotel for a banquet hosted by more Chinese businessmen friends of Mr Dang's. The courses kept coming, seven or eight in all, each one more delicious than the preceding one. I remember frogs' legs fried crisply in batter and an unfamiliar dish of an animal that might have been a pangolin or some iguana-like reptile in a sauce with lemon and herbs. Halfway through lunch Mr Dang asked me whether I ate snake and I told him that I almost certainly could and would, provided I didn't know that it was snake. But when the snake arrived, looking horribly scaly and life-like as if basking in its accompanying 'heating' broth, I couldn't manage even a polite mouthful.

By the end of lunch, one of the waitresses was sitting in Mr Dang's lap and another entire crate of beer – thirty-two cans in all – I counted – had been drunk. Our original plan had been to return to Can Tho for the night but Mr Dang was clearly enjoying himself and suggested that we stay on in Soc Trang instead. The waitress wriggled happily and whispered in his ear. I said that was fine by me but on two conditions: that we visit Dai An, the beautiful Khmer pagoda we had passed the day before and that someone whisk a broom round my room and mend the bed.

An hour later, when it was time to leave, there was no sign of Mr Loc. Nguyen went off to look for him and returned after ten minutes, giggling wildly, and asked me to lend him 15,000 *dong*. I handed the money over and asked what it was for. 'Never mind, never mind,' he said, 'I will tell you later.' He disappeared upstairs and reappeared with Mr Loc in tow. The little man was looking seedier than ever. His clothes were stained with food – he had done full justice to our magnificent lunch – and his hair and face needed a good wash. As he walked towards the car, Nguyen told me that he had found Mr Loc in bed with a 'taxi' girl and without any money to pay her so he had to borrow 15,000 *dong* from Nguyen. Nguyen was delighted because he was sure that Mr Loc would not dare be rude to him again after being caught literally with his pants down. I asked Nguyen why they were called 'taxi' girls. He looked at me as though I was very stupid and said, 'Because they are like taxis. They come when you call them and you only keep them for a short ride.'

Dai An fulfilled the promise of the previous afternoon. Close up it was even more beautiful than it had seemed at a distance in the rain and its shabbiness and air of desolation only served to enhance its romantic appeal. The walls were decorated with frescos of *apsaras*, their original bright colours now faded to a subtle wash, and carved lotuses adorned the gateposts. Six new very young monks were being received into the pagoda. They looked about fourteen; their heads were newly-shaved and each wore a broad sash of white cotton across his bare chest and a silk sarong girded with a golden tassel. An old Khmer woman with a fuzz of iron-grey stubble on her skull asked, in Khmer-accented Vietnamese, if she could come to England with me because things might be better there. Then I was taken to see a blond child. They said that both his parents were Khmer but that his father had been wounded in the war and they wondered whether he might have been given some American blood in a transfusion which would, they reckoned, account for the boy's unusual colouring. When I tried to take a photograph of him, he ran away.

Back in Saigon the following afternoon, we drove down Dong Khoi past the entrance to the Continental. Through the open doors, I could see a wedding party. The bride was gorgeous in a white lace dress with a huge skirt and a train covering half the foyer floor. She had scarlet lips and waist-length black hair which lay in elaborate curls under her veil. The groom wore a tuxedo, cummerbund and bow tie. There must have been over a hundred guests milling around. Nguyen told me that it was a point of honour among Vietnamese couples to make a splash on the big day, even though they might have to spend the rest of their lives paying off the debts incurred.

At the Caravelle I went upstairs to the Fitness Centre on the eighth floor. I felt as if I had been away for weeks. Tu, the masseuse, walked up and down on my back, chattering about marriage and children.

'I think you have many boyfriends,' she said.

'Only one,' I answered.

'Why he not marry you?' she asked.

'Who knows?'

'I think if you have children, you are very very happy,' she said.

'Maybe, maybe not.'

'How old are you?' she asked.

'Thirty-seven.'

'Oh, then you have very young face but body not so young.'

Later that evening I took Chi and a chubby friend of hers called Luang out to dinner. Chi was a little girl of about twelve whom I used to see most days in the square outside the hotel selling old stamps. She was very proper and would usually do up a couple of buttons on my blouse until she felt that I was decent. Her father had died in prison five years before and she supported her mother and siblings by selling stamps and maps to tourists. She said that she would really like to be a tailor.

We went to a new restaurant right over on the far side of town run by a friend of Mr Thuan's. It had a sign outside which read 'We produce and give out hundreds of Vietnamese pure dishes'. The place was completely empty and so far from Dong Khoi that I wondered if business would ever pick up but the girls didn't mind. They said that they hadn't eaten all day and devoured their food in ravenous silence, leaving their plates looking as if they had been licked clean by a dog. Afterwards we rode back to the Caravelle under a full moon. My *cyclo* driver had driven a tank in the South Vietnamese Army and spent five years in a re-education camp after the fall of Saigon. He said, 'I would like to work for my government but the Communists do not like me.' He now wished to get a driving-licence so that he could become a taxi-driver. I had never even seen a taxi in the city but he was probably right: there were bound to be taxis sooner or later. As we rode through the unlit streets, the homeless were preparing for bed on the pavements, tiny fires blazing in the gutters, candles flickering in the dark. Away from the Continental, Saigon's poverty was glaringly obvious, yet the night was wonderfully rich in sights and sounds and smells.

5

Across the Middle Distance

Nguyen was obsessed with the World Cup which was being played out thousands of miles away in Italy, and had drawn up a kind of knockout chart in his notebook. Every morning he would record the name of the winner of the previous evening's match. On the day that we had planned to leave for Dalat there was a particularly crucial semi-final and he begged me to spend an extra night in Saigon. There were television sets everywhere and it seemed unlikely that there wouldn't also be one in Dalat but it was clearly a risk that he was reluctant to take. As I wouldn't be returning to Saigon – or at least not on this trip – I didn't mind staying on. It gave me one last chance to fix the city in my mind and to say proper farewells.

Dalat, capital of Lam Dong province, the first of the three provinces of the Central Highlands, is 215 miles north of Saigon. It was a day's drive on indifferent roads through increasingly dramatic scenery. Suddenly, looming over tiny houses, were huge boulders and steel-grey rivers racing down mountainsides. The thatch-and-bamboo shacks of the plains became neat little clapboard cottages with an Alpine feel to them, and the paddy fields, palm trees and water buffalo gave way to tea plantations, waterfalls and horse-drawn carts as the road climbed to the Cao Nguyen plateau where the city lay. The colours were no longer Mediterranean, tropical and brilliant: the emerald and turquoise faded to spruce green and silver grey. The mountain peaks were shrouded in cloud, the

air turned cool and the skies grey. Nguyen gloomily predicted
'European' weather in Dalat. We drove past a forest which
Nguyen said had been planted by Madame Nhu, wife of Ngo
Dinh Diem's brother Nhu, and the Cruella de Ville of the Diem
regime. The wood, he claimed, was particularly good for gun
stocks.

Dalat was first established as a resort in the 1920s. A French
doctor, Alexandre Yersin, thought its temperate climate would
benefit his European patients who were being driven slowly mad
by the tropical heat of Saigon and the plains. Vietnam's last
emperor, Bao Dai, retreated to Dalat in 1950 when it became clear
that the French had brought him back simply as a figurehead, a
'puppet' emperor and that Diem was really going to run the show
in South Vietnam. There he was able to indulge his passion for
hunting – shooting tigers, bears, deer, polecats and other smaller
animals living in the woods around Dalat. Mr Dang made his own
small contribution to this tradition of slaughter by running down
and killing a couple of dogs and a chicken. As soon as he saw a
clear stretch of road ahead, he would put his foot down, making
no attempt to avoid any animal that was unfortunate enough to
get in his way. After the death of the first dog, when I was looking
shaken and unhappy, Mr Dang muttered something to the effect
that the stupid beast hadn't been looking where it was going. After
the second dog, I told Nguyen to tell Mr Dang that if he killed
any more dogs I would refuse to be driven by him. Nguyen shifted
uneasily in his seat – he was rather in awe of Mr Dang – but
eventually said something tactful in Vietnamese. They were big
dogs, yellow mongrels, and the noise and impact at the moment
of collision were quite something. The second dog in particular
made, I was glad to see, a sizeable dent in the front of the car.
But Mr Dang wasn't the only killer on the roads. Someone up
ahead had run over a chicken and feathers were whirling through
the air towards us. This nonchalance towards animal life and
death was further evidence of the Vietnamese insouciance towards
Buddhism. A committed Buddhist, a Lao or a Cambodian, for
example, would rather nail himself to the stake than run down an
innocent animal.

One of the dogs had clearly done more than dent the car and

we limped into Dalat towards the end of the afternoon, stopping and starting as the engine spluttered and coughed unhappily, refusing to engage in any gear other than first and firing on two cylinders at best. Mr Dang asked me whether I had any views on where we should stay in Dalat. I had – surprisingly. It was, in fact, the only place in Vietnam about which I had been able to form an opinion on this particular subject and I was keen that we book into the splendid old Palace hotel, built in 1916 by the French and apparently little changed since. Mr Dang shook his head and said that it would be expensive and that he knew a very nice mini-hotel (as houses, or, in this case, villas, which have been converted into small hotels are called) run by a friend of his. I insisted that we at least check out the Palace and when I saw its magnificent gothic art deco façade, there was, as far as I was concerned, no contest.

It was wonderful to be cool. It was wonderful to be quiet. I felt myself unwinding like a ball of string as I lay in a hot bath scented with Floris Rose Geranium bath essence and thought about the nature of comfort and how spoilt and soft I was. It was not that I *needed* hot water or clean sheets or whisky or proper lavatories but I found that I never *wanted* them any the less. In Saigon I had bought a history of Vietnam written in the 1960s and, as I lay in the bath, a passage came back to me.

' . . . This cruel, uncertain existence has bred a race of men who are inured to physical and moral suffering and who expect little of life in the way of pleasure or comfort. In addition to chronic malnutrition, public sanitation is rudimentary and disease is endemic . . . '

I remembered reading that Vietnamese soldiers were astonished by the degree of comfort, almost luxury, that their American adversaries seemed to demand as their right. One was quoted as saying ' . . . we even saw helicopters bringing special water for the Americans to wash themselves and we realised the soldiers used nothing Vietnamese . . . ' and the 'ice-machine plants, sixty-five-cubic-foot walk-in refrigerators . . . folding beds . . . filing cabinets . . . barber shops, sports fields, miniature golf courses, swimming pools . . . ' must have seemed equally astonishing to men used to marching for a day on nothing more than a handful of cold boiled rice. I knew what Mr Dang's idea of fun was and I sensed that it was rooted in survival. All his pleasures involved taking a fierce bite out of life: food, sex, the company of friends. His vanities were few and ultimately endearing.

I washed my hair and watched with relief as it dried and reverted to its normal manageable state away from the dripping humidity of Saigon. My room was enormous, a treasure-house of 1930s furniture, the sort of pieces that art deco fanatics in Europe and Manhattan would kill for. It contained two beds with Empire-style mosquito nets, a writing desk, chest of drawers, wardrobe, dressing table, coffee table and a couple of armchairs. A long wide balcony smelling faintly of drains ran the length of the wing and looked out over Xuan Huong Lake, a large artificial lake built by the French and named after Ho Xuan Huong, a subversive nineteenth-century poetess who ridiculed Hue dynastic politics in her verse. In the grounds below, skinny ponies were grazing and small boys were leading other ponies mounted with shrieking Vietnamese tourists while their companions took photographs.

The Palace was a superb establishment. A large creamy yellow stucco building, it reminded me of another deco fantasy in a city that could hardly have been more different, the Corals Gable Biltimore Hotel in Miami. It had a central stairwell giving onto two long dim corridors, the light-bulbs glowing reluctantly in the gloom, and forty-two rooms costing between eighteen and twenty dollars a night for foreigners and some joke sum for Vietnamese guests. Behind the reception desk hung a clock which played a different tune every time it struck the hour. Sometimes it was *Für Elise*, sometimes the Brahms lullaby or other melodies which I didn't recognise. Under the glass of the reception counter were displayed a hundred or so visiting cards and Tim Page's name leapt out at me. I met Nguyen in the bar and he complained about the lack of a 'sympathetic' atmosphere in the hotel.

We went to have dinner in a shabby little restaurant near the market. The *cyclos* of Saigon and the south had been replaced by little ponies and carts – though there were old white Peugeot taxis dating from the Fifties as well – and you would see a horse and cart tethered in the driveway of a house, just as you might see a car parked in Europe or a dug-out moored in the Mekong Delta. Dalat, like San Francisco, is a city of steep little hills and sudden spectacular views, glimpsed through slits between the houses. It was also almost entirely European in style – at least as far as the architecture went. 'Pitlochry with a French accent' was how Andrew Graham, a British diplomat stationed in Saigon in the early 1950s, described it; and it certainly bore atmospheric similarities to the Cameron Highlands, the Malay hill-station where Jim Thompson, the Thai silk tycoon and Lord Lucan of South East Asia, disappeared in mysterious circumstances one fine Easter afternoon in 1967. Dalat was the sort of place which *looked* tame but, like one of those old pussies in Agatha Christie novels, its very cosiness could conceal almost anything.

Mr Dang was in gallant form. He admired my denim jacket and said, 'We have been to the end of the Mekong Delta and now we have come to the heights of Dalat and nowhere have we seen anyone as beautiful as you.' The compliment may have lost a certain something in translation and I looked at him hard to see whether he was pulling my leg but, he was as always, absorbed in ordering dinner. He told me that the Vietnamese expression meaning 'Will you order?' was literally 'Will you go to the market?'

Looking through the open window of the restaurant were two children: a boy aged about twelve carrying his baby sister or brother, a toddler, on his back. He was begging in a patient, resigned, tentative way and, against Mr Dang's express instructions, I gave him 500 *dong*. His youth was painfully touching and I realised that one of the most moving aspects of life in Vietnam was the way in which children were obliged, from a very early age, to behave as if they were already grown-up and to assume corresponding responsibilities. They seemed not so much children as miniature adults and both play and leisure were rare luxuries.

Next morning we went to visit Bao Dai's summer palace. The first thing I saw, having left my shoes at the entrance as if entering a pagoda, was a huge stuffed tiger, its fangs bared. A Vietnamese girl was draped across the beast, posing while her husband or lover took her picture. The villa was full of such scenes. Almost every room contained a stuffed animal and someone posing on or against it. We wandered through the rooms. On the former emperor's desk lay a physician's reference book and an old diary. In the dining room, which could have comfortably seated thirty, there was a rather fine map of Vietnam etched onto glass and illuminated from behind with a tiny pinpoint of red light to mark each major city. We went upstairs into Queen Nam Phuong's bedroom. It would be nice to report that it contained something wonderful or bizarre but there was nothing. Apart from the plethora of stuffed wild life, it was just a very ordinary Thirties villa. Nguyen wanted to know why the house had so many bedrooms. It had seven which seemed modest for an oriental potentate, even one as emasculated as Bao Dai.

Bao Dai was the last of the Vietnamese emperors and the last of the Nguyen dynasty which had ruled from the imperial court of Hue since 1802 when his ancestor Nguyen Anh dislodged the previous incumbent, the emperor Nguyen Quang-Toan, second of the two Tayson emperors. Having seen off Nguyen Quang-Toan after a protracted struggle known as the Monsoon War, Nguyen Anh crowned himself emperor and took the name of Gia Long. Under his rule, a single Vietnamese court governed a united nation that stretched from the Kwangsi-Yunnan border all the way south to the Gulf of Siam. There had never before been a united Vietnam: a thousand years under Chinese rule had been followed by constant attacks from the Mongols under Kublai Khan and, in the sixteenth century, the country was divided between the Trinh in the North and the Nguyen, whose descendants were to become the Nguyen emperors of Vietnam, in the South.

In 1858 the French seized the port of Tourane (later Da Nang) and, between 1860 and 1895, re-divided the country into three parts. Gia Long's successors made various attempts to counteract the process of colonisation but by 1885 when the emperor Dong Khanh was installed on the imperial throne, he had little choice but to co-operate with his colonial masters. As of 1887, Vietnam had 'ceased to exist for all practical purposes, except as a memory and a rallying cry to revolt'. A French decree of the same year established the IndoChinese Union, an administrative entity which eventually came to include Cambodia and Laos. The true ruler of Annam was the French Resident Superior and another Resident Superior governed Tonkin. The colony of Cochin China came under the jurisdiction of a French lieutenant-governor and the entire IndoChinese Union was ruled by a governor-general whose capital was Hanoi. By the time Bao Dai succeeded to the imperial throne in 1925, his emperorship was little more than a formality with more pomp and ceremony than real power.

Vietnam's last emperor was born in 1913 and taken by his father, the emperor Khai Dinh, to France as a nine-year-old boy. He is unlikely to have been received with the enthusiasm and excitement that greeted his ancestor, Prince Canh, Gia Long's eldest son, when he accompanied Pigneau de Behaine, Bishop of Adran, to the court of Versailles in 1787 on a negotiating mission. Then Marie Antoinette was so charmed by the seven-year-old oriental boy that she permitted him to play with the Dauphin and a court musician composed a song in his honour. The Queen's personal *coiffeur* created a *chignon à la cochinchinoise* to mark the occasion.

Bao Dai remained in France after his father returned to Vietnam and he was brought up and educated there, living with the family of a French colonial official and attending a public *lycée*. He did not return to the court at Hue until 1932. From the start there was little chance that he would be able to achieve much politically but one ultimately significant appointment that he did make was to give Ngo Dinh Diem the job of Minister of the Interior. In March 1945, following the Japanese takeover from the French, Bao Dai proclaimed the independence of Vietnam but by the end of August of the same year he had abdicated, after having received a message from the Vietminh demanding his resignation. He complied – remembering, he later claimed, that Louis XVI had gone to the guillotine for resisting the French Revolution – and in so doing, conferred the 'mandate of heaven' on Ho Chi Minh, giving him the legitimacy that, in Vietnamese eyes, had traditionally resided in the emperor.

In 1946 Bao Dai went into voluntary exile, first to Hong Kong and then to a château near Cannes in France where he lived with his wife, beautiful Queen Nam Phuong whose exquisite features I had seen on the old stamps Chi had for sale in Saigon, and five children. He maintained a Vietnamese mistress in Paris and his aides kept him supplied with a steady supply of French courtesans to stave off sexual *ennui*. At the urgent request of the French, he returned to Vietnam in 1949 as head of state, but in 1955 he was deposed by Diem and left Vietnam for good.

I loved Dalat because it was cool and quiet. I adored the Dracula's castle gloom of the Palace. Otherwise, its attractions were almost exclusively for those with a taste for kitsch – not that the Palace wasn't high camp at its best. Bao Dai's passion for big-game hunting had evidently created a demand in the local labour market and there was a thriving taxidermy industry. No beauty spot was complete without a few stuffed polecats or deer and a moth-eaten tiger always took pride of place. At the Cam Ly waterfalls, whose natural magnificence took on a surreal quality with the addition of a couple of large stuffed black bears posing in among the rapids, an old man told me that there were still tigers in the woods. It seemed unlikely, given the number of dead ones in the villas and parks of Dalat, but I told him that it was against the law in most places to shoot tigers. He said it was in Vietnam, too, but they did it all the same.

There were 'English' gardens full of dusty roses, snapdragons, marigolds and sweet-williams – and dozens of honeymooners capturing each other on film. Dalat was full of places with silly – or romantic – names. The city itself was known as the City of Eternal Spring; there was a Lake of Sighs where a Vietnamese-style Romeo and Juliet tragedy had taken place and where you could paddle around in a little boat shaped like a toy dragon, and in the Vallée d'Amour (originally named the Valley of Peace by Bao Dai), tiny Vietnamese 'cowboys' in stetsons, spurs and fringed jackets, pranced around like miniature John Waynes on their little ponies, offering rides and photo opportunities.

All this was amusing up to a point but might easily drive one mad, particularly the photography – and Dalat had been designed almost entirely to cater for this passion. The Vietnamese would equal the Japanese or Koreans in photo-mania were it not for the near-prohibitive cost – four dollars – of a roll of Kodak colour film. It was Nguyen's enthusiasm for fiddling with my cameras that led to me finally losing my temper.

I was becoming frustrated at my inability to communicate with anyone except on the most basic level and, used to travelling and living alone, found the constant presence of Nguyen and Mr Dang something of a trial. We spent all day together and we ate every meal together. They were reluctant even to let me go for a walk on my own, probably because they were convinced that I would get into trouble for which they would be blamed, and also because their instructions were to keep an eye on me. I worried about what they were thinking or feeling and that interfered with my responses to any situation. Mr Dang never got out of the car to look at anything, claiming that he had seen it all before. I worried that they might be bored or not like me and that made me irritable at the same time. After the excitements of the Mekong Delta and a day or two in Dalat, I wanted, in Garbo's famous phrase, to be alone. I was also determined to do something by myself to prove that I still could and to dispel the passivity that I felt stealing over me. I was becoming institutionalised and I didn't like it.

I had therefore told the boys that, like it or not, I was going for a walk and would make my own arrangements for lunch. I doubted that it was beyond me to order a bowl of *pho*. I had been wandering happily around the town, inspecting the market and the cathedral when I came across Nguyen in the street. He had been to the post office to send a telegram to his wife, Minh Phuong, who was to meet us in Da Nang. No-one, except government officials, used the telephone. Almost nobody, even in Saigon, had one.

Nguyen insisted on accompanying me to a café and watched, like an anxious mother, while I ordered lunch. I put my bag containing one of my cameras on a stool next to me and Nguyen, while fussing around me, managed to knock it onto the stone floor. I said, 'Now, look what you have done,' and peered through the lens to discover that the shutter was no longer working. Nguyen's face crumpled as if he was about to burst into tears. He said, 'I can mend it', and tried to take it from me.

We both tugged at it until I said, 'Nguyen, just go away and leave me alone. I don't want you to try to mend it. It's a complicated delicate machine and you'll just make it worse. Now go away and find Mr Dang and let me eat my lunch in peace. Now. Please.' He shuffled off unhappily and my anger gradually cooled.

Late that afternoon I was sitting on the step of the door leading out onto the balcony, painting my toenails with Dior's 'Rouge Mysore' and listening to the news on the BBC World Service. There had just been an item saying that the Vietnamese Government claimed to be improving its record on human rights when there was a knock on the door. Nguyen came in, looking very down in the mouth. He had spent the afternoon drinking with Mr Dang and the men from the garage where the car was being repaired. They had consumed four bottles of Vietnamese vodka and Nguyen was now awash with maudlin self-pity. He said that he had never felt so bad in his whole life about anything as he did about the camera and that he had been so unhappy that he had had to drink himself silly to drown his sorrows. I told him that it didn't matter, that it was an accident, that everyone had accidents, that I had two cameras just so if one got broken I had a back-up, but nothing I said could stem the flood of recriminations.

It was all beyond me. He had some story about not having wished to bump into me in case someone – it was not clear who – should think that we had a pre-arranged rendezvous – though why that should matter, given that he was my interpreter, I couldn't make out. He talked on and on, all through dinner in the enormous empty hotel dining room, moving on from his great sorrow about the camera to what was important in life and his sad desire for a better life in the West. Every time I disagreed with him, he would say that he must have expressed himself badly and that I clearly hadn't understood what he meant. He seemed to find the idea that we might simply have different views very threatening. In *Vietnam Inc*, Philip Jones Griffiths has a chapter called 'The Communication Gap' which is illuminating for anyone experiencing the sort of difficulties that I was encountering talking to Nguyen. I was astonished that he could read Sidney Sheldon with apparent ease, since most of the time he appeared to have the greatest difficulty in understanding a single word that I said.

Part of the problem was that although he was there as my interpreter, he always seemed to be taken aback when I spoke to him – and in English. But then, according to Jones Griffiths, 'It is naturally assumed that any Vietnamese is allowed to "not hear" or to misunderstand when addressed in English . . . '

On our last night, we went out dancing with some friends of Mr Dang in one of the hotels near the centre of town. Couples jived sedately to the Dalat Seaprodex band and two boys attempted a demure tango. I danced a foxtrot with Nguyen who held me stiffly six inches away from him. As we drove into the shadowy silent gardens of the Palace hotel, I saw a couple making love against a pine tree. She was facing the tree, her arms embracing its trunk, her lover pressing himself urgently into the curve of her back.

The road from Dalat to Nha Trang and the coast twisted downwards through the mountains and some of the most beautiful country I had ever seen. We had left early, around five, without breakfast and, as we drove, the dawn broke over the hills and scorched away the mist floating in the rich valleys. Clouds of butterflies flitted in amongst the wild orchids and it was difficult to distinguish between the insects and the flowers. There were shaggy little ponies everywhere and oxen pulling big cumbersome carts loaded with logs or sacks of rice or old car tyres. Sometimes, hanging underneath the ox cart there would be a hammock with a man lying in it, his head swinging only a few inches from the ground, fast asleep while the oxen went on their way. It was cool until we dropped down to the plains where a heat haze shimmered above the baked earth. I took off my jacket as a blast of hot air poured in through the car windows. I could feel the red dust settling inside my collar and my hair started to frizz up.

By then we were driving through what was for centuries the ancient Hindu kingdom of Champa, which was gradually eroded into extinction by the Annamites over nearly five hundred years of on-off fighting with their southern neighbours. By the second half of the fifteenth century, the Annamites had annexed the whole of Champa, which had once stretched from Hue south down to

Cam Ranh Bay and west beyond the Annamite mountain chain into the Mekong Valley of Cambodia and southern Laos. By the end of the seventeenth century, the Chams, legendary enemies of the great building kings of Angkor, had been reduced to no more than just another minority group within the expanding Vietnamese kingdom. Near Thap Cham we passed a couple of restored Cham towers, great solid masses of brick planted squarely on the earth, visible from miles away, their roofs displaying an elegant cockscomb silhouette of brickwork against the skyline. Further down the road were a couple of Cham towers that hadn't been touched for centuries, sprouting spiky cacti from every orifice, their walls as thick as an elephant's torso. Inside they were pitch-black and stinking, apparently having been used for decades as lavatories by man and beast alike.

Around half-past ten, we turned off the road for an early lunch at a restaurant near Cam Ranh Bay. During the war, Cam Ranh Bay, one of the finest natural harbours in Asia, was developed by the Americans as a huge naval base with an extensive port, ship-repair and deep-water harbour facilities and an airstrip. Now the Russians had the use of it and a squadron of Soviet planes was based there but, despite pressure from their main economic and military allies, the Vietnamese declined to allow them a permanent base at Cam Ranh.

Lunch was, even by Mr Dang's high standards, exceptional. We had driven nearly a hundred miles since we left Dalat, all on the most terrible roads, full of pot-holes and hairpin bends, and we were ravenous. The restaurant, a pretty place out on stilts in a sea-lagoon, was owned by a nice man who spoke some English and kept a macaque and a little black-faced gibbon in large spotless cages. He served us clams roasted with garlic, oysters in batter and a wonderful soup of crab, quails' eggs and coriander, washed down with ice-cold San Miguel beer. I thought that it was the most delicious meal I had ever eaten. As we left, I asked the proprietor for the name of his restaurant and his card. I told him that I wanted to put it in my book and here it is: Ngoc Suong, Quoc Lo 1, Cam Ranh, Vietnam. Written on the same card in English are these words which do the place no more than justice:

Sea-Food Restaurant
Polite – Elegant
– Serving Special Dishes
European – Asian
(– Morning: Breakfast, Coffee)
Invite Respectfully

We drove on, refreshed, along a coastal road with a view that was positively Caribbean. Vietnam, in a more tranquil past, was known as the 'balcony of the Pacific' on account of its long coastline. Here the fronds of the palm trees waved languidly in the sea breezes and fine white sands sloped down to limpid aquamarine waters. High up on a hill to the left, a giant white Buddha seated on a stone lotus blossom and surrounded by 'flame' trees, dominated the city of Nha Trang; and down below by the roadside was Nha Trang Cathedral, guarded by an enormous statue of Jesus Christ, His arms outstretched in welcome. The hotel was across the street from the beach and I threw on my swimsuit and flung myself into the water. I had been swimming for literally thirty seconds when a young man doggy-paddled rapidly towards me.

'Hello, how are you?' he shouted across the water.

'Fine, thank you, how are you?' I shouted back, resigned already to having my swim interrupted.

'What your name? Where you from?'

I answered these questions with a sinking heart as another two boys started swimming excitedly towards me. The problem here was not the boys but the fact that they only knew these three phrases which they repeated over and over, giving equal emphasis to each word. Answering the questions was a necessary courtesy but also a waste of time because the conversation had no chance of developing.

I swam back to the shore and took a *cyclo* to the centre of town where there was rumoured to be a foreign-language bookshop. I was now down to my last two books – *Emma* and Stendhal's *Le Rouge et Le Noir* – and beginning to panic about running out. A friend in England had advised me to take the classics because they required greater concentration and I would be forced to read more slowly. This was true but then I ran the risk of becoming absorbed in a world that had nothing in common with the one I was inhabiting.

The bookshop was disappointing. As I eventually learnt, foreign-language bookshops in Laos, Vietnam and Cambodia almost invariably carried only a few Russian books and English language teaching manuals. I bought a copy of *Streamline English*, an Oxford University Press intensive English course for beginners published in Hong Kong. It took the form of various imaginary scenarios accompanied by the appropriate grammar and vocabulary. These included such everyday situations as 'In Prison' (lesson 27); 'Computer Dating' (lesson 29); 'I want you, Fiona' (lesson 30); 'Return From Space' (lesson 44); 'On The Moon' (lesson 61); and my favourite, 'An Interview' (lesson 32). In it, Robin Knight, the television reporter, is interviewing the Duchess of Wessex for the programme 'The English At Home'.

Robin: 'Now, Duchess . . . tell us about an ordinary day in your life.'

Duchess: 'Well, I wake up at seven o'clock . . . '

Robin: 'Really? Do you get up then?'

Duchess: 'No, of course I don't get up at that time. I have breakfast in bed and I read *The Times*.'

Robin: 'What time do you get up?'

Duchess: 'I get up at ten.'

And so on throughout the Duchess's leisurely day which includes dictation to her secretary, a walk with her dog, Philip, an afternoon nap and dressing for dinner.

The course was first published in 1978 and this edition in 1984 – but even so . . . No wonder Nguyen had a rosy view of life in the West.

Nha Trang had the kind of sleepy relaxed atmosphere that you get in small seaside towns. The houses were in faded pastel colours and most of its pretty little streets, fringed with frangipani and flamboyant trees, seemed to lead down to the sea. The air smelt fresh and fragrant, scented with cinnamon from Mount Thien Thai and the incense trees of Van Gia forest. It was a place for lovers and there was no shortage of young couples strolling through the market and along the waterfront. There is a popular song about Nha Trang which goes:

> White sand at night.
> Holding your lover in your arms.
> Listening to the whispering of the waves . . .

Lovers in Nha Trang probably have a more comfortable time of it than those in Dalat.

Bao Dai had five beautiful French-style villas here, each with magnificent views over the South China Sea and Nha Trang Bay. Air Vice-Marshal Nguyen Cao Ky, who was Prime Minister of South Vietnam from 1965–1967, used one of them as a summer house. Ky was a flamboyant figure, an ace pilot who enjoyed nightclubs, cockfighting and fast cars. His second wife was a beautiful stewardess from Air Vietnam who accompanied him on trips throughout the country dressed identically to him in a black flying suit, covered with zippers, dark glasses and a peaked cap. Even by the exceptionally chaotic and corrupt standards of the time, Ky was not much of a politician and he was forced in the 1967 elections to give way to Thieu in return for the largely decorative position of vice-president, a post which he held till 1971. He eventually fled to California where he opened a liquor store in 1975. His house was at the end of a long drive which was being slowly swept by a woman in elbow-length white gloves and a hat with an orange net veil. I paid 2,200 *dong* to the man on the gate but the house turned out to be locked and shuttered.

The sun was setting over the Cham towers of Po Nagar, where the goddess Uroja (meaning woman's breast in Cham) is worshipped. They stood at the summit of a small hill to the north of the city near the road to Da Nang, facing east and with a view of the fishing boats moored in the Cai river which flows into the South China Sea. To the west lay the river, the mountains and the white marble Buddha, gleaming in the rays of the setting sun. The sky was heavy with storm clouds and a brilliant penetrating light brought to life every corner of the ancient brickwork, every dozing beggar, every ripple in the water, every leaf on the trees. Nothing stirred in the lull before the storm.

Back in the open-air café opposite the hotel, Mr Dang had found some friends. Through one of those happy coincidences which filled his life, he had met up with two women who lived nextdoor to him in Saigon. They were visiting relations in Nha Trang, boy soldiers stationed out at the airport. The women were cousins, both aged twenty-six and unmarried, one plump and pretty, the other slender and plain. They ran a business together in Saigon, importing and selling motorbikes from Thailand which they would ride from the Cambodian border across the country to Saigon. There was another older woman at the table. She was my age, divorced with two children and had fled Saigon in a boat with forty-five other people. She said that they hadn't got far, not even to the sea, when the river police had arrested them. She had spent three months in prison and was now waiting to go to the United States. She was spending the time learning French and Japanese. It was odd. She seemed unmoved by her experiences, cheerfully philosophical about her failure to get away and her spell in jail, and the others attached no stigma to her for having tried to leave. It was already clear to me that most South Vietnamese regarded the Hanoi Government with a less than fond eye and that patriotism did not in any way imply a duty to speak well of the North Vietnamese or the Government. We sat under a string of coloured fairy lights, talking and drinking beer and listening to Vietnamese versions of western pop songs, until it was completely dark and the mosquitoes became unbearable.

In 1986 I had met, through the writer Gavin Young, a family of Catholic North Vietnamese from Haiphong. They were the first Vietnamese I had ever come across, 'boat' people who had fled to Hong Kong in the early 1980s and spent four years in a closed camp there. During the entire time they had been allowed out only once, for an afternoon, to go to Ocean Park, a funfair and oceanarium on the south coast of Hong Kong Island at Deep Water Bay. Do's family, which consisted then of his wife, their little daughter, his two younger brothers and his sister, had sailed across the South China Sea with sixty-seven other people in a boat meant to carry twelve. In Hong Kong they lived, all six of them, on a slatted wooden platform, in a space measuring some ten foot square. Do's son had been born in the camp and they called him Dai meaning 'ocean' after the journey to freedom.

Gavin spent years trying to get them out of the camp and to England where Do's mother-in-law was already living. Finally they were granted immigration visas. When I met them, it was December and very cold. They had just arrived and were living in a small council flat in Woking. They had nothing. I borrowed a friend's Volvo station wagon and drove it with Gavin down to Woking, laden with all the things that I had in my flat and didn't need or want: old blankets, a battered card table, some rugs, saucepans, clothes that would otherwise have gone to the Oxfam shop and a portable Sony television set. They liked that best.

Do's wife had prepared lunch for us: tiny delicately spiced Vietnamese spring rolls, rice, soup – I can't remember what else. The television set was immediately plugged in and turned on. After lunch, photographs were taken to mark the occasion.

Over the years, I saw the two teenage boys, Hu and Hao, once or twice a year. They were very keen on football and in the summer they used to come to stay with Gavin in Cornwall and we would cross at Exeter St David's station as I left and they arrived but lately they hadn't found Bude exciting enough. Sometimes Gavin would bring them to lunch or dinner with me in London. They always said that they missed Vietnam and wanted to know if I had any pictures of it. Every Christmas I got a Christmas card from them. Recently I realised that the rental I had paid on the television set would have been enough to *buy* four or five such sets and wrote to the rental company asking to buy the now old and outmoded set. The company declined, saying that it was their policy not to *sell* television sets but to *rent* them. I wrote to the Vietnamese apologising but asking for the return of the set as it was patently absurd to continue renting it *ad infinitum*. I got a charming letter back explaining that the set had gone wrong some eighteen months before and so they had thrown it out and replaced it with a new 22-inch screen model. They were awfully sorry. I explained the situation to the rental company who said that they were prepared to accept £80 for the non-existent set.

In 1988 there were 68,520 Vietnamese refugees. Today, despite attempts at forcible repatriation and the policies of countries like Malaysia and Thailand who force 'boat' people attempting to land back to sea, the tide of Vietnamese refugees has still not been stemmed and at the latest count, the figure was 110,866. Not all the 'boat' people have been political refugees; many were fleeing the desperate poverty into which Vietnam has been forced since the end of the war in 1975. The economic embargo imposed by the United States (and its allies) as a punishment to Vietnam for winning the war continues to this day and has caused terrible suffering and hardship. The 'boat' people are, in part, a direct consequence of that vindictiveness.

The story of Gavin's Vietnamese friends had a relatively happy ending – although being forced to flee your homeland in terror must be a nightmare from which you never quite recover. But not all 'boat' people, whether political refugees from the South or economic migrants from the North who launch their precarious vessels by night from the outlandish splendour of Ha Long Bay end up in a place as safe and cosy as Woking or Orange County. And even those who do survive to make a new life, still suffer the pains of separation and displacement. Trinh Cong Son wrote a song for those people. It goes like this:

> Do you still remember
> or have you forgotten?
> Remember Saigon's falling rain
> and sudden sunshine
> Remember the familiar streets,
> remember the footsteps
> Remember the street lights
> which stayed awake every night
> to light for you the green domes
> of tamarind leaves
> Do you still remember
> or have you forgotten?
> Remember the two seasons
> which still come and go . . .
> You have gone

but this place is still the same
The leaves are still green
on the small streets . . .
Remember the rivers
joining streams and canals . . .
On the streets,
the pouring rain, soaking feet
the water, flooding from the rooftops
turning the streets
into rivers and streams . . .
Do you still remember
or have you forgotten?

Two hundred and fifty or so miles along the road to Da Nang, we stopped for a night in Quang Ngai, capital of Nghia Binh province, once two former provinces of central Vietnam, Quang Ngai and Binh Dinh, before the 1976 reorganisation of the provinces. Quang Ngai is the jumping-off point for Son My, a group of four hamlets, one of which is called My Lai, a name that sends a chill down the spine, just as the words 'Belsen' or 'Jonestown' do.

During the Franco-Vietminh War, the whole area around Quang Ngai was a Vietminh stronghold and some of the fiercest fighting of the Vietnam War also took place here. Son My was at the heart of a region nicknamed 'Pinkville' by the Americans on account of its known Vietcong sympathies. There, in March 1968, hundreds of civilians were murdered in cold blood by the soldiers of Charley Company of the First 20th American Infantry Battalion in a routine search-and-destroy operation.

The events of the My Lai massacre bear re-telling. Shortly after 7.30 a.m. on 16 March 1968, the Year of the Monkey, one hundred and twenty men and five officers entered Son My and started rounding up and shooting the villagers. There was no enemy fire and they met with no resistance. When they 'broke for lunch', over 400 people had been killed, many shot while they lay cowering in ditches. A number of women were raped and gang-raped. The soldiers also shot the water buffalo, the pigs and the chickens. They threw the dead animals into the wells to poison the water and torched the houses. Some of the soldiers, sickened by the wholesale slaughter of innocent people, refused to take part in the carnage but their refusal did not deter the others. By the time Charley Company had finished for the day, over five hundred people had died and the village had virtually ceased to exist. A large plaque at the My Lai massacre museum (known as the Son My Memorial) details the dead and lists their names: 173 children of whom 56 were babies, 60 old people, 89 adult males and 182 women, seventeen of whom were pregnant.

The My Lai massacre occurred some six weeks after the Tet offensive which took place on the evening of 30 January 1968 when nearly seventy thousand Communist soldiers launched an offensive of 'extraordinary intensity and astonishing scope'. Violating a truce which they themselves had pledged to observe during Tet, the lunar New Year and the most important holiday of the lunar calendar, they surged into more than a hundred cities and towns, including Hue, Da Nang and Saigon where nineteen National Liberation Front commandos succeeded in entering the United States embassy compound and occupying the interior of the compound for nearly six and a half hours. Television audiences back in America were treated to the extraordinary and shocking sight of the mission co-ordinator, George Jacobson, leaning out of the chancellery window with a pistol in his hand, and scenes of furious battles and summary executions on the streets of Saigon were broadcast to bemused viewers in Minnesota and Arkansas. General Nguyen Ngoc Loan, brutal chief of South Vietnam's national police, was filmed personally executing a Vietcong prisoner in broad daylight near Saigon's An Quang temple and the report went out the next day on NBC's evening news bulletin.

Once the Allied forces had stopped reeling from the unexpectedness of the attack, they responded with the 'fury of a blinded giant' and bombed, shelled and strafed the densely populated districts of the cities as if they were the scarcely populated jungle.

By the fourth day of the battle, Allied planes had flattened large sections of Cholon and Gia Dinh, the extensions of Saigon.

The Tet Offensive came as a major shock to the Americans, both at home in the United States and in Vietnam. Despite a broadcast by General Westmoreland, the then Commander-in-Chief of the United States combat forces, saying that the Communists had 'very deceitfully' taken advantage of the Tet truce 'to create maximum consternation' but that their 'well-laid plans went afoul', there is no doubt that 'maximum consternation' was indeed one of the effects of the offensive. Neil Sheehan wrote, 'The financial and human costs of Westmoreland's war of attrition were so high that when the 1968 Tet Offensive exposed it as a fiasco, the inevitable result was a psychological collapse and a domestic political crisis of historic proportions.' The Tet Offensive must inevitably have helped to create a climate ripe for the My Lai massacre. In an introduction to *Dispatches*, David Leitch wrote: '1968 was the year when the War, and not a few of those involved in its sharp end, went comprehensively mad.'

For the Americans, one of the problems of the war in Vietnam was not just the enemy but the nature of the enemy. The Vietcong were fighting a guerrilla war in a country they knew intimately. The Americans were not. They complained endlessly that the Vietnamese all looked alike. How could they be expected to tell the difference between friend and foe, between civilian and soldier? And their mission was not to win terrain or seize positions, but simply to kill: to kill Communists and to kill as many of them as possible . . . This led to the practice of counting civilians as Vietcong. 'If it's dead and Vietnamese, it's VC, was the rule of thumb in the bush,' wrote Philip Caputo who was one of the first marines to go to Vietnam.

And then they couldn't see the enemy nor could they find the enemy to shoot back at. Lieutenant William Calley, platoon leader of Charley Company's 1st Platoon and the only soldier actually to be court-martialled and convicted, was originally charged with personally killing 109 Vietnamese in the hamlet of My Lai. He was eventually found guilty of the premeditated murder of at least twenty-two, including babies. An unappealing-looking man with cold fishy eyes who now runs a jewellery store in Columbus,

Georgia, he said after his trial, 'My troops were getting massacred and mauled by an enemy I couldn't see, I couldn't feel and I couldn't touch . . . ' The soldiers were frustrated men in an alien and hostile land, watching their comrades being felled by invisible snipers and blown up by invisible land-mines. Most of the time their enemy seemed to have no name other than Communism, no face other than the stereotypical yellow mask of the 'gook', of whom, like a dangerous wild animal, the only trace was his lethal spoor.

Caputo wrote: 'Out there, lacking restraints, sanctioned to kill, confronted by a hostile country and a relentless enemy, we sank into a brutish state. The descent could be checked only by the net of a man's inner moral values, the attribute that is called character. There were a few – and I suspect Lieutenant Calley was one – who had no net and plunged all the way down, discovering in their bottomless depths a capacity for malice they probably never suspected was there.' Calley who appears to have been a sadist, was sentenced to life in prison but his sentence aroused a storm of protest among Americans who could not understand why their boys were being punished for doing their job. President Nixon intervened and Calley's sentence was commuted to three years, served mostly as house arrest in his apartment at Fort Benning with visiting rights for a girlfriend.

We arrived in Son My in the early morning. The scene was idyllic, like a beautiful dream of rural life. The sun was climbing slowly up into the sky, the fields were lush and verdant, the irrigation canals glinting through the fine green stalks of the young rice. It was market day and farmers were taking their crops and animals to market along a path bordered by groves of elephant grass and bamboo. One old man had an enormous pig crammed into a long frail-looking basket balanced on the back of his bicycle. The pig was the size of a ten-year-old boy and must have weighed at least seventy pounds. It looked like a fat lady in a dress three sizes too small as it lay across the mudguard, its body bulging through the wicker casing and flopping down on either side of the wheel. There were children playing by the roadside in the shadow of the coconut palms and women working in the paddy fields, bending and straightening in a rhythm that seemed as old as life itself. So must My Lai have looked on the morning of 16 March 1968 – before so many lives were ended, ruined and changed for ever.

Mr Dang told me that earlier that year, a division of Korean troops had killed over three hundred people at Binh Hoa, a village ten miles from My Lai, but he said nobody cared as much because they weren't American soldiers. I asked if we could go there but was told that it wasn't on the programme.

There were two things that set Son My apart from every other village in Vietnam. One was a kind of massacre theme park surrounding the little museum that, complete with lists of the dead, recounted in words and ghastly photographs which had been taken at the time by an American Army photographer, the story of that dreadful day. The park was full of statues of weeping women cradling dying children, victims frozen in stone for ever at the moment of agony and death. It was sad and it was awful. It was also too much. It seemed to be saying 'Don't think anyone will ever, ever be allowed to forget' and the statues themselves were so totally devoid of any real beauty or artistic merit that they failed to move.

The other anomaly was a large modern hospital building, set back from the road on the outskirts of the village just past a gateway decorated with reliefs of the wounded and dying. The hospital was built with money from an American organisation called Hope and opened in May 1990. When I walked round it that morning, there wasn't a stick of furniture in the place, let alone any equipment. They were still waiting for equipment and more money from Hope.

Hoi An was a pleasant change from My Lai with its blood-stained memories. One of the oldest towns in Vietnam and the site of the first European settlement, it lies less than twenty miles south of Da Nang on the banks of the Thu Bon river. In 1535 a Portuguese adventurer called Antonio Da Faria established a settlement there. He hoped to make Faifo, as it was then called, a major Portuguese enclave like Goa or Malacca but it never took off. In the early seventeenth century, the Jesuits set up a mission there and the great French Jesuit, Alexandre de Rhodes, devised *quoc ngu*, the romanisation of the Vietnamese written language. But long before either the Portuguese or the Jesuits arrived, Hoi An was a thriving Cham seaport and even after the beginning of the fourteenth century when Cham influence in the region was starting to be undermined by the Vietnamese, it remained for centuries a trading centre used by a whole variety of merchants of differing nationalities including Japanese, Chinese, Dutch, Spanish, French, Thai and Portuguese. But it was the Japanese and the Chinese who were to leave behind the most enduring heritage: the Japanese built the exquisite little covered bridge that spans a stream that once divided the Japanese from the Chinese quarter of Hoi An; and the Chinese a number of houses and assembly halls. Today some 1300 of Hoi An's population of 60,000 are ethnic-Chinese.

Visiting Hoi An was like entering a time machine. I often had that sense in Vietnam and even more so in Laos but here, as I wandered round the pretty quaint little town, with its old houses with their tiled roofs curving upwards and its narrow streets, I was going back not twenty or even fifty years but centuries. It was like stepping onto the set of an oriental costume drama, directed with loving attention to detail, and it had almost nothing in common with anything else I had seen in Vietnam.

Mr Dang had set aside a couple of hours on his whistle-stop tour of South Vietnam for Hoi An. It was nothing like enough but I was too tired after all the driving to argue with him. It was also becoming difficult to concentrate. In the two days since we left Dalat, we had driven hundreds of miles over bad roads and in incredible heat. The journey had taken a physical toll and My Lai an unexpectedly high emotional one. I had also been suffering, more or less constantly since the Mekong Delta, from a mysterious stomach ache. I was having terrible cramps but not an upset stomach in the usual meaning of the term. I thought that part of the problem might be the lavatories. Vietnamese standards of cleanliness were lax, to say the least, and it often seemed preferable not to go at all. I had suffered in silence for a week or so but eventually, in Nha Trang, flushed with embarrassment, I had had to ask Nguyen to accompany me to a chemist for something to deal with the problem. I was given a little tube of chocolate-brown pills and been told to take one, not more, last thing at night. I had been doing this and, sure enough, there would be a great unblocking when I got up at dawn but, as the day progressed, the pains would return in full force. Nguyen and Mr Dang would dart anxious looks at me as I stifled groans and, in Hoi An, as we emerged from visiting yet another Chinese pagoda – this one with an extraordinary fountain of writhing dragons in the courtyard – Mr Dang rushed to buy me a soothing frozen yogurt. It slid down agreeably enough but didn't do much for my stomach ache. We piled into the car and drove on to Da Nang.

I found certain Vietnamese place-names almost painfully evocative. They made me yearn for something: something unknown, probably unreal and certainly unattainable. Da Nang was one of them. Before I went to Vietnam, I would lie in bed at night in London chanting, like a mantra, the names of places I had heard and read about: Saigon, Da Nang, Hue and the Perfume River, Mekong, Dien Bien Phu, Ha Long. I couldn't wait to reach Da Nang.

Da Nang, the fourth largest city in Vietnam, was where the first American marines had come ashore on 8 March 1965. During the war, it became a garrison town with a huge concentration of Americans second only to that of Saigon, stationed in and around the city. It was a boomtown teeming with whores, pimps, black marketeers and camp followers where the GIs who couldn't get to Saigon or Bangkok would come for 'R-&-R' – rest and recreation, also known as 'I-&-I' – intercourse and intoxication. Da Nang was nicknamed 'Rocket City' because of the frequency of the artillery fire aimed at the airbase whose vast airfield stretched almost the length of the city. Then you could buy jackets with the words *Da Nang – I've Served My Time in Hell* sewn onto the backs.

Now it looked dusty and fly-blown and had one of the highest unemployment rates in the country despite attempts to attract foreign investment and claims that economic reforms were being implemented. There was a large port which served as the main seaport for southern Laos and the former United States consulate had become Da Nang's Museum of American War Crimes. I walked down the street from the hotel and changed $100 into *dong* in a little shop that sold whisky and Russian vodka. Mr Dang was always offering to do this for me but it was one of the few chances I got to assert my independence. The old woman in the shop didn't have $100 worth of *dong* and asked me to sit down and wait for a few moments while her daughter ran round the block.

A small boy was playing a video game in which a single soldier alone in the jungle shot down a succession of enemy soldiers. The higher the body count the bigger the score. The game was American-made but I couldn't work out what nationality the lone sniper was supposed to be nor the defeated enemy. I bought a bottle of Johnnie Walker Red Label as a present for Mr Dang and went back to the hotel. He and Nguyen were sitting in the lobby with Mr Minh, the man from the Da Nang branch of the Department of Foreign Relations. After my experiences in the Mekong Delta with Mr Loc, I had said that I wanted to have as little as possible to do with bureaucrats and we had managed to avoid them in Dalat and Nha Trang. But Da Nang was where the American journalist, Michael Morrow, had been arrested for spying and everyone was still a little edgy. I gave Mr Dang the whisky and he got up and walked across to the bar to check that it was the same as what they were selling in the hotel. He also looked to see that the seal was unbroken and told me that I had been given a poor rate for my dollars. He clearly thought that I was totally incompetent. I said I was too tired to go out with them and went to lie on my bed in my air-conditioned room – oh, heavenly air-conditioning – and wonder whether I would ever be able to move again. I seemed to have been in Vietnam for ever.

Upstairs in the restaurant I ordered a bowl of crab soup. The waiter was in a mood for conversation. He began predictably enough by asking me how many children I had and then how old I was. Then he wanted to know what my monthly salary was. He told me that he earned 100,000 *dong* (about sixteen dollars) a month.

'How much television do you watch?' he asked.

'Not much.'

'I think English people are very fat,' he said.

'Well, yes, certainly fatter than Vietnamese people,' I answered wearily.

'Yes, very football fat.'

'Oh, you mean "fan"?'

'Yes, fat, very fat.'

But the World Cup had, thank God, finally come to an end with, to Nguyen's disappointment, West Germany as the winners. He supported Argentina and its coke-sniffing star player, Diego Maradona. I spent a dreadful night in my air-conditioned room with its pale blue walls and crimson velvet curtains and had a series of paranoid erotic dreams which left me aroused and ashamed. Between each one I woke briefly to find the bed more and more dishevelled, the neon still flooding through the gaps in the red curtains and the noise outside unabated. The ice cream vendor with his tinkling bell seemed to work through the night and there was another bell like an alarm going off to add to the soft roar of the Hondas, the rumble of the trucks and dozens of horns at volumes ranging from a muted sound like a fart to the full-blown blast you get when someone has his hand jammed down hard. The air-conditioner juddered like a washing machine in the death throes of the spin cycle and had been so badly installed that there was a three-inch gap on one side which enabled hot smoggy air and neon light from the street to pour into the room at eye-level. Shortly before dawn, I fell asleep again and dreamt that my car, my beloved beautiful old yellow Karmann Ghia, had been stolen in London.

The next morning Mr Dang and Nguyen looked bleary-eyed too and Nguyen whispered to me that they had had to buy thirty beers at a cost of 120,000 *dong* for Mr Minh. They had got back to the hotel at midnight but didn't go to bed till three because Mr Minh wanted to bring a 'girlfriend' in for Mr Dang and the hotel objected. The argument, which Mr Dang eventually lost, went on for three hours. Nguyen said, 'I was again the middle man.' This wasn't the first such occasion. One night in Dalat, they had had to climb in through the window of the hotel because everything was locked up when they rolled in at four. Nguyen told me that

his wife always worried when he went off on trips with Mr Dang.
I wasn't surprised. It was rather like being on the road with Don
Giovanni, and Leporello's famous 'catalogue' song came to mind.

> . . . In Italy six hundred and forty,
> in Germany two hundred and thirty-one,
> a hundred in France,
> ninety-one in Turkey; but in Spain
> already a thousand and three . . .
> . . . women of every rank,
> of every size, of every age . . .

I also couldn't understand the etiquette involved. Mr Dang and
Nguyen were sharing a room. Was Mr Dang going to have it off
with the 'girlfriend' while Nguyen turned a blind eye and a deaf
ear or what? And where did this leave the famous Vietnamese
pudeur which forbade videos of the Lambada lest the dance
inflame the young? Nguyen had told me that about fifty per cent
of 'respectable' Vietnamese girls slept with their boyfriends before
marriage (though he managed to look both blank and horrified
when I asked about homosexuality) and certainly Madame Dai
had suggested that the old practice of concubinage had by no
means ceased. Housing conditions were inevitably cramped but
even so, I couldn't make it out at all and Nguyen always squirmed
when I tried to press him for details so I didn't like to insist.

We set off for the beach. The guide book had raved about a
beautiful stretch of sand called Non Nuoc and I had had visions
of a long lazy day by the sea: swimming, sunbathing, enjoying a
leisurely lunch washed down with a few ice-cold beers – but no
such luck. Mr Minh had selected the nearer town beach for our
morning bathe. Though it was only just after seven, the place was
packed. We picked our way across damp brown sand and over
broken bottles, tin cans and old plastic bags. There were some
little piles of excrement – human, by the look of it. I found a few
square feet of relatively clean sand, settled myself and opened a
paperback lent me by Mr Minh. It was a dreary big blockbuster

called *Saigon* by an English writer called Anthony Grey, to whom one of the waitresses at the Caravelle had asked me to post a letter. Within minutes I was surrounded by children shouting, with mind-numbing monotony, 'How are you? What your name? Where you from?' Mr Dang and Nguyen were soon frolicking in the tepid green sea, splashing each other and squealing with laughter and mock-terror like teenage girls. By ten o'clock, it was time to leave – not a moment too soon in my opinion – and I remembered that the Vietnamese don't like to get 'black' in the sun.

Later that afternoon, as a storm was whipping through the dunes, we drove out to Non Nuoc, which the Americans used to call 'China Beach'. There the sands ranged for deserted golden miles north and south of the Marble Mountains and the sea was a beautiful clear pale blue. Floating in the water were huge round baskets woven from strips of bamboo covered with pitch, called *thung chai* – *thung* meaning 'basket' and *chai* 'pitch' – and used by the fishermen to travel from shore to boat and between boats. The beach was so large that there could have been a thousand people on it and it still wouldn't have been crowded. I asked irritably why we couldn't have come there in the morning instead of the filthy town beach. I can't remember the answer but the real reason was probably something to do with the oriental passion for crowds or rather blank incomprehension of the joys of solitude. The point of any outing is social and that takes precedence over all other considerations. We sat and watched the storm brewing and the *thung chai* bobbing on the waves. As the sky darkened, the fishermen in the basket-boats lit little lanterns and the water suddenly sparkled and shimmered with the reflection of the tiny orange flames, like a piece of silky material covered in sequins. An old Australian was drinking beer and eating marinated squid with a crowd of young Vietnamese men with whom he was doing business – something to do with the import of building materials. We fell into desultory conversation, marvelling at the amount of beer the Vietnamese managed to drink and wondering how they paid for it. He said that he thought that they spent every penny they earned on the stuff. He had been in Hanoi for nine months and was fed up with being referred to as the 'foreigner' or the 'capitalist' or even the 'capitalist foreigner'. He said that he had tried to explain to the Vietnamese that there were politer ways of referring to people from overseas but to no avail. As we talked, the rain began to fall thick and fast in drops the size of coins and the few solitary figures on the beach came running for cover in the restaurant.

There were probably lots of wonderful sights to see in Da Nang but none of us seemed to have the energy for them. Nguyen and I got halfway up Thuy Son, the largest of the Marble Mountains, which is riddled with hidden pagodas and Buddhist monasteries, before collapsing from exhaustion.

'Let's go down, Nguyen,' I said. 'I can't go on and I really don't care if I never see another statue of Buddha again.'

'It is up to you,' Nguyen replied and we turned back.

Mr Dang had driven round the foot of the mountain intending to meet us when we came down the other side but we were too tired in the blistering heat of the midday sun even to walk along the road to catch up with him. Nguyen gave two hundred *dong* to a small boy to go and fetch him while we sat in a café drinking coconut water and fending off hawkers trying to flog hideous little marble ornaments.

We did, however, manage two visits to the beautiful Museum of Cham Sculpture, where it was wonderfully cool and soothing. Built in 1915 by the Ecole Française d'Extrême-Orient of Hanoi, the museum has the finest collection of Cham sculpture in the world, much of it from around Da Nang, for centuries the centre of the kingdom of Champa. Cham art is similar to Khmer and accordingly distinguished by an influence that owes more to India than to China, but is heavier and earthier, consisting largely of massive three-dimensional figures carved out of sandstone. Cham portrayals of human features reveal distinctive physical characteristics: thick lips topped by wide moustaches, flat noses, heavy-lidded eyes and eyebrows that meet in the middle. The museum contained some 300 pieces in all: images of Shiva, Brahma and Vishnu; lithe *apsaras*, monstrous *lingas*, great winged *Garudas* and pudgy *Ganeshas*, their elephant trunks resting on their fat bellies; giants and monsters, all the gods, goddesses and semi-divine creatures of Hindu mythology, beautifully displayed in a simple white single-storey building consisting basically of a series of open-air alcoves. My favourite piece was a tenth-century *apsara* from Tra-Kieu, site of the fourth-century Cham capital, Sinhapura, the 'Lion Citadel'. She was carved of a wonderful honey-coloured stone, her graceful limbs arranged with apparent ease in the sensuous motions of a dance, her head tilted to one side, her almond eyes closed, her beautiful full lips curving only very slightly.

Nguyen's wife and son were due to arrive any day and the antici-pation was having an effect on him. Mr Dang was different too. The further away from the south we were and the further north we went, the less interested and the more withdrawn he became. He had fewer friends here, fewer drinking companions, fewer women. We were all tired and our time together was drawing to an end. The closeness that had grown up between the three of us over the weeks was dissipating and I felt increasingly alienated from them both. A lethargy and indifference had descended on us all. It didn't seem to matter much what we did. The adventure was almost over and a new chapter was about to begin.

6

Hue and History

I liked Minh Phuong. She was pretty and competent and serene. Her dainty presence showed us up for the load of roughnecks we had become and she was a necessary civilising influence in her graceful *ao dai*, her porcelain complexion sheltered from the sun by a striped red umbrella. Nguyen's son was a grave polite little boy of seven with big eyes and blackened teeth like his father, slightly precious in the way that only children can be and, like his mother, immaculately clean and tidy. His name was Minh.

'After Ho Chi Minh?' I asked.

'Oh, no,' Nguyen answered, 'I would not dare.'

We picked them up at Da Nang airport and set off immediately for Hue along Highway One which runs the length of the country all the way from the Cambodian border in the south to the frontier with China in the north. Minh Phuong and I sat in the back of the car, the others in the front. We drove through wonderful country where the mountains seemed to be saved from tumbling into the jade-green sea only by the road. This was Hai Van or the Pass of Clouds, the start of the massive bulk of the Annamite Cordillera. When you look at a map of Vietnam, you can see that this marks the beginning of the narrowest part of the country – only fifty or so miles from the Lao border. Everything was very intense and clear and fresh: the blues and greens of the water, the sky and the hills and even the air seemed to be coloured, a bright yellow-white, the colour of pure clean heat. We rounded bend after bend and round each corner, there would be yet another more dazzling scene. At one point, we looked down on an exquisite little

village, set in a bay on a peninsula, its church and spire giving it
a Mediterranean air. From a distance it was idyllic, palm trees
swaying in the breeze, white sands stretching down to turquoise
waters, fishing junks picturesquely moored. It beckoned irresistibly and we motored on down there for lunch. Close up, it was
less charming. There were flies everywhere and a strong smell of
rotting fish from the catch put out to dry in the sun. Hanging
from a faded patchwork awning was a string of tiny sea horses.
It was wonderful to see these creatures, if not alive, at least in the
flesh, which had before been the stuff of near-mythology. Minh
Phuong who had been carsick on the drive, insisted on wiping all
the bowls and the chopsticks with a roll of lavatory paper that
she produced out of her bag and she and the boy fanned the flies
away – to no effect – while we ate oysters and a fish full of tiny
sharp bones. Nguyen said that Minh was terrified of germs. After
lunch, Mr Dang lay down in a nearby hammock and went to
sleep. He had, as usual, been flirting with the women who ran the
place and one of them, who spoke a little English, told me that
Mr Dang was a 'very naughty man'.

That evening, in Hue, we attended a cultural show, a performance
of traditional music in the town hall given by four wrinkled old
men and one young man wearing long twilight-blue silk tunics
over white trousers, and hats of the same blue. One old man with
a lute-like instrument sang a song whose title he announced in
French. It was called *La Nostalgie de l'Amour* and was all about
nostalgia, separation and peace. There was a delicate monotony
about the music and, compared to Miss Tao in the Mekong Delta,
it seemed very cerebral and very passionless. Already I thought
Hue was awfully civilised, keeping up ancient mandarin traditions
of culture. If South Vietnam was earthy and North Vietnam tough,
then the atmosphere in Hue – the country's intellectual heart
where there are twelve schools of higher learning – was exquisitely
rarefied.

Afterwards we dispersed to our separate accommodations, I to
the Perfume Hotel on the banks of the river of the same name
and the Vietnamese, in the interests of economy, to a nearby

guesthouse. It was the first time since the beginning of the journey that I had slept somewhere different from Nguyen and Mr Dang and it marked a change in our relationship. We could all have stayed at the Perfume Hotel but it was quite expensive and I couldn't really afford to pay for Nguyen's family as well. As it turned out, I would have done better to join them in the lavender-coloured guesthouse as the Perfume Hotel was a dump.

I got up at dawn the next morning and went to explore the remains of the Imperial Citadel. By half-past seven, the heat was stifling. Hue has the highest rainfall of any city in Vietnam and was incredibly humid even by Vietnamese standards. I spent an hour or so wandering round the shabbily beautiful ruins. Remembering the garishly-restored Ming Tombs in Peking, the thought briefly crossed my mind that it was perhaps just as well that there was still not enough money in Vietnam to repair the damage inflicted first by a fire in 1947 and then by the Tet Offensive in 1968 when the Vietcong occupied the city for over three weeks.

During the Tet Offensive, many of the inhabitants of Hue had Vietcong soldiers actually living with them in their houses, trying to convert them, teaching them Communist songs. They resisted conversion but they and their city paid a terrible price. Of a population of 140,000, some 90,000 were turned into refugees. Possibly as many as 3,000 civilians were killed (the victims had been shot or clubbed to death, or buried alive) and 4,000 wounded. Much of the commercial centre of the city and of the Citadel were destroyed. The streets stank of decomposing corpses. An American marine described the scene that confronted the Allies as they re-took the city: 'My first impression was of desolation, utter devastation. There were burnt-out tanks and trucks, and upturned automobiles still smouldering. Bodies lay everywhere, most of them civilians. The smoke and stench blended, like in some kind of horror movie – except that it lacked weird music . . .'

Enough remained of the Citadel to give an idea of what it must have looked like. The wounds inflicted on the grey stone had softened and healed over the years and much of the damage lay hidden under creepers and greenery. A thick carpet of floating lotus blossoms covered the moat surrounding the ramparts of the Citadel and through the gateway stood the Palace of Supreme Harmony. Beyond stretched a grassy expanse where most of the original buildings had been flattened, leaving only a few bricks and stones.

This was once the Forbidden Purple City or the Great Within, the private living quarters of the emperor's family, his eunuchs and his beautiful concubines. Hue is renowned for the beauty of its women and certainly they all seemed to take far greater pains with their dress and appearance than elsewhere in Vietnam. It was all overgrown in a rather charming and romantic way and I couldn't make out from the map in my guide book what was, or had been, what. It was far too hot, anyway, for serious sightseeing. I walked slowly through the ruins, fanning myself with my notebook and thinking about Vietnamese history or rather Vietnamese attitudes towards their own history.

I had noticed that it was as if nothing had existed before the war, as if modern Vietnam, like Venus, had sprung into life fully formed. True, the streets were named after Vietnamese heroes like Le Loi and Trang Hung Dao and you could visit villas that had once belonged to Bao Dai but nobody ever seemed to *know* anything about anything that had taken place before the late 1950s. I couldn't really blame Nguyen. He was born in 1957 and had lived his whole life under first the Americans and then the Communists. He was educated in that he could speak English – up to a point – but, in reality, he knew nothing. Mr Dang was older and more experienced but he had learnt his lessons in the school of life. A Chinese scholar once wrote: 'The people of Vietnam do not like the past', and it might well be that they have little reason to do so. In addition to what may be an understandable ambivalence towards their own history, the Vietnamese have had to face certain practical difficulties in this area. In the fifteenth century when the Chinese conquered Vietnam for the second time, they carried off all the archives; and after World War Two, the imperial library in Hue was demolished resulting in the scattering of valuable ancient documents all over the city like discarded bits of waste paper. The Vietnamese historian Hoang Xuan Han described rescuing documents from the market where they were being used to wrap up food. Other papers dealing with recent history were destroyed when the presidential palace was burnt during the coup which overthrew Diem in 1963. Even so, there seemed to be a widespread indifference to historical fact. For instance, I asked about the fate of Queen Nam Phuong, Bao Dai's beautiful wife. I was told variously that she had died of cancer in 1930, that she had fled to the United States and that she was living in France with the former emperor. (In fact, she died in France in August 1964.) I found increasingly that I believed almost nothing that I was told. All history, or rather the answers to any questions about the past, smacked of myth, legend or hearsay – but when it came to which teams were playing in the World Cup, everybody knew the answer.

That evening we took a boat out on the Perfume River and spent a couple of civilised hours with Mr Que discussing literature and current events. Mr Que was a local poet and songwriter whose favourite British authors were Byron, Shakespeare (he particularly liked *Othello*) and Somerset Maugham who, he said, 'wrote much about the fate of the human being'. Mr Que had 'played his part in the sad and happy incidents of the city of Hue'. He had spent a year in prison on Con Dao in 1972 for protesting against the South Vietnamese Government and earlier, in 1963, when he was sixteen, he had taken part in the Buddhist protests against the Diem regime.

What became known as the Buddhist Crisis began in Hue one day in May 1963 when a company of Civil Guards, commanded by a Catholic officer, killed nine people, eight of them children, and injured fourteen others in a crowd protesting against a new decree that forbade the flying of the Buddhist flag on Buddha's birthday. Diem's elder brother, Thuc, was Archbishop of Hue and South Vietnam's leading Catholic prelate at the time. The discrimination against the Buddhists, including this latest decree, was largely his doing.

The initial protest and violent consequences in Hue were followed by a series of demonstrations and, most dramatically, by the suicide of an elderly monk named Quang Duc who was doused with petrol and set alight while seated in the lotus position on a busy Saigon street. The protests and suicides went on throughout the summer until 20 August when some 1,400 monks and nuns were arrested in pagodas all over South Vietnam. In Hue where the movement had originated and where the Buddhist leader Trich Tri Quang held court, about thirty monks and student followers were shot or clubbed to death and the great statue of Buddha in Hue's main Tu Dam pagoda was smashed. Diem then closed the universities in Hue and Saigon and effectively silenced the Buddhists, but the Americans were sufficiently impressed by the whole business and Diem's inability to conciliate dissident groups in the face of a growing Communist challenge, to give their support to a coup engineered by a group of senior insurgent generals that brought down the Diem regime and led to the assassination of Diem and his brother, Nhu, later that year. In 1966 the Buddhists, again mobilised by Trich Tri Quang, re-surfaced in like manner to protest against the military regime of Generals Thieu and Ky and to demand elections for a civil government with a fresh wave of demonstrations and self-immolations.

I would have liked to question Mr Que more closely about his experiences but he seemed to prefer our conversation to follow a more courtly path. Nguyen kept saying, 'Mr Que would like to serve you a song' and then the poet would break into song or verse. One of the poems he recited was made up on the spur of the moment. I had asked him how he felt about the collapse of Communism in Eastern Europe. His response was, I thought, somewhat oblique.

> everyone likes flowers
> and we have to respect
> each other for living
> everyone is a musical instrument
> and we look to each other
> for our hope
> everyone is the river
> and the river meets together
> with the big sea at the breakways
> everyone is a star
> sparkling in the open sky
> everyone is a poem

to praise our earth happily
everyone is a sun

He recited this – well, let's be frank – nonsense in a sort of plainsong chant, adding that the events in Eastern Europe could be attributed to 'not keeping the beautiful things of the world'. 'What is beautiful will live for ever, what is ugly will be destroyed,' he said. He told me that he made only 40,000 *dong* a year from writing and had to be supported by his friends.

Mr Que was the artistic director of the Hue club of traditional music and told me that he had composed twenty songs in the traditional style. He was also a member of the local kite-flying and flower-collecting clubs. All in all, he seemed to be fairly typical of Hue and it was no wonder that Mr Dang looked impatient and macho in this city. Hue was, however, the only place in the whole country where it was possible to imagine mandarins in silk robes paying for white herons to be released across the sky at dusk for the aesthetic gratification of their guests which was once one of the high points of life in old Vietnam.

Now the mandarins have long gone and those with a taste for the finer things in life have to be content with such gentle and harmless pleasures as kite-flying and flower-collecting. I thought Mr Que was a bit of a bore and Nguyen's renditions of his poetry left a great deal to be desired but initially I found the rarefied atmosphere of Hue rather soothing after the rigours of the rest of South Vietnam – and I knew from past experience that the North would be even tougher. Back at the hotel, a woman with heavy purple eye make-up and a matching low-cut evening frock was singing *Jambalaya* in Vietnamese to the accompaniment of a noisy band of electric guitars. The noise was unspeakable. I sat out on the terrace as far away from the loudspeakers as possible and watched the sun's last rays stroke the waters of the beautiful Perfume River where prostitutes still ply their trade in the *sampans* moored close to the riverbank. I was told that the police had tried 'many ways' to stop it but the old combination of money and sex proved irresistible. I still had stomach ache, now compounded by menstrual cramps, and I felt depressed, irritable and awash with self-pity. Nguyen had disappeared back to his family and, even though I had been longing to be alone, I found myself resenting their cavalier desertion.

The next morning soon after six, I walked across to the guest-house to meet Nguyen and the others. We were going to visit the mausoleum of the Emperor Minh Mang The Light and The Decree of Heaven, who succeeded the great Gia Long. Everything had to be done early before the heat became unbearable. They were sitting outside on little low stools under a banyan tree drinking coffee and eating 'gâteaux folkloriques', tiny sweet cakes made of jelly which looked like wet black stones wrapped in banana leaves and which Miss Van had brought as a present. The cakes, if I understood her correctly, had some kind of sexual significance, with the different ingredients denoting the man and the woman.

Miss Van was a history teacher who was to accompany us to the tomb. She had been supposed to escort me round the Imperial Citadel but had failed to show up. Now she was dressed for the occasion in an apricot silk *ao dai*, with a delicate pattern of flowers woven into the silk, worn over a pair of white silk trousers and high-heeled silver sandals. Minh Phuong wore an embroidered scarlet *ao dai* and high white sandals. Both women had pale pink frosted polish on their toenails. In the interests of comfort, I had decided to ignore Vietnamese standards of modesty which demanded that every inch of skin be covered and, as a result, I felt a little under-dressed in a cotton skirt, a sleeveless tee-shirt and rubber flip-flops.

The mausoleum lay some seven miles to the south of the city and was reached by taking a little rowing boat across to the left bank of the Perfume River. It was a beautiful mausoleum in a beautiful setting, consisting of a series of graceful towers and courtyards reached through slender ornamental gateways topped with ceramic lotus buds and decorated with flower designs. All around were ponds brimming with white lotuses. Miss Van told me that the site had been chosen deliberately so the mountain behind would represent the emperor's head, the lotus ponds his arms and the main stretch of land where the buildings stood, his body. Minh Mang who ruled from 1820–1841, was the fourth son of Gia Long by a concubine. He was interested in science and technology and invented a water wheel that would pump water through a conduit into his palace so that coolies would not have to carry it. He was also an admirer of such western products as glass, English gunpowder and French brandy – but not of French attempts to convert the Vietnamese to Christianity. He had read the Old Testament in Chinese and told his officials that he found it 'absurd'. In 1825 he issued a decree outlawing the dissemination of Christianity and then embarked on a persecution of those who had embraced the faith, which included the execution of Roman Catholic missionaries.

As we left, the caretaker waded through the mud to pick me two lotus blossoms. They exuded a faint slightly bitter perfume like that of green Chinese tea. When I remarked on it, Miss Van told me that sometimes dry tea was placed inside the flower to imbue it with the scent of the lotus. Back at the Perfume Hotel, I put the blooms straight into water but they wilted quickly, their great heavy heads drooping over the side of my tooth glass.

Despite its beauty, I found Hue ultimately depressing. Minh Mang's mausoleum in all its splendour, the lovely seven-tiered octagonal pagoda of Thien Mu built on a little hill overlooking the Perfume River, the haunting ruins of the Imperial Citadel, even the Hue Museum of Antique Objects, they all seemed so remote from present-day Vietnam. Even their beauty meant nothing. The dusty museum was filled with exquisite objects made of carved ivory, mother-of-pearl, jade, amethyst, coral, crystal and *cloisonné*. There were flowers carved in rose-quartz and little gold bowls with delicate designs etched onto them but not even Miss Van knew anything about any of these treasures. Each monument, each *objet d'art* was perceived merely as an emblem of a hateful past. And the longed-for future lay in the status symbols of modern capitalism: televisions, video recorders, cameras, anything marked 'Sony'.

I was also apprehensive about the journey north. In my original application to the Vietnamese embassy in London, I had asked to travel some of the route from Saigon to Hanoi on what is known as the 'Reunification' train – so-called because it runs from North to South Vietnam and thereby unites the country. I like trains and

I thought it would be fun and make a change. But, as chance would have it, just before leaving England I read an article by Richard West entitled 'Rough Ride to Saigon' which cast a shadow over my enthusiasm. West had taken the train in the opposite direction, all the way from Hanoi to Saigon, and had not enjoyed himself. The journey had been uncomfortable, dirty and at times frightening. This was hardly encouraging particularly as West, an experienced foreign correspondent who knew Vietnam well, had been travelling with three other people including a Vietnamese guide. I would be all alone as I was due to say goodbye to Mr Dang and Nguyen in Hue – which was where I had hoped to pick up the train. All the same, I was determined to do it if it was at all possible.

By the time we reached Hue, I had given up the whole idea. Both Mr Dang and head office in Hanoi, who would often telephone me at dawn to discuss my plans, insisted that it was out of the question for me to travel alone on the train, claiming that it was dangerous and complicated. At one point Mr Dang had suggested a compromise, that Nguyen and I go by train from Nha Trang to Da Nang – a comparatively short journey – but that didn't work out either and when we got to Hue and heard that the very train we were to have taken had crashed *en route*, killing thirty people, it seemed just as well.

It had been decided in Da Nang that I would return there by car and catch a plane. I didn't seem to have any choice and had accordingly bought an air ticket from a girl in a canary-yellow *ao dai*. Any disappointment I might have felt was assuaged by the prospect of a blissful day on China Beach. But, suddenly, on the evening before we were to return to Da Nang, Mr Dang announced with a broad smile that he had succeeded in getting me a place on the night train to Hanoi. The journey would take twenty hours but he knew how keen I was to go by train, so he had pulled every string possible in order to please me.

'But you told me that it was too dangerous,' I said.

'No, no, you'll be just fine,' he answered cheerfully.

'What about the train that just crashed?'

'The brakes failed.'

'Well, how do we know that the brakes will be all right on this train?'

'It's a different train and anyhow there aren't any mountains on this leg of the journey so you'll be perfectly OK. Of course, if you now don't *want* to go on the train . . . '

I didn't *want* to go by train *at all*. I wanted to spend a day lying in the sun on the most beautiful beach in the world. I wanted to have a decent night's rest in the seaside hotel, lulled to sleep by the sound of the waves. But I couldn't say so – not just because Mr Dang might have gone to some trouble on my behalf (though a little voice inside my head kept suggesting that he had had enough of this job and was eager to see the back of me) but also because I felt it was my duty to endure this potentially ghastly experience. Otherwise I would feel guilty and a coward and I'd almost certainly regret it.

We had a magnificent farewell dinner of shrimp, squid and a huge spiced fish wrapped in rice paper in a restaurant set in the middle of a lake covered with lotus blossoms. This had once been the Emperor Tu Duc's fishing lodge. Tu Duc, Minh Mang's grandson, was a man who enjoyed the pleasures of the flesh. At his court every meal consisted of fifty dishes prepared by fifty chefs and served by fifty servants. His tea was made with the dewdrops that had gathered overnight on the leaves of the lotuses. He was immensely fat, had 104 wives and countless concubines but never succeeded in fathering any children. One theory is that he became sterile after contracting smallpox but perhaps he was just too fat. Before I came out for dinner, I had heard on the radio that the United States had changed its stand on Cambodia and was going to withdraw its recognition of the coalition government (which included the Khmer Rouge) at the United Nations. This was bound to have implications for Vietnam which was desperate for the financial embargo imposed by most western countries to be lifted. Soon there might be money to restore the Imperial Citadel.

The train arrived in Hue an hour late – around eight. It was already very dark and its arrival was quite dramatic. The station was lit only by oil lamps and a few flickering bulbs powered by an erratic generator. Men, naked to the waist, their muscular chests gleaming with sweat, leant out of the windows as the train clanked into the station. I kissed Mr Dang and Nguyen goodbye, thanking them for everything and promising to look them up when I next came to Saigon, and climbed aboard. In preparation for a night among thieves and vagabonds, I had stashed all my remaining dollars in an elaborate leather money belt and I was terribly hot. There were two other westerners on the train: an enormous Scandinavian and a neat handsome Australian in a solar topee and a green shirt open to the waist to reveal a splendid pelt of black curly hair. He was sharing my compartment along with two utterly silent Vietnamese women who were already installed in the upper bunks. The train had no lighting so once we had pulled out of the station, we were plunged into pitch black. There was no glass in the windows and the night roared past. The breeze was refreshing enough but it was virtually impossible to talk because of the noise. I offered Bruce, the Australian, a swig of whisky from my flask and settled down to read *Emma* by torch- light. After ten minutes, I gave up and rolled onto my stomach, reasonably confident that no-one would be able to get at my money belt and rob me.

We woke around six when it got light and Bruce unearthed a sausage of Hue pâté wrapped in banana leaves which had been in his rucksack. The end had been gnawed by a rat during the night. He hacked off the tooth-marked section with my penknife and handed me a couple of slices to have for breakfast with the bread rolls and sweet black coffee I had bought in the restaurant car. The Vietnamese passengers were tucking into bowls of *pho* cooked on the spot over an open fire. We were passing through an increas- ingly drab and charmless landscape, flat and arid with only the odd volcanic crag to break the monotony. By eight, we were drinking cans of warm Tiger beer cooled and diluted with shards of ice – I had long given up worrying about my bowels – and Bruce was telling me *all* about himself.

He had been teaching an English course in Hue for three weeks and was now returning to Hanoi where he was living. He came from Perth and had been in Vietnam for over a year. He was gay and in love with a young Vietnamese tour guide called Houm who lived in Saigon. He said that he was planning, if necessary, to adopt Houm legally as his brother so that they could live together. It seemed highly unlikely that he would be permitted to do this but he assured me that it was possible. He told me that because he often didn't see Houm for eight or ten weeks at a stretch, he was driven by frustration and desire to be unfaithful to him with boys in Hanoi. The noise of the train was deafening and Bruce had to shout for me to be able to hear what he was saying. It was as if he hadn't talked to anyone for months. Out it all poured like water from a burst pipe: accounts of blow-jobs, sex in secret places with strangers, and all the clichés of gay promiscuity. He described going to a room about six foot square which had a tiny loft above it and waiting in the loft while four Vietnamese men queued below to have sex with him one after the other. He said half the men he slept with were married but they referred to themselves as 'sisters', the 'seven sisters of Hanoi'.

'One evening,' he said, 'Houm and I had been out. When we came back to the hotel, a young man followed us up to our room. I thought he and Houm wanted to talk so I offered him a beer and they started chatting. Then Houm translated what the stranger was saying. He said that he had never before been offered a beer by a foreigner and how nice I was. Then he offered to give Houm some money if Houm would let him sleep with me. I told Houm it was up to him. I said I didn't particularly want to sleep with the stranger, I'd rather sleep with him but, if he wanted the money, I'd oblige.'

It seemed an extraordinary conversation to have with someone with whom you were supposed to be in love (though perhaps no more extraordinary than the one we were having) but it did at least demonstrate a crude grasp of the facts of life. Money is important, particularly in a country as poor as Vietnam. In the event, Houm didn't want him to sleep with the stranger though the latter later claimed to have had sex with Bruce – twice – while Houm was back in Saigon. If a word that Bruce said was to be believed – and I wasn't sure how much was boasting – all the boys in Saigon and Hanoi were just longing for him. He said he liked them because they were soft and hairless, and that they adored his hairy chest – and presumably the fact that he was a foreigner. He told me that Houm wore lipstick and the *cyclo* drivers in Saigon nail polish. He said one of these *cyclo* drivers was called 'Big Penis' which, he insisted, in the face of my total incredulity, was a common Vietnamese first name, but that Houm teased him by calling him 'Little Penis'. I sensed that he wanted me to ask for details of the size, etc. of these penises so that he could elaborate but I couldn't quite face it. I thought he was a bit sad and hopeless, a randy misfit who had allowed vanity, lust and loneliness to blind him to reality. I had spent enough time in Vietnam to know that many Vietnamese were desperate for a different kind of life and it seemed highly probable that much of his attraction for the men he slept with lay in what they might hope to get from him one day: money, contacts, an entrée to a new life. Or perhaps he really was irresistible and Hanoi was full of secret gays, dying to come out.

7

Hanoi Again

We arrived in Hanoi around two which meant Bruce had had a good six hours to share the details of his sex life with me. Despite Mr Dang's telephone calls alerting the Ministry of Information to my arrival, there was no-one to meet me and I had to struggle the length of two platforms and across the tracks festooned with suitcases, and swearing like a trooper. Bruce had told me that when his mother had travelled from Saigon to Hanoi, the train had hit and killed a cyclist on the line as it pulled into Hanoi station. There were rats scurrying under the carriages of the stationary trains and piles of old tyres and scrap iron all over the place.

Outside there was pandemonium and a crowd of what appeared to be at least a thousand people fighting for *cyclos*, pushing and shoving each other into khaki jeeps and all yelling at the tops of their voices. Most of them were dressed in black or that pervasive drab olive-green I remembered from my last visit. It was fiendishly hot and humid and the muscles in my back and shoulders were protesting violently against the weight of the cases. Bruce disappeared into the maelstrom waving and shouting, 'See ya later at the Billabong Club', and a terrifying seven-foot *cyclo* driver with a complexion like petrified lava grabbed my bags and flung them into his vehicle. I handed him Mr Dang's letter to the Ministry of Information and told him to take me to the address on the envelope. I figured that we could argue about the price when we got there.

We reached the Ministry as a slender middle-aged woman in

trousers was getting into a station wagon. She was Mrs Thuc and she was just leaving for the station to meet me. My train had apparently arrived an hour early. On her instructions, I gave the giant 20,000 *dong* (over three dollars) which seemed excessive, and we went inside to discuss plans.

At dinner in Saigon, Madame Dai had told me that there was nothing in Vietnam to compare with Angkor or even the *wats* in Laos. She had said, 'The only things we have that are really extraordinary are the tunnels of Cu Chi and the Bay of Ha Long'.

The tunnels of Cu Chi are near Saigon and were where hundreds of members of the National Liberation Front had lived and worked underground while waging a guerrilla war in the South. They are now something of a tourist attraction but I was too claustrophobic to go down a tunnel and so had had to make do with reading about them. The Bay of Ha Long was a different matter. I had first heard of it through *The Quiet American* in a scene where Fowler is taken by a French airman to see the view at sunset. 'He said, "We will make a little detour. The sunset is wonderful on the calcaire. You must not miss it," he added kindly, like a host who is showing the beauty of his estate, and for a hundred miles we trailed the sunset over the Baie d'Along. The helmeted Martian face looked wistfully out, down the golden groves among the great humps and arches of porous stone, and the wound of murder ceased to bleed.'

We left for Haiphong and Ha Long Bay at dawn the next morning. Mrs Thuc was to be my guide in the North and I was looking forward to spending some time with a woman. There was another advantage: unlike Nguyen, she spoke excellent English. This car, a station wagon once owned by one of the Eastern-bloc embassies, was more comfortable than Mr Dang's and the driver, Tam, appeared to have seen fewer Clint Eastwood movies but, by now, I was chronically tired from weeks of bad sleep and stomach ache so it didn't make much difference. We stopped around seven in a fly-blown roadside café for bowls of *pho*. Mrs Thuc and Tam ate hearty breakfasts. I had coffee. Between mouthfuls, Mrs Thuc talked at length about artificial limbs, the pros and cons of plastic, aluminium and wood. The farmers prefer wood – it is more solid and not as sweaty as plastic. She was also a mine of information about family planning (two children per couple is the prescribed maximum) and birth control (the IUD, the pill and condoms are the methods of choice). She confirmed reluctantly that there were cases of AIDS in Vietnam – she didn't know how many – but made a *moue* of distaste when I asked about attitudes towards homosexuality.

Ha Long Bay was wet and windy. The weather reminded me of days on the west coast of Ireland. The fishing junks with their ox-blood sails were writhing on the waves and the spectacular crags were almost invisible in the spray. There was no question of going out on the water and we went instead for a damp walk round Bai Chay, a grimy little coal-mining town across the bay from Hong Gai where we were spending the night. Three muscular old men in tattered trousers rolled up to the knee and sleeveless tee-shirts revealing sinewy arms and legs were gathered round a huge, almost totally bald cock. I asked Mrs Thuc to ask them what was the matter with the bird, what disease he was suffering from to make him so featherless.

'He's a fighting cock and he has to have very few feathers so that there is nothing for his opponents to grab hold of,' one of the old men said. The bird was named Tia Hong, meaning 'Red Pink', after the livid colour that suffused his scrawny bald torso. They were very proud of him. He was worth, they said, between 50,000 and 60,000 *dong* and could earn them as much as one million *dong* in a fight – if he won – but they had to spend a small fortune on getting him ready for fighting: 100,000 *dong* worth of special food, Vitamin B and medicine. I said that cock-fighting had long been outlawed in England and they shook their heads pityingly at the kill-joy nature of the law-and-order merchants in my country. They told me that the Cubans imported cocks to Thailand and Hong Kong but that their cock was Vietnamese and due to fight again next Sunday. Cock-fighting had been popular for centuries in the East. Errol Flynn was supposed to have bailed himself out of a tight financial spot by organising cock-fights in

Macao and as early as the fifth century it was a favourite sport in the ancient Mon-Khmer kingdom of Funan in the lower valley of the Mekong.

One of the men spoke French and had been a soldier in the French Army, fighting against the Vietnamese. He and his father had worked for the Frenchman who used to own the coal mine.

'Once I was rich and a bourgeois. Now I am a peasant and sixty and life holds nothing more for me,' he said. 'I love my fatherland and I have warm feelings towards it but I am not satisfied with the present situation. I would like the freedom to make money.' At this Mrs Thuc gave him a sharp look and I half-expected the secret police to appear and carry him off.

That night an electric storm raged over Ha Long Bay. Lightning streaked the sky, thunder crashed, traffic roared past my window and the red and green lights of the café next door flashed on and off all night long. Sleep was, at best, elusive. At four o'clock my alarm went off and I tiptoed along the corridor to wake Mrs Thuc for our boat trip. The previous evening I had expressed a desire to see the dawn break over the bay and we were supposed to go out on the water. We peered out into the pitch-black and listened for a few moments to the wind howling. It didn't seem quite the weather for boating. I stumbled back to my room, took a Valium and went back to sleep till seven. At half-past seven Mrs Thuc and Binh, the local man, came to discuss plans. The ceiling in Mrs Thuc's room had sprung a leak during the night and her bed had been soaked. Tam had had bed bugs. Nobody was very satisfied. Binh returned with the news that no boat was available till eleven and then it would cost thirty-five dollars. It was pouring with rain and there wasn't a rock in sight. It was difficult to know what to do but I thought it would be a waste to have come all the way from Hanoi and not even tried to see the bay from the water so it was agreed that we would meet downstairs in three hours.

I had a crippling stomach ache which I thought might be eased by a visit to the bathroom but, when I got there, it was as if a typhoon had hit the place. Someone, or perhaps an army, had had diarrhoea everywhere: lavatory bowls were overflowing and wads of soiled paper littered the floor. I couldn't understand it. These were modern bathrooms, nicely tiled in pale blue and with proper cisterns, not the holes in the ground that you often found. Why were they in this revolting state? My spirits were at an all-time low. The whole business was worse for women, of course, though Mrs Thuc seemed to take it all in her stride.

When we had stopped for breakfast on the road to Haiphong, I had gone to use the lavatory there at her suggestion. That too was a nightmare. It was right next to the pigsty where a large sow was comfortably snorting and grunting through her breakfast. The floor was covered with excrement and the stench was appalling. The pigsty was spotless by comparison. But I never heard anyone comment on such things, let alone apologise or complain. Perhaps it was considered bad manners, perhaps no-one thought it was important. In the great scheme of things, it wasn't really. Vietnamese babies never wore nappies, just little shorts with a large slit in the appropriate place and probably grew up to have a much healthier attitude towards bodily functions. But having been brought up in a society that had elevated potty-training to an art form, this apparent total disregard for basic hygiene – and the sensibilities of others – was just a little hard to take. I was also genuinely puzzled by this insouciance in the face of serious squalor because the Vietnamese were scrupulously clean and neat in their clothes and appearance. Perhaps the explanation had something to do with the fact that lavatories seemed to be something of a novelty or, at any rate, rarity (there were, as far as I could discover, no public lavatories: people use the bushes or fields or even the sidewalks) and an etiquette – or perhaps a technique – had yet to be developed to deal with them.

I was feeling far too queasy to linger there and returned to my room where I resorted to the somewhat medieval practice of using a tin basin which I had found under the bed and hurling the contents out of the window. Everyone else's behaviour was so squalid that joining in seemed to be the only way to cope. But not even that eased my stomach ache and soon after eight, I went down to the Intershop where I bought a bottle of Black & White Scotch whisky from a girl in a gold lamé jumpsuit. I lay on my bed, curled into a foetal position, rubbing my stomach, staring out at the rain, sipping whisky and wondering whether it would be possible to be more miserable. It seemed unlikely. I had with me a book of poems written by Ho Chi Minh when he was in prison. One of them was called 'Endless Rain'.

> Nine days of rain, of sunshine but one day:
> Really the sky above has shown no feeling.
> Tattered shoes, muddy road, legs caked in clay!
> Still, endlessly we must keep slogging on.

By eleven, the sky had cleared sufficiently for the boat trip to be possible. We set out in a kind of old tug which ploughed doughtily through the waves in between the massive rock formations that jutted out of the bay. Close up they were quite extraordinary – huge, dramatic and fantastic, rearing up out of the sea, like mythical beasts. A fine mist lay over the water and often it was not possible to see more than a few yards ahead so that these strange shapes would suddenly appear through the haze. The only sound we could hear was the low rumble of the engine. At one point, the boatman cut the engine and we drifted silently through this forest of stone. There were few other boats on the water and they were junks, the wonderful fan-silhouette of their dried-blood sails etched against the skyline. An old tanker was sinking slowly into the bay, its deck half-submerged, its masts rotting and rusting in the damp air. Ha Long means 'where the dragon descends to the sea' and it was easy to believe that this was the home of a dangerous prehistoric animal. It was from this beautiful and eerie place that hundreds of 'boat' people, economic migrants from the impoverished North, set precarious sail for Hong Kong every year. They would leave while it was still dark, negotiating the crags in their fragile over-crowded and barely seaworthy vessels, hoping not to be caught and stopped, hoping to survive the journey.

As we glided through the silent waters, a soft rain blew in our faces and Mrs Thuc reminisced happily about the BBC and television directors with whom she had worked. She seemed to have been involved with almost every programme ever made about Vietnam including one on the Mekong River written and presented by William Shawcross. I said that he was a friend of mine and she looked disapproving.

'Ah, yes, William Shawcross,' she said in the manner of a stern headmistress recalling a talented but ultimately disappointing pupil. 'At first, we liked William Shawcross very much. He was a good friend to Vietnam and he wrote a good book about Cambodia but, in that programme, he showed that he was not a true friend to Vietnam. We thought that he understood us and our problems but he does not. So when he applied for a visa again, we had to say "No".'

We stayed that night in Haiphong in a pretty old French villa, built in the 1920s, that had been converted into a guesthouse. The rooms were enormous with high ceilings, big windows, damp-stained *eau-de-nil* walls and scarlet satin bedspreads. When I came upstairs after dinner, my bed had been turned down and the mosquito net arranged. A cheerful plump old woman called Quang had proudly demonstrated the efficacy of the hot water tap and, as I stood under the shower, I simultaneously revelled in the comfort and despised myself for caring about such things. Later, snuggled into clean white cotton sheets, I read a couple of chapters of an old Ed McBain that I had borrowed from the British embassy library in Hanoi and, soothed by the familiar characters of the 87th Precinct, fell into a deep contented sleep.

I woke around six to the sound of heavy rainfall. The room smelled faintly of mildew. I had been dreaming of an old lover and the dream brought back all the feelings of love and hurt and loss that I thought I no longer felt for him. It made me wonder whether one ever really gets over anything. During the weeks in Vietnam, even though I had so rarely been alone, I had nonetheless spent hours sunk in introspection and often, like a drowning man, found my whole life passing before my eyes. It seemed as if, at some point or other on the trip, during those endless hot hours in the car, I had examined, in unwelcome detail, every aspect of my past. None of it was reassuring. Every failure, every missed opportunity had been held up to scrutiny. Perhaps it was time to go home.

I opened the shutters and looked out at the drenched dawn. The guesthouse had a lovely little garden in the courtyard, full of palms, hibiscus and vines. Quang was wheeling her bicycle out into the main street, her conical hat swinging from the handlebars. She saw me leaning out of the window and waved and made eating gestures with her hand to indicate that breakfast would soon be ready. I turned back to face the room and the solid bourgeois furniture of an earlier era and felt obscurely comforted by it. Downstairs, in the dining room, I complimented the manageress on her establishment. She accepted my praise with a deprecatory smile, apologising for its shabby state and said that there was no money to replace or repair anything. I told her that I liked it, that in Europe we liked old things – if not old people – and realised, as I was speaking, that a taste for old things is a luxury, which you can indulge only when you can afford to buy new things.

After breakfast, we went for a brisk tour of Haiphong. The city, which was a small market town until the French took possession of it in 1874 and turned it into a major port and industrial centre, was laid out like any French provincial town with wide tree-lined boulevards and solid prosperous-looking mansions set back from the road in their own gardens. It lay on the left bank of the Cam river and had a pretty opera house of which an American writer wrote in 1927: ' . . . a fine theater in which bewildered companies try to feel the thrill of art in a climate like a sponge dipped in hot water.'

But its calm bourgeois façade was deceptive: Haiphong had had a turbulent history. In 1946 French troops fighting the Vietminh stormed through the city, 'demolishing whole neighbourhoods of flimsy structures' and killing what a French admiral at the time estimated as 'no more' than six thousand people (this figure was later revised to between five hundred and a thousand). Then, in December 1972, in an effort to force the North Vietnamese back to the negotiating table, Richard Nixon gave the signal for an operation which became known as the 'Christmas Bombing'. B-52s and other aircraft 'carpet bombed' the heavily-populated sixty-mile stretch between Haiphong and Hanoi in the most intensive bombing campaign against North Vietnam of the entire war, with nearly three thousand sorties flown and some forty thousand tons of bombs dropped. For eleven whole days, breaking only for Christmas Day itself, the skies over Haiphong were alive with explosions, the flares turning night into day.

We walked around the harbour into which nine hundred submarine mines had been released in 1972. It was quiet and almost deserted except for a series of huge cranes straddling a tram track like giant insects poised to strike and a mountain of scrap metal waiting on the quay to be shipped to Japan.

We looked at the market and failed to find a scarlet bedspread like the one in my room at the guesthouse. I bought instead a couple of pairs of clear plastic sandals which, I thought, might set a trend back in England. Mrs Thuc was very pleased and told me that they were a 'speciality' of Haiphong.

We visited a factory. Mrs Thuc had made it very clear that I absolutely had to visit a factory. The choice was between refrigerators, canned fish and carpets so I had opted for the last. We drove through the pleasing rain-sodden streets with their soothing colonial mansions and visited a carpet factory where nimble-fingered Vietnamese women hand-wove exquisite designs in subtle shades for export to the West. The factory was built by a Frenchman in 1929 but since 1954 had been under Vietnamese management and ownership. I liked the carpets which were very beautiful but had less enthusiasm for the vice-director's form speech about productivity. We sat in an upstairs room and drank tiny cupfuls of bitter green tea (I hated this tea but always ended up drinking it to stave off the boredom of these briefings) while he reeled off a litany of statistics, his voice plumbing new depths of monotony as he intoned the year's figures for levels of productivity and medals awarded for industry, fraternity and quality. Outside in the courtyard was a statue of three figures, two women and a man. He told me that it symbolised the tradition of the workers in the carpet factory who had combined fighting and working, and the co-operation between the farmers, the factory workers and the intellectuals. There was nothing spontaneous or genuinely enthusiastic in what he said and I found him and our time together in his little upstairs office rather depressing.

I had noticed that in the North the party line was trotted out at every possible opportunity and that, though I liked to think that I supported and admired the party line, my heart sank whenever the old clichés were brought into play. I liked the Vietnamese, both the idea of them and the reality, but more than liking them, I admired them. I admired their fierce courage and resilience. I admired them for being so tough. I admired the genuine egalitarianism that I sensed existed in the country, the way that they had been united by a common goal against a common enemy. I liked the way that the Vietnamese people really did seem to see themselves as a family and I was moved and impressed by their actual family relationships. I found their patriotism heartening. I knew that I was both being romantic and over-simplifying but I detected a spirit of comradeship amongst them that was very appealing. But I hated it when they started preaching. It made conversation impossible and it made me want to argue with them though I felt that, by and large, we were on the same side. Mr Dang had never bothered with all that. He was a free spirit and immune to any laws other than his own. Nguyen was too busy worrying about his family and the future to have time for speech-making though fear drove him ostensibly to toe the party line. But Mrs Thuc often spoke like an automaton. All I had to do was press the right button and out would come the spiel. She had a slogan for every occasion. I preferred her when she was coveting my umbrella, a tiny telescoping one that I had bought in Paris and promised to give her when I left.

Back in Hanoi after a five-hour drive, I dumped my things at the Army Guesthouse where I was billeted and took a quick bath in preparation for a visit to the Billabong Club. This was where ex-patriots, mainly Australian as the name would suggest, gathered on Friday evenings to drink and assuage the pangs of homesickness. Bruce, my gay acquaintance from the train, had told me to come along.

Even at the best of times, I dislike large gatherings and particularly large gatherings of strangers so going to a bar or club on my own was not something I would normally do by choice. But here I felt that I had no choice. I might meet somebody who would tell me something I needed to know. Like the train journey from Hue, it was my duty. And I wanted, for an hour or two, not to be a foreigner, to be with people whose native tongue was English.

The *cyclo* squeaked to a halt outside a large shabby villa – all villas in Hanoi were shabby – down the road from the British embassy. As we pulled up, so did a gleaming black motorbike, liberally festooned with chrome, and an elderly man wearing a crash helmet climbed off. The helmet alone would have been enough to mark him as a westerner – no Vietnamese wore a helmet which was why so many were killed in road accidents. As his head emerged from its shiny carapace, I recognised him as the Australian building contractor whom I had met on China Beach. We walked round the back of the Australian embassy to the Billabong Club and he signed me in and bought me a can of Foster's before going off to speak to a friend.

Bruce was deep in conversation with a ferrety little man who looked familiar. I walked over to them. Bruce didn't look particularly thrilled to see me and I suppose that he regretted his intimate outpourings on the train. The other man was an aid worker whom I had met at Bangkok airport weeks before. Then he had mistaken me for a woman from ODP (Overseas Development Programme) and rushed over to greet me. He seemed annoyed when I turned out not to be his friend but we fell into the kind of casual conversation you make at airports. I had asked to visit his project in Saigon but he was so unfriendly that I never bothered to go. He was no more affable now. He clearly resented what he perceived as my presumption in planning to write about a country that he thought I couldn't hope to know or understand as well as him. I quoted André Gide's famous remark to him: 'You either get to know a country in twenty-four hours or twenty-four years', and his face grew mottled in the dim light of the Billabong Club. I only said it to tease him. I was having quite enough problems of my own working out what I knew and felt about Vietnam. I felt that I had, as it were, learnt basic Vietnamese and the longer I stayed in Vietnam, the less I adapted, the more foreign I felt. Each day affirmed my difference. Yet, surrounded by my own kind with their puffy, multi-coloured faces, I felt desperately out of place too. My eye was no longer attuned to western faces; my own shape, size and colouring were a constant surprise to me. I expected and wanted everyone to be slender and delicate with smooth ivory faces and straight dark hair and dark eyes that managed somehow to be simultaneously liquid and opaque.

I left the Billabong Club and caught a *cyclo* back to the Army Guesthouse. I was reasonably sure that I wasn't going to meet anybody nice to take me to dinner at the Piano Bar or dancing at the International Club – these were the ex-pat delights promised me by Bruce. At the hotel, the receptionists were staring intently at the television where a video of a thriller called *Dead Calm* was showing. I had seen it on a flight to Bangkok and been too terrified to watch much. It's one of those movies where the dead homicidal maniac won't stay dead. There was a pair of middle-aged Italians watching too. One was drinking twelve-year-old single-malt whisky from a half-bottle of duty free. The other looked grey with fatigue and could barely keep his eyes open. The man with the whisky offered me a glass and I sat down. They were from RAI, the Italian television station, and were finding Vietnam gruelling. The tired one, who was the cameraman, said that he had worked all over the world, in Africa, in Eastern Europe, everywhere, but Vietnam was the toughest place he had ever been. He complained about the hotel which, by my current standards, ranked with the Oriental in Bangkok, and the sanitary arrangements, and looked at me, saying, with a shudder, '*E per una donna, dev'essere incredibile!*' The next day they were taking a jeep up to the Chinese border and asked me if I wanted to go with them. I would have loved to but knew that it would be impossible to get the necessary permissions in time. It was not on my programme. Nothing spontaneous was.

The Red River was very high and still rising. Much of Hanoi was flooded and my driver, Tam, was unable to come to work because the water had reached chest level in his house and he had to move out. There were dozens of people camping in makeshift homes on the pavements near the hotel: cooking, sleeping, getting on with their lives under flimsy sheets of plastic draped over wooden poles. I couldn't understand why the houses weren't built on stilts like they were in Malaysia and Thailand. Mrs Thuc said that it was because there the rainy season lasted for six months of the year but in Hanoi the monsoon only blew for three or four months from June to September and the people preferred to live in houses on the ground and move out when the rains came. It might also have had something to do with the typhoons that regularly buffeted the eastern coast of Vietnam. Rather like the wolf in the fairy story, these typhoons would have no trouble huffing and puffing and blowing the house down. But the sight of all the homeless ensconced on the sidewalks was a further reminder of the climatic hardships of life in Hanoi: freezing and damp in the winter, torrid and sodden in the summer. As the historian, Joseph Buttinger, wrote: 'One would be hard put to say whether the people in the Red River valley have been victimised more by invading armies, by the swollen waters of the Red River in the many years of excessive rainfall, or by the equally calamitous droughts.'

Mrs Thuc took me to see the Army Museum. Something about the place affected me and I began to sneeze furiously. I sneezed seventeen times in a row – something of a record. The museum was full of items celebrating the Vietnamese triumph over the Americans including a ghastly cross made up of photographs of captured US pilots 'confessing'. Their faces were gaunt and terrified and I found the combination of these haunting images and the cross particularly grotesque. I said as much to Mrs Thuc who looked at me with a mixture of impatience and incomprehension and said briskly, 'But now they all lead normal lives.' Remembering the never-ending stream of stories of young American soldiers who, one way or another, had had their lives changed for ever by the experience of Vietnam, I silently begged to differ.

The museum contained endless relics of Ho Chi Minh, including a strange mosaic of Ho on horseback in a landscape composed of tiny shards of Chinese porcelain ('very precious porcelain' said Mrs Thuc) and a photograph of him as a young man with a beautiful clear face shining with intelligence and idealism. His oft-quoted maxim 'Nothing is more precious than Independence and Freedom' was written in large letters above one of the photographs.

That afternoon Colonel Le Lam (Vice-Director in Charge of Art) of the Vietnam People's Army Studios arranged for me to see some archive footage of the Battle of Dien Bien Phu. I wanted to go to Dien Bien Phu itself but, in case it literally wasn't possible because of the weather, Mrs Thuc had suggested that I see some old films made at the time. Even if the plane managed to take off and land, we would only be able to stay a day and it would cost eighty dollars for me and forty dollars for Mrs Thuc. I was advised not to go. I could, she pointed out, see films of the battle far more cheaply. The films didn't make much impression, just lots of soldiers running and shouting, and generals, including General Giap (who, fourteen years later, was the architect of the Tet Offensive), pointing at maps and nodding sagely, but it was wonderful to see Ho Chi Minh animated. Again I was struck by the beauty and asceticism of his features. The French soldiers were tall and handsome, just like one's dream of a Foreign Legionnaire, some of them with film-star good looks like Mel Gibson or Robert Redford – but it was impossible to get any real sense of place. There were no aerial shots of the valley, no panoramas – the Vietminh had no aircraft – just close-ups of bunkers and tanks and guns. I watched the flickering black and white images on the screen for about forty minutes and then had had enough.

We left soon after dawn for the airport. When I came downstairs, the receptionists were watching *Dead Calm* for the tenth time, the smooth creamy ovals of their faces unruffled as the killer, his knife dripping blood, hove crazily into view.

The plane, weather permitting, was supposed to take off around eight. It wasn't raining and the road, though riddled with pot-holes and crammed with bicycles, ancient buses, jeeps, and the usual Noah's Ark-load of water buffalo, pigs, chickens, ducks and mangy dogs, had a convivial air to it, rather like a travelling circus. It was hard to believe that it was along this road that I had endured such terrors on my first visit to Hanoi. At one point a bus had veered off the tarmac down a steep bank, no doubt swerving to avoid a cyclist or a gaggle of geese, and its nose was inches away from a large circular pond made from an old bomb crater. The passengers had all got out of the bus and were attempting to push it back up the hill or, at least, prevent it from sliding any further down. A rope had been attached to the rear bumper of the bus which looked as if it might give way at any moment and a lorry was trying unsuccessfully to drag it back up onto the road. The wheels of the bus were spinning helplessly in the mud and traffic was at a standstill. We couldn't move and I got out to have a better look. I was struck as always by the cheerful stoicism of the Vietnamese. No one was cursing or looking at his watch. There was none of the hostility and pent-up rage which is the inevitable accompaniment to any delay or traffic jam in the West. Everyone was interested, concerned, even excited. Mrs Thuc said that the plane would wait for us.

In the event, it was we who waited for the plane. For five dreary hours, we sat at Noi Bai airport waiting for the fog to lift in the hinterland of Dien Bien Phu ('Phu' means administrative centre and Vietnamese maps refer to it simply as 'Dien Bien' meaning big frontier). When Graham Greene went there for twenty-four 'doom-laden' hours in January 1954, barely two months before the start of the battle that was to put a decisive end to France's intervention in the affairs of Indo-China, he wrote of a 'heavy fog' that ' . . . filled the cup among the hills every night around ten, and . . . did not lift again before eleven in the morning'. One could perhaps be forgiven for imagining that years of experience – and fog – might have encouraged Mrs Thuc or even the pilot to take this factor into account when specifying the probable hour of our departure but apparently not. We finally took off around one.

Mrs Thuc used the time to continue to fill me in on the party line. Her conversation was larded with phrases like 'puppet soldiers' and 'imperialist oppressors'. She described how an American teacher had been expelled from Hanoi because her classes were not 'good for socialism' and then said that it was anyhow a bad idea for Americans to teach English because they didn't speak good English: it was best to learn English from the English and, in their absence, the Australians. The Italians who were coming with us to Dien Bien and who spoke little English, dozed on the hard wooden bench.

In an effort to change the subject, I asked about the 2,273 US soldiers who were still officially listed as missing in action (MIA). Their unaccountable absence remained one of the principal reasons for America's refusal to 'normalise' relations with Vietnam. Since 1985 when *Rambo: First Blood, Part II* first hit the movie screens, there had been a plethora of movies and books on the subject. *Rambo: First Blood, Part II*, yet another swaggering vehicle for Sylvester Stallone, earned over $100 million in the United States and broke box-office records in Thailand and China where 'hatred of Vietnam amounts to a national frenzy'. It also fed the stereotype of the Vietnamese as a race of pitiless little yellow devils. In an article in the *Times Literary Supplement*, Richard West wrote: 'The MIA obsession is both a cause and effect of America's psychological failure to come to terms with the Vietnam War. It confirms the idea of the Vietnamese as a race of satanic cruelty who are holding on to the MIA to sell them for ransom.'

Mrs Thuc said: 'There are none here now. We gave them all back after Liberation and the Vietnamese people are very angry that we didn't make the Americans pay any money for them.'

There had been endless 'sightings' of American GIs in Vietnam which caused great excitement but there continued to be no hard evidence to support claims that there were still American prisoners-of-war in Vietnam. West summarised the present situation as follows: 'Of course, the Vietnamese can never prove what happened to the MIA. They probably do not know and certainly do not care. If they had ever wanted to use the MIA as hostages or bargaining counters, the chance to do so has long passed. Surrounded by enemies, of which the most dangerous is Communist China, and no longer aided by the Soviet Union, Vietnam desperately wants to be friends with the United States.'

*

The little plane circled down to land through thick snowy clouds. I hadn't managed to fasten my seatbelt which had been tied into knots to shorten it for tiny Vietnamese waists. No-one else was bothering with seatbelts and the child next to me burst into noisy tears when I tried to strap her in. Dien Bien lay below us like an illustration for a Vietnamese edition of *How Green Was My Valley*. England is supposed to be so green but I felt that I had never before seen *real* green until the velvety verdancy of the valley of Dien Bien unfolded before my eyes. It had that secretive quality that valleys often have, hidden away among the blue-green mountain peaks. We touched down on a landing strip made of ridged metal grid, originally laid by the Japanese in the 1940s. The heart-shaped basin was ringed by soft rolling hills, green again, very green. In the fields women were transplanting rice – the opium cultivation of the past is no longer permitted. Water buffalo rolled in pools of terracotta mud. Dragon-flies floated on the breeze. The air was sweet and clear after the steamy Turkish bath heat of Hanoi. Mrs Thuc said: 'The French chose this place to decide their destiny.'

Whether or not the French envisaged the Dien Bien Phu operation to be as potentially decisive as it turned out, the battle of Dien Bien Phu 'marked virtually the end of any hope the Western Powers might have entertained that they could dominate the East'. Dien Bien, a large village in the centre of a prosperous opium-growing district, had been selected as the base of operations because of its proximity to the Lao border, which is only ten miles away. At the time, the old Lao royal capital of Luang Prabang was considered to be under threat of attack from the Vietminh. The French had just signed an agreement which committed them to protecting Laos. But the defence of Luang Prabang presented practical problems: the town stood in the middle of forests in the peak-lined valley of the Mekong, and the airfield was inadequate. The wisest course of action was deemed to be to bar the way to Luang Prabang in the basin of Dien Bien, over a hundred miles away to the north-west.

The battle of Dien Bien Phu was begun by the Vietminh on the night of 13 March 1954. Though fighting continued for nearly two months, by 28 March, the French knew that they could not win. They were trapped in the valley which their pilots had nicknamed the 'chamber pot'. They finally surrendered on 7 May 1954 and their defeat marked the end of the French colonial empire in Indo-China.

The French, being more realistic or philosophical than the Americans, appear to have come to terms with this defeat. Vietnam was full of French tourists, two of whom were staying at the Army Guesthouse in Hanoi while they completed the formalities for the adoption of a tiny Vietnamese baby. The French were anxious once more to do business with the country that had served them so well in the past. The only credit card accepted in Vietnam was Visa, introduced by the Banques Françaises du Commerce Extérieur. The only non-Far Eastern or non-Eastern-bloc airline to have an office in Saigon was Air France. A major movie epic was being made of the battle of Dien Bien Phu, filmed, not at the scene of the original confrontation which was too large and too far from Hanoi, but at Xuan Mai, thirty miles from the Vietnamese capital. The cast would include over eighty French soldiers and the British actor, Donald Pleasence, was to star as an American journalist. General Giap, the hero of the hour, inexplicably would not be featured. *L'Amant* had just been adapted for the screen and Catherine Deneuve's cool blonde beauty was soon to have to learn to cope with Hanoi's damp heat for *Indochine* – the movie. How many of America's myriad Vietnam movies could have been filmed *in situ*? The French, as old Mr Thuan, the restaurateur in Saigon, pointed out, were in Indo-China for nearly a hundred years and knew and loved it well. They married Vietnamese, Cambodian or Lao women. Their relationships went deeper than those enjoyed by the majority of American servicemen on 'R & R'. Their rule was by no means entirely benign but they integrated far better than their American and Russian successors. They lived there in peace as well as in war.

But while the French might cherish fond memories of Indo-China – Greene wrote: ' . . . in Indo-China I drained a magic potion, a loving-cup which I have shared since with many retired *colons* and officers of the Foreign Legion whose eyes light up at the mention of Saigon and Hanoi' – the compliment was not returned and the Vietnamese seemed fairly indifferent to the French. The little museum at Dien Bien catered almost exclusively to Vietnamese chauvinism. One French visitor had left this peevish message in the visitors' book: *'Nous trouvons très regrettable que le monument au souvenir des morts français ne soit pas entretenu.'*

We spent barely two hours in Dien Bien. We had to take off for Hanoi before it grew dark and the fog rolled down the mountainsides once more. Gun-metal-grey storm clouds were gathering in the sky. The Italian cameraman hurriedly filmed rusting tanks, bunkers like abandoned foxholes and a small boy astride a mortar. A long-haired youth in shorts and a shirt with the sleeves ripped out, a rifle slung over his shoulder, patrolled the red-dirt tracks. The cameraman walked backwards away from him, filming excitedly, and fell into a pot-hole. Water buffalo wallowed ecstatically in pools, their clumsy grey bodies all but submerged in the reddish mud, their splayed nostrils sniffing at the sky. Dragon-flies hovered in the balmy air. As the plane rose into the sky, the figures below – the women bending and stretching in the rice fields, the men with their olive solar topees on their bicycles, the children clambering over the old tanks, the water buffalo – all got smaller and smaller until they were just tiny insects floating in a sea of green. The clouds closed over the valley like water after the parting of the waves and Dien Bien vanished from sight.

8

A Postcard from Phnom Penh

The night before I took the plane from Saigon to Phnom Penh I dreamt that I was dying of leukaemia. I did not want anyone to know. I met an old friend at a party but he said that he was too busy to talk to me. Finally, to get his attention, I told him about the leukaemia. He stopped what he was doing and poured us both a large brandy.

I woke up crying in my room at the Caravelle. It was half-past two and very dark – the darkest hour of the night. The hotel's air-conditioning plant roared like a furnace on the other side of the courtyard across from my room.

I am looking at a colour postcard of Phnom Penh that I bought at the airport the day I left. It was the only view of the city I ever saw on sale. The few other postcards were of the Royal Palace or the National Museum, portrayed in lurid and unnatural colour. This postcard shows a characterless modern city whose main landmark is the undistinguished façade of the Hotel Monorom. It makes Phnom Penh look like any other late twentieth-century city. It is, I suppose, intended to encourage tourism from which Cambodia hopes one day to make money.

I stayed at the Monorom for five days in 1989 when I first went to Phnom Penh. I had gone with a group of American film people from Hollywood to write about the first screening in Phnom Penh of a film called *The Killing Fields*. The film tells the true story of American journalist Sydney Schanberg's attempt to learn the fate of his Cambodian interpreter whom he had to leave behind after the fall of Phnom Penh to the Khmer Rouge in April 1975. Dith Pran, Schanberg's interpreter, like almost everyone else in Cambodia at the time, was sent by the Khmer Rouge to the countryside. There he endured terrible privations until finally he escaped from his captors and fled to Thailand.

The film is therefore also about what has become known as the Cambodian holocaust, the gruesome period when Pol Pot, the self-styled 'Original Khmer' and his followers, the Khmer Rouge, ran the country. During their reign at least one million people died, if not actually at the hands of the Khmer Rouge, from the famine and disease which raged as a consequence of their policies. Such policies were intended to 'recreate' the past greatness of the Angkor period ('If we can build Angkor,' declared Pol Pot, 'we can do anything'). Forced labour was used to construct a network of canals in imitation of that which existed at the time of Angkor, and which had harnessed the monsoon waters to create a constant water supply to provide for 'the permanent irrigation of rice fields'. But the reintroduction of such brutal work methods had actually dragged the country back into the dark ages and had led to the death or flight of most 'intellectuals', including doctors and anybody who spoke a foreign language. Refugees fleeing to Thailand told stories of how anyone wearing spectacles was killed and how there were no dogs left in the country because they had all been eaten by starving people. Under Pol Pot, Mao Tse-tung's dictum 'Politics is war without the bloodshed' went hideously wrong.

When Norman Lewis visited Cambodia in 1950, he wrote: 'Cambodia. It was a place-name always accompanied in my imagination by tinkling percussive music.' Now the name of Cambodia is linked in the world's imagination – when the world remembers Cambodia – to the sound of the cries of the tortured and starving.

As recently as 1960, Cambodia seems to have been a reasonably cheerful peaceful little country under the 'coddling, dictatorial rule' of an eccentric and egomaniacal sovereign, Prince Norodom Sihanouk, who had succeeded in gaining independence from the French in 1954. Cambodia had been a French protectorate since

1863. Sihanouk had many faults, not least of which was an unpredictability ('mercurial' is the adjective usually chosen to describe Sihanouk) that made him difficult to trust, but he was determined to keep his country neutral and out of the escalating chaos of the Vietnam War – and had gone to the lengths of breaking off diplomatic relations with the United States in 1965. In March 1969, the Americans, convinced that the NLF guerrillas of South Vietnam were taking refuge over the Cambodian border, began to send B-52s on bombing missions over Cambodia. Meanwhile, mounting dissatisfaction with the blatant corruption, favour-swapping and patronage of Sihanouk's rule led, in March 1970, to a successful right-wing coup, instigated by the Army and the urban middle class and now widely believed to have had the tacit support of the United States, which deposed him and placed the unreliable and inefficient General Lon Nol at the head of the country. With a ghastly inevitability, Cambodia slid slowly into chaos. Lon Nol's government was corrupt beyond belief and shored up by American aid. Between February and 15 August 1973 the Americans launched a six-month intensive bombing campaign during which they dropped 257,500 tons of bombs on Cambodia, nearly twice as many tons of bombs as they had dropped on Japan in World War Two. The guerrillas, whom Sihanouk had nicknamed the 'Khmers Rouges' ('khmer' simply means Cambodian and 'rouge' was a comment on their political leanings), gained increasing control of the country. People were starving. The Americans, recognising that they had backed a loser, pulled out at the beginning of April 1975, leaving the field clear for the Khmer Rouge. This group of sadistic and ruthless men who emptied the cities and drove the people to the countryside like pack animals, controlled Cambodia from 17 April 1975, which they proclaimed 'Year Zero', to 7 January 1979 – for a period, as every Cambodian you meet will tell you, of exactly three years, eight months and twenty days. In January 1979 the Vietnamese invaded to put a stop to Pol Pot's raids along their common border by which means he hoped to regain for the Khmers that part of the west Mekong Delta that centuries ago belonged to Cambodia and was once known as Kampuchea Krom, meaning 'lower Cambodia'. A former Vietnamese ambassador to Bangkok who went in with the so-called

Liberation Army compared the city they found to Oran, the Algerian town which is the horrific setting for Camus's *La Peste*, saying, 'There were rats in the streets, corpses everywhere.'

Pol Pot and his cohorts retreated to Thailand and the Thai-Cambodian border\ where Pol Pot, like Sihanouk, was given a residence in the Thai province of Trat. There they were able to lick their wounds and regroup with the help of financial aid and arms from the Chinese (who had also provided Sihanouk with a home in Peking after he was deposed) and other governments opposed to the Vietnamese/Soviet-backed regime in Phnom Penh. The United States, still smarting from the loss of the Vietnam War, refused to recognise the new government and declared the invasion illegal. From 1982, Cambodia's seat at the United Nations was held by the self-styled Coalition Government of Democrat Kampuchea, a tri-partite comprised of the Khmer Rouge, the Khmer People's National Liberation Front (KPNLF) and the Sihanoukists (Armée Nationale Sihanoukiste – ANS) led by Sihanouk. (From 1979–1981, the seat was held by Democratic Kampuchea, Pol Pot's regime, but after the Vietnamese invasion, Sihanouk threw his lot in with the Khmer Rouge.) Until 1990, it was this group that was recognised by the West as the legitimate government of Cambodia, rather than the Vietnamese-backed government of President Heng Samrin and Prime Minister Hun Sen, which sat in Phnom Penh and actually governed the State of Cambodia, as the country was renamed in May 1989. Under Pol Pot, the country was known as Democratic Kampuchea and initially under the Hun Sen government, as the People's Republic of Kampuchea.

The Vietnamese overstayed their welcome, remaining for almost eleven years until September 1989. During this time and even after their withdrawal, Cambodia was a battleground where what was effectively a civil war was being waged. The Khmer Rouge regained strength and provided the military might of the resistance coalition. Thousands died or were hideously mutilated by land mines and thousands more lived miserable lives in refugee camps along the Thai-Cambodian border. The largest Cambodian city outside Phnom Penh was Site 2, a camp housing approximately two hundred and ten thousand supporters of the KPNLF.

Attempts at peaceful solutions came and went but the Khmer Rouge's insistence that they be included in any settlement always led to a breakdown in talks. Finally, in October 1991, an agreement was signed in Paris by all four factions which established a United Nations-monitored Supreme National Council (SNC), embodying Cambodian sovereignty, headed by Sihanouk and comprising delegates from all four factions. Its stated role was to advise a UN body which was to organise elections to be held in early 1993 and to implement the Paris Peace Agreement.

But, at the time of my return to Cambodia in 1990, the Paris Peace Agreement was still in the future and any possible peaceful solution to Cambodia's problems had yet to be agreed upon.

I settled into the Hôtel Asie where there was no hot water and a plague of red ants in the bathroom but it only cost eight dollars a night so I could afford to keep my room there for the length of my stay in Cambodia. I liked the Asie. It was right in the centre of town; the receptionists and chambermaids were delightful and there was a mangy old white tomcat with one of those sawn-off tails common in South East Asia who was prepared to sleep with me. (Malaysian legend has it that a princess slipped her ring onto a cat's tail while she went swimming and knotted it for safety.) My room had a double bed, a wardrobe chattering with termites, a desk for my typewriter, a large refrigerator and a tiny room containing a shower and lavatory made for people much slimmer than me. I was always getting trapped between the lavatory and the door. But otherwise it was fine.

The Cambodians were more relaxed – or perhaps less organised – than the Vietnamese when it came to foreign visitors. Madame Sun Saphoeun at the Ministry of Foreign Affairs agreed to my every request and sent her nephew to be my guide and interpreter. Im Sophy was a handsome dark-skinned man of thirty-five whose English, unfortunately, was so bad that I sometimes found it difficult to tell what language he was speaking. Otherwise, he seemed nice enough. I wanted to go to Angkor, Kampot and Kep, the now-deserted seaside resort which the French used to call Kep-sur-Mer and where Sihanouk had maintained a villa and built a casino. A journalist friend in Bangkok had also suggested that I ask to visit Ratanakiri and Mondulkiri, the two provinces that border Vietnam and which few foreigners get to. Sophy (pronounced Soapy) wrote all this down and disappeared back to the Ministry for the necessary permissions. He said there would be no problem.

Phnom Penh looked healthier and more prosperous even since my last visit fourteen months before. It was the season of *kak-then*, a kind of fund-raising festival where people take offerings of food, clothing and money to the monks in the pagoda. On the sidewalks all over the city, there were bright fringed parasols in bands of yellow, pink and green, shading tables laid ready for eating and loudspeakers booming with high whiny music. Every so often, the traffic would come to a standstill while a float bearing a multi-tiered parasol swaying with the motion of the truck and shading a poster showing scenes from the life of the Buddha, would make its way slowly through the streets. People would process around the city, the women in embroidered *sampots* (like a Lao *sin*), some with gold thread, carrying hundred *riel* notes attached to long sticks and presents of food and new robes for the monks, wrapped in orange cellophane. The children, dressed in their best clothes, carried posies of marigolds which matched the monks' robes. Men in monkey masks would suddenly begin capering as I walked past, holding out a plate for me to put some money in.

Mme Sun Saphoeun told me that the central market 'with its strange yellow spaceship building' was known as '*le marché jaune*' because of the quantities of gold it contained. It was indeed brimming, not only with gold and silver and precious stones – sapphires from the mines in Pailin in the west of the country, rubies from Burma and emeralds from India – but also with electronic goods, clothes and cosmetics imported – or smuggled – from Thailand. In a pavement stall, I found an old Omega apparently in perfect working order and bought it for forty dollars. The vendor would have preferred to trade it for my new quartz Seiko but, after similar encounters in Saigon, I wasn't convinced that the Omega would go on working once I got it home. In the delicatessens on the Boulevard Achar Mean, so named after the first Cambodian known to have joined the Indochinese Communist Party, you could buy jars of Russian caviar – Sevruga and Beluga – for twenty-three dollars, Stolichnaya vodka, Hungarian wine and Johnnie Walker Red Label whisky. A gold lamé dinner jacket with narrow black lapels was a strange sight in the window of a little tailor's shop. There were many more westerners on the streets and in the restaurants than in either Saigon or Hanoi, or even in Vientiane. They were mainly aid workers attached to one of the many non-governmental organisations based in Phnom Penh. Taking me for one of them, a man in a camera repair shop filled with rusting Leica parts, tried to interest me in buying or renting an apartment in an old French villa. He wrote a courteously-worded little advertisement for his services in my notebook. It ended with the words '*Prix raisonnable, la confiance surtout*'.

But there were still rats in the gutters – usually dead ones, thank God – and in the last three months there had been three and a half thousand cases of dengue fever in the city, and a procession of parents carrying their feverish children in their arms to the hospital. There were begging amputees on every street corner and, at night, a curfew sent everyone scurrying indoors by nine o'clock. I found the curfew more restful than alarming. As in Vietnam, the days began very early and by ten at night, I was usually ready for bed. While Sophy organised flights and permissions, I explored Phnom Penh either on foot or by *cyclo*. From the comfort of my seat in the *cyclo*, I toured the decaying *quartier français* where once the petty bureaucrats and businessmen from companies with names like the Union Financière d'Extrême-Orient and the Société Anonyme Franco-Khmere d'Exportation du Caoutchouc (rubber) enjoyed an easy life in the tropics.

'*C'était le quartier le plus calm,*' said Sok Sann, an elderly *cyclo-pousse*, who hung around outside the Asie. The French phrases evoked vividly an era when all was tranquil but now the once-gracious mansions of the old colonial officials were green with slime, their roofs gaping, their windows shattered. In front of each house a miniature shanty town had grown up: rickety shacks roofed with corrugated iron or bamboo, low fires smoking, piles of old rubber tyres for re-cycling, the odd pig snuffling through the mounds of rubbish, mangy yellow dogs chasing stringy chickens and everywhere the smell of open sewers.

'Former' was a word much in use in Phnom Penh. 'This,' the *cyclo-pousse* would say, 'is the *former* American embassy, now the Department of Fisheries, and here is the *former* Ministry of Religion, now Foreign Affairs, and here the *former* Monument of Indpendence, now of Victory.' The former French embassy from which Schanberg and the others were finally evacuated in 1975, had become an orphanage, and then there were all the 'formers' that had just ceased to exist: the offices of companies like Cathay Pacific and Citroën, now deserted and desolate, small monuments to a prosperity that had long since given up the ghost. The Russians had profited from all this. As Sok Sann put it rather sourly, 'The Russians very lucky. They build nothing but they can live everywhere they like in the nice buildings in my city,' and then he pointed out a lean-to near the old French embassy where he lived with his wife and three children.

It rained most afternoons for a couple of hours. Often I would be coming back from some far-flung corner of the city, perhaps Tuol Tom Pong market where you could sometimes find old English or French books. The choice was limited: Sihanouk's collected speeches for five dollars, Philip Roth's *Good-Bye Columbus*, Fodor's Guide to Morocco, and an astonishing number of books about Jackie Onassis and her two marriages. As the rain started, the driver would put up the hood and fling an old bit of plastic over my knees but I always ended up soaked. In my hotel room, I could hear the rain drumming on the corrugated iron roofs of the houses opposite. When the rain stopped, the inhabitants would move the sheets of tin apart to let in some light and the cats would come out to sunbathe.

In the evenings I usually went for dinner to the Bayon restaurant on the corner of the Boulevard Achar Mean and the little side street where the Asie was. The restaurant took its name from the cluster of towers at the heart of Angkor Thom, the Bayon, an unnerving temple-mountain from every tower of which the face of Jayavarman VII looks out in all four directions at once. The food was nothing special but I liked the old man who ran it. He looked Chinese and spoke French with exquisite courtesy. One evening as I came in, he was holding an enormous black snake by the tip of its tail. Its head had been cut off and its blood was draining slowly into a bowl. He came over and recommended snake soup but I ordered an omelette and a salad with sweet green tomatoes. Outside a little group of amputees had gathered to beg. As I left, I gave each one some money and the first one, whose legs had been blown off at the groin, swung himself round on his hands to the end of the receiving line. When he saw that I recognised him, we both laughed. He couldn't have been more than twenty. I thought it was pretty good to be able to laugh like that without any legs.

One Sunday morning I took a *cyclo* to the Royal Palace. Small naked brown children were splashing in the waters of the Tonle Sap river and couples were strolling in the wide boulevards and along the riverfront. My guide book had held out the prospect of a ride on an elephant but there were none to be seen.

The Royal Palace, which consisted of a number of different buildings, all housed in an enormous walled courtyard, was originally built in wood in 1866 on the site of the ancient citadel of Banteai Kev. The present palace was re-built in brick in 1913 by King Sisowath, Sihanouk's great-great-uncle, and, though Khmer in style, was designed largely by French architects. Its various buildings included the Throne Hall; the Royal Treasury; the Silver Pagoda; the Pavilion containing a huge footprint of the Buddha; the bell tower; the Chan Chaya, meaning the Shadow of the Moon, the pavilion where Cambodian classical dancers would perform and from which the king would address his people; and an exquisite and anomalous little house in *belle époque* style which had been a gift to King Norodom from Napoleon III. It had been given originally by the Emperor to Queen Eugénie and then dismantled and sent to Phnom Penh in 1866.

It is something of a miracle – and a mystery – that the Khmer Rouge, who murdered nineteen members of Sihanouk's immediate family including his favourite son and daughter, chose to destroy neither the palace, where Sihanouk was kept under house arrest between 1976 and 1979, nor the National Museum, and the former remained to this day, an astonishingly opulent sight in contemporary Phnom Penh where few buildings were intact, let alone in a decent state of repair. The roofs of the palace were covered with green, gold and blue tiles which glinted in the sun, creating a literally dazzling effect, matched by the sumptuousness of the royal apartments.

A plump young woman with a cheerful moon-face called Miss Rasmey (meaning 'sunrise') showed me round. In the throne room was the royal hammock – or possibly litter – suspended from a scarlet and gold pole from which the king and queen would supervise the first planting of the rice. Then came the coronation throne, complete with ceremonial parasol, on which the king was permitted to sit only once in his life, and another even more splendid structure for the queen, made, said Miss Rasmey, 'like a ship floating in the sea', which was covered with a sort of canopy topped with a gilded model of a *wat* and which could be ascended by three different little staircases of ten red and gold steps each. There was a day-bed for 'when the King is tired of talking', several gilded sedan chairs and bundles of fine bamboo sticks, apparently for the royal policemen to beat 'disorderly persons three times'. Off a hall on from the throne room were the royal bedrooms, one for the king, one for the queen, each with an extravagantly gilded bed. During the seven days following the coronation ceremony, when the king and the queen were required to sleep separately, they spent their nights here, moving afterwards to the royal residence.

The walls were decorated with scenes from the Ramayana (or Reamker, as the Khmer version of the epic is called), the air was thick with incense from the joss-sticks burning in front of a golden Buddha and the whole effect was utterly gorgeous. Miss Rasmey pointed out the 'chatting room' where the king would recline under a seven-tiered parasol and perhaps discuss the future with the royal fortune-teller. She drew my attention to the building set aside for 'the king's dresses' and another pavilion which she described as the king's dancing hall and not to be confused with the afore-mentioned Pavilion of the Shadow of the Moon which sat over the entrance to the palace complex. This was a rectangular structure, open on all sides to the elements, the roof supported by little winged caryatids oddly reminiscent of Busby Berkeley chorus girls, and the stair rails adorned with slithering *nagas*, where the king himself, the queen and favoured guests would dance.

The Silver Pagoda or Wat Preah Keo (Pagoda of the Emerald Buddha), in the adjacent courtyard, was equally splendid. It had originally been built in wood in 1892 by King Norodom who admired the *wat* of the same name in Bangkok which had been built to house the so-called emerald Buddha looted by the Siamese from the Laos in 1778 at the sack of Vientiane (the Siamese were busy that decade – they burnt down Phnom Penh in 1772). In 1962 Sihanouk re-built the Silver Pagoda in its present form and gave it a solid silver floor consisting of 5,281 pieces of silver, each weighing one kilo. As usual, we had to take off our shoes at the door and I enjoyed the novel sensation of solid silver under my bare feet. We wandered round, looking at faded sepia photographs of Sihanouk's ancestors and presents bestowed on him and them by foreign heads of state and Miss Rasmey reeled off statistics, such as 9,584 diamonds and ninety kilos of gold – which I dutifully wrote down but I have no recollection what they applied to. In that respect, nothing seemed to have changed since Norman Lewis's visit some forty years before. Then he commented: 'Whenever a Buddha happened to be of solid gold, the guide, padding relentlessly in the rear, inevitably announced the exact weight of the metal that had gone into its construction.'

Napoleon III's gift was a sorry sight in the midst of all this gleaming green and gold. Most of its windows were broken, the pink marble steps that led to the front door were cracked and chipped and the delicate wrought-iron bannister was rusty. But a few panes of stained glass still remained, bearing Napoleon's crest and the letter 'N'. Two Cambodian teenage boys followed me into the building. They said that it was the first time they had ever been inside because it looked so shabby. They asked me whether I could get them permission to visit the Silver Pagoda which was only visitable with special permission from the Ministry of Information and Culture – as a result of which few Cambodians ever went there.

I found the Royal Palace astonishing. Compared to Versailles or even Buckingham Palace, it was a modest affair but it was extraordinary to remember that, only twenty-five years before, Sihanouk, as a *deva-raj* or god-king, had been living here, making good use of his dancing hall, reclining beneath his seven-tiered pagoda, holding public audiences from the Shadow of the Moon pavilion overlooking the Tonle Sap river, ruling over the Cambodians to whom he liked to refer as his children or 'my little people'.

As laid down in the 1954 Geneva Accords, Sihanouk had held elections in 1955 (unlike Diem in South Vietnam). He formally abdicated from the throne in favour of his father, Suramarit, and then established his own political party, the Sangkum Reastr Niyum (meaning 'popular socialist community'). It won – though it seems likely that the results were rigged. In any event, the elections were certified as 'correct' by the International Control Commission (established at Geneva to oversee the implementation of the agreements). Sihanouk then had the best of both worlds. 'To conservative Cambodians, he was still the god-king. To radical Cambodians, he was the democrat who had won independence and given up the throne.' He continued, unsurprisingly, to behave exactly as if he was still king, and the court – and court intrigue – remained the focal point of Cambodian society. Renouncing the throne changed nothing and Sihanouk enjoyed a considerable advantage over his predecessors: his kingdom was no longer under the control of a foreign power.

It was never difficult to understand why Sihanouk would like to return, not simply to Cambodia, but also the Royal Palace in Phnom Penh. Not for him the insignificance that befell China's last emperor, Pu Yi, nor even the uneventful and obscure retirement that Bao Dai enjoys to this day in France. Sihanouk claims to be the only living human being to have met Queen Elizabeth II, Mao Tse-Tung, Haile Selassie, Tito, Nasser, Khrushchev and De Gaulle of whom he wrote: 'On the surface we seemed to be so dissimilar – the tall, austere French general and the short, gregarious Cambodian king – yet we were kindred spirits with much in common ' – and he clearly has never had any intention of renouncing his position in world affairs. To this end, he has managed – even in exile – to dominate Cambodian politics for the last thirteen years, either from the lakeside palace built for him in

Pyongyang by Kim Il Sung or from the old pre-war French embassy in Peking in which the Chinese installed him.

But, as I wandered through the lavish apartments, the notion that Sihanouk might one day return to his palace in Phnom Penh and once more address his children from the Pavilion of the Shadow of the Moon had a surreal quality. In the West, if we retain any affection for our monarchies, it is a kind of tolerant amused fondness such as that accorded to an eccentric old aunt. We don't really take them seriously. But in neighbouring Thailand, where the monarch is also considered a *deva-raj*, the clarinet-playing King Bhumipol is still waited on by chamberlains crawling on their hands and knees and *lèse-majesté* is an offence punishable by imprisonment. However, no-one complains and the Thais adore their king. Perhaps it wasn't surprising that the Cambodians should wish to revert to a time – the so-called Golden Age – that the events of the last twenty-five years must make look very rosy indeed?

Tourists in Phnom Penh in search of contrast and different kinds of statistics can check out Tuol Sleng, the 'museum of genocidal crime' or the 'killing fields' of Choeung Ek. In the former, an interrogation and torture centre whose name means 'Hill of the Poison Tree', some 20,000 people were detained and tortured by the Khmer Rouge before being taken to Choeung Ek to be executed. When the Vietnamese Army arrived in 1979, they found just seven people alive in Tuol Sleng, a former primary school and *lycée*. Fourteen others had been tortured to death as the Vietnamese troops were closing in on the city. Elizabeth Becker wrote: 'If a regime can be understood by the institutions it creates, Democratic Kampuchea should be remembered through Tuol Sleng.'

There were still blood stains on the floor of Tuol Sleng and hundreds of photographs of the victims, including several westerners who were unlucky enough to find themselves in Pol Pot's Cambodia at the time. Many of those who died were members of the Khmer Rouge cadre who were suspected of disloyalty and treason and consequently tortured by their own comrades to extract 'confessions'. There was a grim list of the methods of torture used and a series of paintings by a prisoner who survived illustrating the different methods. The school notice boards were used to post rules for victims, instructing them not to cry out loud while being tortured, to answer questions directly and to follow other awful rules while awaiting their deaths. Here, we are told, 3,314,768 people were *'tués et disparus'*: there were 141,868 *'invalides'* and 200,000 orphans.

An Italian tourist in jeans and Gucci loafers was posing for photographs in the torture chambers. He asked his guide to take the snaps. The guide obliged and then pointed to one of the photographs on the wall. It showed a middle-aged man with an expression of patient suffering. 'This,' he said, 'is my brother-in-law. He was a professor.'

The former 'extermination camp' of Choeung Ek lay ten miles or so south-west of Phnom Penh. Those who had survived Tuol Sleng were taken there at night by the lorryload and then bludgeoned to death in order to avoid wasting precious bullets. Towards the end of 1980, the camp was discovered and 8,985 corpses found, many headless, many of naked women and children. Today the scene was both ghastly, with a *stupa* piled high with the skulls of the dead, and oddly pastoral. Gawky young oxen with spindly legs were grazing on the narrow walkways between the mass graves and a nearby tree was festooned with loosely-woven baskets to catch the ripe lychees as they fell.

9

Gardens of Stone

The plane to Siem Reap took off late – as did all planes in modern Cambodia. A very old woman was the last person to board. Supported by two stewardesses, she moved like a sleep-walker, very slowly and stiffly as if any sudden movement might cause her to break into tiny pieces. Her face had a death-mask quality; it was chalk-white, stretched over the bones, unwrinkled.

We flew up the country towards Thailand over the airstrip built for the Khmer Rouge by the Chinese in Kompong Chhnang and over the vast milky-brown expanse of the Tonle Sap, the Great Lake, whose waters, fed to bursting point by the Mekong, miraculously reverse during the rainy season and start to flow north. It was still the rainy season and, all around the Tonle Sap, huge tracts of land were submerged under water. Other areas looked parched and dry and Sophy told me that rice production was down by thirty per cent that year because of lack of rain. An hour or so later we landed at the tiny airport of Siem Reap. If you knew what to look for, you could pick out Angkor Wat from the air.

The plane was crowded. Dangerously so. Like a bus at rush hour, there were people standing in the aisle and crammed into the small space at the rear of the aircraft near the luggage. There were only two flights a week to Siem Reap and never enough seats to meet the demand. My ticket and *laisser-passer* were in the name of Nicholas Charles – whoever he might be. For some reason, no ticket had been issued in my name so Sophy had simply taken the one destined for Nicholas Charles. I never found out what happened to him or his plans to visit Angkor.

I was travelling with Sophy and a Scots journalist called James Pringle, a short chubby man who had been the Reuters bureau chief in Saigon during the Vietnam War and was married to a Cambodian woman whom he had met in Phnom Penh in the early 1970s. There were also a couple of earnest, bearded and bespectacled Americans in shorts and sandals with backpacks and eager dreary expressions, and the Italian tourist whom I had seen modelling Gucci fashions at Tuol Sleng the previous afternoon. All the other passengers were Cambodians who, being small and neat, could sit three across in seats that would barely fit two westerners.

The Americans, like the Italian, had come up on the usual tourist deal – that is effectively for only half a day during which you are taken to see the Bayon at Angkor Thom and for a quick squint at Angkor Wat in the blazing heat of the midday sun, then back to the Grand Hotel d'Angkor for a four-course lunch, followed by the return flight to Phnom Penh around two. I had done this with the American film people and, though it was obviously better than nothing, it was frustrating. But Siem Reap was not really geared for tourists and the very real threat of guerrilla activity round the ruins of Angkor, which lies only 150 kilometres from the Thai border (Siem Reap means 'Siamese Vanquished' in Khmer) and the camps housing the resistance groups, meant that the Phnom Penh Government was reluctant to let foreigners just wander around. The Americans were, however, hoping to strike some kind of deal with the local authorities and get permission to stay till the next flight in four days' time.

The Grand Hotel d'Angkor, formerly the Grand Hotel des Ruines, was a large cream stucco building of no great architectural merit which looked similar to the Palace hotel in Dalat – but shabbier. It had been built in 1937, presumably by the French, and, like Angkor itself, bore witness to a time when Cambodia was both happier and more prosperous. In the 1950s and 1960s, foreigners could travel reasonably easily and freely round the country and there were three luxury hotels in Siem Reap and daily flights from Phnom Penh. Seaplanes were able to touch down on the waters of the Baray Occidental, the enormous reservoir to the west of Angkor, where the head, shoulders and a couple of arms of the beautiful giant bronze statue of Vishnu *'plongé dans le sommeil cosmique'*, now in the National Museum in Phnom Penh, was found. Then you could also drive up from Phnom Penh in a day, now considered far too dangerous, even if the roads were navigable. Up until the 1930s the journey between Phnom Penh and Siem Reap had to be made by boat, across the Great Lake and along the Tonle Sap river, as there was no road. Nowadays goods were still transported by water but the journey was long and slow, taking two days and one night, and not without risk.

Sihanouk used to give lavish soirées in the ruins of Angkor, entertaining foreign visitors like De Gaulle, Princess Margaret and Jackie Kennedy – who arrived in 1967 by helicopter – with displays of fireworks and classical dancing by the light of the moon and flaming torches. Jackie Kennedy is said to have lisped, in her breathy baby-girl voice, that visiting Angkor was the fulfilment of a childhood dream. My parents spent three days there in 1953, exploring the overgrown ruins, not seeing another soul for hours. My mother remembers oddly little about their visit, perhaps because she was too excited after the French army pilot allowed her to take the controls of the little Beechcraft in which they flew back to Phnom Penh.

Because of the years of war in Cambodia, I never believed that I would ever get to Angkor, let alone be able to spend any time there. It had become one of those places which people of earlier generations had once visited and now talked about nostalgically, like Shanghai in the old days or Berlin before the Second World War. I had thought that Angkor existed only in dreams and distant yearning memories and it was both disturbing and wonderful to be there.

The Grand Hotel had all the grace, charm and disadvantages of such places. There was electricity for a couple of hours round lunchtime and from six to nine in the evening. The modern Japanese air-conditioners were therefore largely ornamental and, after curfew at 8.30, there was little to do but lie and sweat under a mosquito net. The cavernous bathrooms recounted a small history of their own: the bidet, the hot and cold taps, the hot water tank, all revealed that the plumbing had once been worthy of the twentieth century. Now only a thin trickle of cold water could be coaxed from the showerhead and the cistern required constant attention.

As we checked in, a procedure that involved completing a predictable multitude of forms, Sophy asked me if I wanted a room to myself or whether I would 'sleep' with Jim Pringle to whom I had been cheerfully gossiping on the flight up. I was taken aback and rather offended by the question, interpreting it as some kind of comment, if not specifically on my morals, on the morals of western women in general, and said sharply, 'No, of course not. He's a married man,' adding, as if it made a difference, 'and his wife is Cambodian.'

Afterwards I wondered whether I had overreacted and he was merely trying to save us money. I knew that it was usual for Cambodians to share rooms – there was rarely enough space or money to avoid this – but I didn't know whether men and women who were not related or married, ever shared the same room without a chaperone.

In the vast dining room, we were the only guests. The Americans, having come to an arrangement with the authorities, had disappeared in the direction of Angkor, and the group of army officers who were occupying most of the hotel, took all their meals in another room. Sophy pushed bits of European food disconsolately round his plate and asked whether we could order Cambodian food in the evening. Beer cost two dollars a can, which was more than double the price in the market. After lunch, we went shopping and laid in a supply of beer and mineral water which I arranged to store in the hotel's only fridge, a huge ice chest, where the meat for our next meal was also kept, protected by a padlock and chain. It became a regular feature of our stay that we would return, fainting with heat and exhaustion from the ruins, and I would then have to hunt for the keeper of the key.

Around half-past two, Mr Huy appeared and presented us with his card which, he said, he had made himself. On a small square of cream cardboard was neatly typed:

Tiger Balm

Huy – My
Giude Angkor
Siem Reap
Combodia

We drove down the Avenue Union Soviétique, formerly the Avenue General de Gaulle, past the shell of the ballroom built by Sihanouk and destroyed by Pol Pot, towards Angkor Wat. Mr Huy talked all the way in fluent but appalling English. His accent was so strange and so thick that it was, at first, almost impossible to tell when he was speaking English and when Khmer. The same applied when he spoke French. When he was pleased or excited, he would make a strange sound, a cross between a hum and a moo – of approval – which would begin low and go up in volume and pitch as his emotion increased. He was a slender, good-looking man of fifty with an amused mischievous face who had first become a guide in the time of Sihanouk. Then there had been thirty-six French-speaking guides at Angkor. Now there were two.

It soon became clear that Mr Huy knew everything about Angkor which he described as an 'allegory of creation'. Every stone, every column, every *bas-relief*, every *apsara* – the king's celestial concubines – was dear to him. He loved the ruins and he was keen to learn the correct English word for each architectural term. How did a cruciform differ from a cross, an arch from a lintel, a pillar from a column? He was particularly exercised as to the choice of words to describe the garments of a particular *apsara* on the wall of one of the inner courtyards of Angkor Wat. She was wearing tiny shorts so I suggested 'panties' and he began racing up and down the long stone galleries of Angkor Wat, chanting 'Panties, panties, panties', his voice rising in a crescendo of excitement and approval.

Nothing that you will have read about Angkor, no photograph, can begin to prepare you for the vastness, the complexity and the beauty of the city created by the Khmer god-kings during their centuries of manic building. Angkor is infinitely more ambitious and more varied than Versailles – though comparisons between the megalomania of the Khmer god-kings and that of the Sun

King are irresistible. Angkor rivals the Great Wall of China in vision – the mere mention of the latter is supposed to have reduced Boswell to tears – and it is as moving and beautiful, though far more austere, as the Burmese plain of Pagan where there are over 2,000 temples and pagodas within thirty-five square miles. I read somewhere that all the temples of Ancient Greece could be accommodated in Angkor.

Angkor Wat, the temple, tomb and observatory of Suryavaram II, was begun in 1113 at the start of his reign and completed after his death in 1150. The historian David P. Chandler describes it as 'the largest, perhaps the most beautiful, and one of the most mysterious of all the monuments'. It is nearly a mile square and supposed to be the largest religious edifice in the world but size is not everything. The plan of the temple of Angkor Wat is rigorously geometrical. Its central temple-mountain, which rises to some one hundred and thirty feet, is surrounded by a containing wall, each corner of which is marked by a tower. These four towers are repeated by a further four at the corners of the four galleries communicating, by covered passages, with the central shrine. Almost every inch of internal wall is covered with carvings. The massive symmetrical edifice of Angkor Wat with its distinctive silhouette of five central pinecone-shaped towers is the symbol on the flags of both the Government and the resistance groups and a rallying point for most Khmers. In Khao-I-Dang, the sad little refugee camp on the Thai-Cambodian border where UNHCR-accepted refugees (United Nations High Commission for Refugees) were waiting in the almost inevitably vain hope of finding asylum and a new life in Australia or the United States, I had noticed that a large model of Angkor Wat was being built and a huge painting of the temple on cotton hung as the backdrop.

But in the flesh, as it were, Angkor Wat was almost, if not too big, certainly too much – in the old hippy sense of the phrase. It could seem, particularly in the harsh light of the midday sun, intimidating, hostile, remote. It was necessary to develop a *rapport* with the buildings, a sense of intimacy, before you could feel at ease and no tourist on a half-day whirlwind tour up from Phnom Penh could hope to do that.

*

Mr Huy darted ahead, like one of the dragon-flies which were buzzing and gliding in the afternoon sun. Every few moments he would come across some tiny exquisite detail of the *bas-relief* and shout for us to come and see. Jim Pringle and I wandered slowly along behind him, cool in the great stone heart of Angkor Wat, scarcely able to believe our luck. There we were alone in one of the most fantastic buildings in the world: alone and not part of a group of shuffling Japanese or German or French tourists. It was enough to make one drunk with excitement. Sophy trailed behind. He had told me on the plane that he had been to Angkor at least thirty times and it was no big deal for him.

The carvings on the *bas-reliefs* were charming. There were monkeys and elephants; dancing girls; peasants and fishermen; and kings – all life was here, divine and secular. But it was really the space and the symmetry of Angkor Wat that moved me. I loved its long galleries, the shadows of the pillars falling across the ancient stone floors, its courtyards and its empty pools where now only old monks lingered and small children played. I liked the cattle grazing among the broken masonry and the stoical water buffalo basking in the mud.

We stayed there till sunset, watching the forbidding grey sandstone soften and come alive and slowly glow gold as the sky turned rose madder and a sweet soft blue and then purple and orange. The air grew piercingly clear and luminous, filled with the sound of bird calls and the rasp of the crickets and the guttural croak of the frogs and the pure high notes of tinkling cowbells. There were swifts wheeling in the sky, bats flitting through the galleries and children singing in the distance. Nature and art combined in perfection. Mr Huy said, 'It is like the poetry.'

We climbed the narrow worn steps up to the top of the central tower where once a gold statue of Vishnu had stood. It was time for evening prayers and suddenly, as an owl hooted somewhere in the forest, a troop of saffron-clad monks ran up the steep flight of stairs, sure-footed in their bare feet, to pray as the last rays of the sun bathed the towers of Angkor Wat in a flood of golden light.

As we walked out into the setting sun along the splendid broad stone causeway, Mr Huy reminisced wistfully about the good old days under Sihanouk. He talked of De Gaulle's visit to Angkor and the fireworks and torchlit processions and crowds of happy people that marked the occasion. 'When Sihanouk returns to power, the first person he will invite to Cambodia is Mitterrand,' he said. In a muddy pool half-covered with water hyacinth, young monks were bathing. The haunting silhouette of Angkor Wat was reflected, tremulous, in the water, and, as they laughed and splashed, ripples shattered the reflection.

That evening we had a meeting with the men from the Provincial People's Committee. Jim wanted to find out to what extent the people in and around Siem Reap felt themselves to be menaced by the Khmer Rouge and how real the threat was, so around eight o'clock, we put out packets of American cigarettes and cans of cold Heineken and sat waiting in the Grand Hotel's gloomy lounge with its tired 1950s décor and its angular sofas and arm-chairs protected by lilac and turquoise plastic slip-covers. Mr Leng Vy, who was both the Deputy Secretary of the Provincial Party Committee and the Chairman of the Provincial People's Commit-tee of Siem Reap-Oudar Meanchey province, came accompanied by two other men, one of whose job was to take notes of Sophy's translation both of our questions and their answers and check for accuracy. Sophy's limited skills as a translator cannot have made for an easy job.

Mr Leng Vy was a small man of forty with a look of Mickey Mouse who had been a teacher under Sihanouk and Lon Nol. He spoke of Siem Reap as '*the* province of Cambodian history' and Angkor as the 'soul of Cambodia'. He too had heard the Voice of America broadcast, which Mr Huy had relayed to us that afternoon, claiming that the Khmer Rouge had received twenty-four tanks from the Chinese, and said, 'This is the strong point of the enemy but also their weak point because they cannot receive gasoline for the tanks.' He added that the enemy (which is how government officials always describe the Khmer Rouge, avoiding the term 'Khmer Rouge' because, as Sophy explained to me one day, both Heng Samrin and Hun Sen had once belonged to the Khmer Rouge) had been planning for months to capture the capital of Siem Reap but that at present they were only active in the remoter areas.

He talked of the carpentry and textile industries and of milk production; of the eighty thousand tons of fish that the Tonle Sap had yielded that year which was more than the previous year, and of the fear of drought. He said that almost every village now had a school and that there were three hundred beds in the hospital but still a shortage of medicines. He described plans for a school to educate doctors and pharmacists, and said that he hoped 'but so far in vain' for some result from all the peace initiatives.

The interview proceeded slowly and rather drearily in this fashion. Poor Sophy was less than equal to his task and every so often the note-taker from the PPC would intervene and correct him – which made him even more nervous and ineffectual.

After they had gone, taking with them the unopened cans of beer and the packets of cigarettes, Sophy disappeared into the night in the direction of the market where he now took all his meals with his brother. Jim and I repaired to the dining room where we were once again the only guests. An enormous dinner of cold *hors d'oeuvre* and *steak haché* with fried potatoes was placed in front of us. I was fairly sure that, as befitted the French traditions of the establishment, the meat was horse-meat but I tried not to think about it. We asked whether, by any unlikely chance, there might be a bottle of wine tucked away somewhere, left over from the days when foreign dignitaries would put up at the Grand Hotel. The elderly waiter, himself something of a relic of former times, having been there since 1956, produced a bottle of 'Tourisme', the optimistically-named *vin du pays*. It was a filthy brew, tasting rather like corked communion wine, but it made a welcome change from the monotonous and slightly metallic taste of beer. A middle-aged Cambodian whom Jim knew came in to say 'hello' and we offered him a glass. He used to work for Cathay Pacific which, in the old days, had weekly flights from Hong Kong to Siem Reap via Phnom Penh. Jim pointed out that if the last twenty years hadn't happened, the people of Siem Reap would be very well-off, what with the tourist trade generated by Angkor and the abundant natural resources of the Tonle Sap. Instead their hospital was full of amputees and the lives of the people were constantly threatened by drought, disease and malnutrition – as well as the war.

One morning we drove out to a small fishing village near Phnom Krom on the banks of the Tonle Sap, the 'Sprawling Sea of Sweet Water', as Mr Huy described it, and took a boat out on the lake for a couple of hours. During the rainy or 'fertile' season the Tonle Sap swells to fifteen metres deep and shrinks to only two metres in the dry season. It was now the end of the rainy season and the lake was brimming. The water, which from the sky looked the colour of milky coffee, close-up was opaque and almost black in parts, and then a wonderful steel-grey blue. I saw a snake swimming, its head just clearing the surface, and masses of fish. The Vietnamese who live in Cambodia traditionally fish while the Cambodians farm, and there were families of Vietnamese fishermen, living in dirty rickety houses built on stilts out on the lake. These, often half-submerged in water, had crude bamboo fishpens attached to them, where they fattened up fish for sale. To amuse us, they threw handfuls of food into the water and suddenly the whole pen was alive and boiling and foaming with fish fighting each other to get to the food. One fisherman reached into the squirming mass and pulled a fat silvery fish out by its tail. It fought against his hand and he threw it back into the water.

Among the carvings on the *bas-relief* at Angkor Wat were scenes of fishermen on the Tonle Sap, their oars jammed by the volume of fish in the lake. Henri Mouhot, visiting the 'great lake Touli-Sap' in the second half of the nineteenth century, wrote: 'Above all, the great lake is a source of wealth to the whole nation; the fish in it are so incredibly abundant that when the water is high they are actually crushed under the boats, and the play of the oars is frequently impeded by them.' Unfortunately, the Great Lake no longer seemed to be a source of wealth to the whole nation and the Vietnamese fishermen and their families now living in conditions of grisly poverty and squalor had little in common with the characters in the carvings, but at least there still appeared to be plenty of fish.

We drifted slowly out across the water. There were large black crows perched on sinking and abandoned shacks, waiting to swoop on a fish or a snake. They had an ominous watchful quality, like the birds in Hitchcock's film, and matched the depressing lifestyle of the fishermen. The contrast between the beauty and fecundity of the Tonle Sap and the obviously difficult and dreary lives of its human inhabitants made me uneasy. It seemed to hint a greater imbalance even than was obvious; a disharmony in nature that mirrored the troubled situation in which Cambodia found itself.

Back on shore, Jim produced a wallet of photographs of his lovely wife with Princess Monique, Sihanouk's wife, and showed them to the villagers. I think he was trying to find out how they felt about Sihanouk but they didn't appear to do much more than evince polite interest. In a little house along the road, a number of elderly women, probably mostly widows, with beautiful ravaged faces and collapsed betel-stained mouths were dancing slowly, waving their hands like leaves in the wind. At the back of the room a group of musicians was playing soft haunting percussive music. Suddenly one old lady with a shaved head, began to shriek and fling herself about the room. The others ran to soothe her and hold her in their arms. I asked Sophy what was going on. He said he wasn't sure but muttered something about 'taking the soul of another'.

Most days we explored the ruins. It made me feel a little guilty because it didn't seem like work but it was too good a chance to miss so we wandered around Angkor Thom, all over the Bayon and along the Terrace of the Leper King and the Terrace of the Elephants; we looked at Takeo, Preah Khan, Baksei Chamkrong and a host of other monuments and temples whose names I never got. Mr Huy was so filled with energy and enthusiasm that he never seemed to get hot or tired and so we rushed from one place to another and, after a while, the wisest course seemed to be to absorb the atmosphere of the place rather than to try to make sense of specifics. Each carving was exquisite but after I had seen a few hundred or thousand, they all merged into one.

The Bayon, the thirteenth-century temple-mountain in the exact centre of Angkor Thom, was perhaps the most intriguing. It was smaller and less imposing than Angkor Wat, more ramshackle and less restored. Built by Jayavarman VII, the Leper King, the Bayon's most disturbing feature is the face of Jayavarman himself in the role of *bodhisattva*, with its enigmatic half-smile, which looks out from every facet of the fifty-four towers (representing the provinces of the ancient Khmer empire). Someone was always watching over you at the Bayon. Sihanouk, never known for his reticence, was in the habit of projecting himself as the reincarnation of Jayavarman VII and had his profile 'photographically compared' to that of the great building emperor. Sihanouk's identification with Jayavarman may not have been entirely wishful thinking. According to David Chandler, Jayavarman VII 'stamped the entire kingdom with his personality and his ideas of kingship as no other ruler was able to do before Norodom Sihanouk in the 1960s and Pol Pot in the late 1970s'.

Other than Angkor Wat, I liked best the tenth-century Hindu temple of Prasat Kravan. I saw its reflection first, quivering very slightly in a murky pool choked with water hyacinth and lotus blossom. Its five towers in mellow brick and simple unornamented design came as something of a relief after the wild excesses of Ta Prohm. Of the latter Norman Lewis wrote: 'Ta Prohm, built to house the image and the divine essence of the Queen Mother and 260 attendant and lesser deities, required for its service 79,365 persons, of whom about 5,000 were priests. The gold plate used in this temple weighed five tons and the temple establishment lived upon the revenue of 3,140 villages.' As I struggled through the hideously overgrown undergrowth and breathed in the foul smell of rotting vegetation, the phrase that sprang irresistibly to mind was 'Pride comes before a fall'. Once diamonds and emeralds studded the walls where the queen's sarcophagus had lain in state. Now a damp mass of roots and creeper, armies of ants, leaf mould and fallen masonry marked the spot. Trees with roots like the tentacles of a giant octopus enveloped and engulfed smaller buildings. One little pavilion was so compressed by the roots of a *fromager* tree that it looked as if a giant hand was pressing down upon it. The French writer, Elie Laure, described it thus: 'With its millions of knotted limbs, the forest embraces the ruins with a

violent love.' A love that would soon destroy the ruin if left to
its own devices.

Mr Huy skipped lightly through the wreckage, shouting gleeful
warnings against cobras and the deadly little emerald green Hanuman snake. There were bats and scorpions and millipedes, and
soldiers in green uniforms which camouflaged them so that, when
they suddenly appeared through an archway, it came as a shock.
We were endlessly having to buy cartons of *Liberation* cigarettes
to distribute to the impossibly young soldiers and policemen
whose job it was to guard the monuments from vandals and
guerrillas. They whistled to each other when one or other disappeared to investigate a noise and their soft whistles would echo in
the stone corridors. The sunlight filtered through the vegetation
casting a watery green light over everything and creating an effect
similar to being under water – and equally unwelcoming. I hated
the way that the jungle had reclaimed the buildings and I also
disliked Mr Huy's apparent relish at the destruction wrought by
both nature and man.

Over the years more than two thousand heads had been chiselled
or sawn off various statues. At Preah Khan, the great temple of
the Sacred Sword built by Jayavarman VII in the late twelfth
century to honour his father, the heads and faces of many of the
apsaras had been gouged out of the stone walls where they stood
in relief and, as recently as January 1990, five massive heads of
demons had been stolen from the magnificent approach to the
south gate of Angkor Thom. The heads were so heavy that six
men would have been needed to lift each one. The thefts therefore
must have been organised at a relatively high level and were carried
out apparently by the soldiers and policemen of both the Government and the resistance coalition. The heads or other fragments
are smuggled to the Thai border and then sold for a fortune to
unscrupulous collectors.

In 1923 André Malraux, later Minister of Culture in Paris under
De Gaulle, went to the exquisite and remote little temple of Banteay Srei and there cut out of its lovely pink sandstone a ton of
the finest statues and cornices. He was arrested in possession of
the treasure as he tried to leave Cambodia and sentenced to three
years' imprisonment, but he never actually went to jail. Malraux

does not appear to have felt any shame or guilt over his actions which he describes, in his novel, *La Voie Royale*. When my parents visited Angkor, there was a notice in the lobby of the Grand Hotel describing the Malraux incident and warning those who might be tempted to follow his example.

Mr Huy said that he had heard that some of the heads had been recovered after twenty thieves had been arrested. They were coming up for trial in a month. When questioned on the subject, Mr Leng Vy had said rather dispiritedly, 'We must develop the spirit of the people living round the temples to protect the culture and history of the Cambodian people.' But I thought it likely that the threat of punishment and imprisonment would prove a more effective deterrent.

Banteay Srei, still – even after Malraux's looting – extraordinarily beautiful and considered to be the most perfect of Khmer temples, was now unvisitable. The road was passable only with a jeep or something similar, and was too dangerous. We would have had to take a large armed escort costing hundreds of dollars. Houghton Broderick wrote of the temple: 'Alone, in its setting of forest, Banteay Srei glows cool under the heat. Great butterflies like black velvet swoop and flutter about the shrines.'

Next time, I thought, next time, and contented myself with a final visit at dusk to the tranquil ornamental lake of Sras Srang, the Pool of Ablutions, which faces the unfinished temple of Banteay Kedi. In the 1960s Sihanouk had sought to turn Sras Srang into a kind of amusement lake, such as you might expect to find in Dalat. With characteristic vulgarity, he had scattered *pedalos*, those clumsy brightly-coloured little boats, like aquatic dodgem cars, on the lake, for courting couples to take out on the water. They must have accorded horribly with the quiet dignity of the stone lions and *nagas* which flank the steps by which the king would descend into the water. But now there were only floating carpets of the all-pervasive water hyacinth and clouds of mosquitoes and a few small children on the cadge for sweets or cigarettes. The mosquitoes were biting fiercely and I got out a little tin of Tiger Balm to put on the bites. Mr Huy took the tin, looked at it and said, shaking his head, 'Very poor quality.'

*

Driving back from the ruins in the half-light, we saw a man lying in a bloody heap on the road. The people standing around him said that he had been there for over an hour because they had no means of moving him. We stopped and lifted him into the front seat of the minibus to take him to the hospital. He was unconscious, with blood seeping from his mouth, and his head lolled alarmingly. Like most young men in Cambodia, he was wearing an olive-green uniform and I thought that perhaps he had had a run-in with some Khmer Rouge. In fact, his bicycle had hit a pothole in the road and he had gone over the handlebars and landed on his head. I wanted to go with him to the hospital but Mr Huy firmly dropped us back at the hotel.

That evening we had an extra hour of electricity. A Japanese television crew had arrived to film a 'spectacular' at Angkor Wat. The lobby was full of expensive Japanese equipment – lights, cameras, generators, all the latest in Japanese technology – and crates of drinking water and Sapporo beer flown up in a specially-chartered plane from Phnom Penh. At dinner that night, the dining room echoed with the polite sound of Japanese voices. There must have been at least twenty of them, all seated at one long table. As Jim and I sat in our usual corner, I thought of Mr Huy saying one afternoon as we clambered through the ruins and undergrowth, 'When I come back in the next life, my first choice is to be born Japanese, then American, and then French.' The Japanese, according to journalists in Bangkok, were already investing millions of *yen* in Cambodia, buying up vast areas of land and smuggling timber over the border to Thailand. Here they had drained the bathrooms of every last drop of water but at least there was light – and air-conditioning till ten. It cost seven dollars an hour to run the generator.

I was grateful for the air-conditioning. Outside my window the night seemed even more leaden and swampy than usual. I fell into a deep sweaty sleep and dreamt that I was blind. I was blind because it was literally impossible for me to open my eyes. My eyelids were too heavy.

On our last morning, we left the ruins alone and went instead for a look at modern Cambodia. We were taken to see a group of 'misled' people: men who having seen the error of their ways in supporting one of the resistance groups, had given themselves up to the government soldiers. There were thirty-nine such people in Siem Reap at present but only three were Khmer Rouge because 'the Khmer Rouge has very strong discipline and few recant'. In a classroom in a school, we were introduced to eight or nine young men, most of them barely more than boys. One man stood out from the others. He was leaner and older with a guarded watchful expression and short hair. He sat quietly, neither smoking nor fiddling with the defused land-mine that lay on the desk in front of him. His name was Sath San. He was thirty-four. At the time of his defection in October 1989, he had been commander of Brigade 58 which operated in Kompong Thom, halfway between Siem Reap and Phnom Penh. He had been a long-term member of the Khmer Rouge which he had joined in Banteay Srei district in 1972 and whose philosophy he outlined briefly: 'We struggle for national liberation. We punish the aggression of Vietnamese troops. The Vietnamese will cut our throats and kill us.'

It was not clear why he had defected. Jim thought that he must have fallen out with his comrades, that internal politics must have played a part in his decision. It is tempting to say that he looked different, more ruthless and sinister than the others, identifiably Khmer Rouge. I don't know whether he really did. I am looking at his photograph now. He looks unhappy. That much is certain.

We left the 'misled' people and drove to the civilian hospital where a team of six doctors and nurses from Médecins Sans Frontières was working. They performed, they said, an average of fifteen amputations a month – and this was only in the civil hospital. Far more could be expected in the military hospital where the soldiers and policemen were treated. Half the activity of the hospital was surgical because of the war and the main cause of damage was land-mines. One of the problems was the difficulty in getting people to the hospital. Often amputations were necessary that could have been avoided if the victim had been seen quickly by a doctor. But poor or non-existent roads and the lack of an efficient transport and communications system meant that the wounded often lay for days before receiving treatment. The other single largest problem was cerebral malaria which was a cause for concern throughout Cambodia. MSF provided the medicines and drugs but the patients were brought food by their families.

We walked through the hospital. The walls were peeling and the patients lay in hot rooms, without air-conditioning or fan, on iron cots covered with coconut matting. More often than not, a *krama,* the all-purpose Khmer red-and-white checked cotton scarf, served as a sheet or cover. On every side, there were scenes of terrible suffering and distress, endured, on the whole, in silence and with good humour and courage. Your eyes would travel either down the body from the beautiful courteous smiling face – Cambodians are almost always beautiful and smiling – to the leg that suddenly stopped short at the groin or knee. Or perhaps you would start at the bandaged stump and then wander up the body till your eyes met those of the unfortunate victim who would smile warmly and accept your gift of cigarettes or soap or sweets. I had some little lipsticks in my pocket as well but I left them there. They seemed too frivolous for this place. If he – or she – was physically able, he would press his hands together and bow his head in the *sampeah,* the traditional gesture of respect and gratitude.

Only the wounded children had forgotten their manners. They were too bewildered and too hurt. There was one little boy aged about ten, his face obscured by bandages, who had been wounded by a mine while looking after water buffalo. He was lucky: he hadn't lost a limb, only an eye. Near him lay a woman who had been wounded by artillery fire thirty-five miles from Siem Reap. She had been in the hospital for four months. In another room, a father and daughter sat together on an iron bed: he was the chief of a village thirty miles away and had been wounded by AK-47 bullets when fourteen or fifteen Khmer Rouge came into his village one night to steal food. His wife had been killed in the attack; he had had an arm and a leg amputated and his other leg was badly damaged; his twenty-year-old daughter had lost a leg after her foot had been hit by bullets and gone gangrenous. He used to earn three hundred *riels* a month (about fifty cents); now he did not know what he would do. His three-year-old grandson sat between his mutilated mother and grandfather, whimpering uneasily.

10

Cambodia's Wounded

One man to five. A million men to one.
And still they die. And still the war goes on.

from *Cambodia* by James Fenton

Sophy had hired his uncle, an elegant taciturn man called Chea
Samol, as our driver. He drove a pick-up truck which belonged
to his employer, an officer in the Army who never seemed to
require his services. We all three had to sit in the front because
there were no seats in the back and, after a few hours on the road,
I developed an ache, that soon became chronic, in my left shoulder
from having to keep my elbow resting on the window sill. That
arm also got very sunburnt.

One morning we set off from Phnom Penh for Kompong Speu
province which lies in the south-west of Cambodia between the
Cardamom Mountains and the Elephant Mountains. A few
months before a camp had been established there to house some
seven-and-a-half thousand people from Trapaing Cho commune
in the Aural district who were being menaced by the Khmer
Rouge. This stormy beautiful area, dominated by the massive peak
of Mount Aural, Cambodia's highest mountain, was among the
most infertile in the country and a stronghold of the Khmer Rouge
whose bases of operations lay along the Thai-Cambodian border
to the north-west, and to the south-west of the country.

As we drove along the dusty red road to the camp headquarters, we passed a large gathering of people, clearly a demonstration of some kind. A man standing on a makeshift platform was shouting into a microphone. People were shouting slogans and waving banners. A young man in a white shirt and jeans carried a placard on which was written in large capital letters 'ABSOLUTELY AGAINST THE RETURNING OF THE GENOCIDAL REGIME OF POL POT'. Others bore slogans with messages in Khmer and French, the latter and the English presumably for the benefit of foreign journalists, like myself, who apparently visited the camp in droves every day.

The people in this camp were there because they lived in fear of the Khmer Rouge. All but three hundred families from their commune or district had been prepared to leave their homes and walk for forty miles to the relative safety of the camp site. It had taken a week to move all the people. Chum Trouk, the district chief and a former soldier in the army of General Lon Nol, had survived after 1975 by taking off his uniform and pretending that he was a civilian. He said that those who had stayed behind had not wanted to. They had remained because they had relatives working for the Khmer Rouge whom they would almost certainly soon be forced to join, probably as porters carrying food to the border and arms and ammunition back into Cambodia. They would not have been allowed to go on living in their village.

Sitting at a long table in a bamboo hut, Chum Trouk described the way that the Khmer Rouge operated. 'When the Khmer Rouge soldiers came to Trapaing Cho, they used the same phrases as before: they said they would "liberate the country from the Vietnamese and build a free regime". Then they started to disrobe the monks and mobilise the people to collective work. If our people had stayed in Trapaing Cho, their living conditions would be no better than in the camp and here they feel more secure. There they were afraid that the Khmer Rouge would kill them. Also by being here, we can cut the source of supply of people to Pol Pot – the Khmer Rouge take men between sixteen and forty-five and women to be porters to the border area. They ask the people to buy them batteries, medicines, hammocks and groceries, and pay them in US dollars. The widows are especially vulnerable because they are the poorest and the Khmer Rouge are rich because they receive US dollars from the United States.'

The camp was on an expanse of land that had been forest until the arrival of the refugees. Now it was untidy scrub, arid and infertile. Women (nearly five thousand of the camp's inhabitants were women) and children squatted in the dirt in flimsy huts that more often than not consisted of just a platform under a palm-leaf roof. They looked dispirited and ashamed, even the children. They also looked alarmingly thin. Because of the drought, it was now too late to plant rice and they were having to rely on whatever the Government and aid organisations provided. They said that they were hungry, that they had received no rice for two months and that they could no longer go into the forest to look for firewood to sell for money to buy rice and wild potatoes to eat because of the danger of land-mines. They also ran the risk of encountering Khmer Rouge soldiers in the forest who would either kidnap them or try, in Chum Trouk's sinister phrase, to educate them.

I had always been puzzled as to how, after the miserable years that followed the fall of Phnom Penh in 1975, the Khmer Rouge had any success at all in recruiting. It seemed unlikely that even the most naive and gullible peasant would swallow a word of their ideology. Everyone feared the Khmer Rouge, no-one trusted them and I never met anyone who was prepared to countenance, with any equanimity, their return. The more articulate and educated among the people, like Chum Trouk, said that they recognised that in order to achieve peace, they had to accept the inclusion of the Khmer Rouge in any settlement. But they didn't like it and they worried about the presence on the Supreme National Council of Khieu Samphan and Son Sen, both of whom were Pol Potists from the bad old days. However, I soon realised that winning hearts and minds was not something the Khmer Rouge were really bothering with. What 'success' they enjoyed was achieved through a combination of fear, intimidation, bribery and anti-Vietnamese propaganda, and often the peasants were simply too weak to resist. They were also extremely well-organised and highly-disciplined.

The little hospital at Kompong Speu appeared to contain only two kinds of patients: drained new mothers with damp matted hair and huge mauve shadows under their eyes, lying on filthy beds in post-natal gloom and exhaustion, barely able to nurse their tiny babies – and very young men without legs and arms. The only doctor, a weary Cambodian in green operating overalls, said that they were on the front line of battle against the Khmer Rouge and often the only way to save life was to amputate. The number of land-mines strewn around the countryside was estimated to be between 600,000 and four million and every day there were hideous accidents. He added that the hospital was assisted by an Australian aid agency but the turnover of Australian doctors was very high and the latest one had just gone to Bangkok for a holiday. He said that they kept the dispensary locked and wouldn't let him have a key. From his tone, it was clear that there was a history of resentment and misunderstanding but I thought it was best not to enquire too closely.

When I had first arrived in Cambodia from Saigon, I had met a pretty, elegantly-dressed woman in her early forties at the airport. No-one had turned up from the Ministry of Foreign Affairs to meet me and I was standing, a little lost and very hot, when she offered to help me. She was there in some professional, rather than personal, capacity but her offer was no less welcome. She recommended the Hôtel Asie, which was considerably cheaper than the Monorom where I had been planning to stay (and just as comfortable – or uncomfortable), and took me into town in a yellow bus with a couple of men from East Berlin who were making a film about the airforces of the Communist countries of South East Asia. She said that she would come to see me later. She did and, over the days that followed, slowly we became friends, real friends. She was intelligent, sensitive and entertaining. We were of an age and both women, and we managed, by some miracle, to transcend the usual barriers of language (she spoke fluent French and reasonable English), culture and experience. Her friendship made me realise how much I missed friends, particularly women, with whom I could talk freely, when I was away, and made all the difference to my time in Cambodia. Her name was Somaly.

Somaly was a widow with two daughters. She came from a family of seven children, three boys and four girls, whose father had spent his life working for foreigners, mainly the French. At the time of the fall of Phnom Penh, he was employed as the accountant at the rubber plantation and factory at Chup near Kompong Cham in central Cambodia – which the French had built in 1927 and where Somaly had spent her adolescence. Theirs was a comfortable *bourgeois* existence. Life was good on the rubber plantation, full of perks. Every day they were given two big loaves of bread and could order butter and jam and cloth to make clothes, calico and poplin. In 1975 Somaly was twenty-nine. Her daughter, Pranita, then her only child, was two. Her husband was a pilot with Air Cambodge, formerly Royal Air Cambodge, and she worked in the administrative section of the same airline and was studying law part-time. One of her sisters was married to a general in the Lon Nol army.

When the Khmer Rouge marched into Phnom Penh, Somaly, her husband and daughter were taken to the countryside, to Kandal province just south of Phnom Penh. In January 1976, nearly nine months after the Khmer Rouge takeover, Somaly's husband was taken away to prison. She was allowed to visit him three times and then not any more. Months later she learned that he had been killed.

During the day, like everyone else, she toiled away in the fields. Her daughter who was too small to work, was cared for by the elderly women who also did the spinning and weaving. The women were often hungry and would get the children to steal food. Somaly was terrified because she knew that if her daughter was caught stealing, she would be killed, even though she was too small to know any better.

One day Somaly was bitten by a scorpion. She became feverish and very ill and was taken to what passed for a hospital during the Khmer Rouge period which the Cambodians always refer to as 'Pol Pot time'. As she lay delirious on the filthy floor, with only an old and dirty *krama* to cover herself with, she dreamt that she was in the hospital in Phnom Penh where she had given birth to her daughter.

'J'ai rêvé de draps blancs où j'ai accouché Pranita et de mon mari qui m'à porté dans ses bras de la salle d'accouchement'.

She had been very much in love with this husband who had carried her in his arms from the delivery room and I guessed from things that she said that this had been a happy and passionate marriage. She once told me that her husband had been born under the sign of the Dragon and that he would joke that, as a result, he was *'très puissant'*, which has the double meaning of 'powerful' and 'potent'.

One afternoon in late 1978, while Somaly was out working in the fields, a couple of cadres came to talk to her. They said, 'Angkar [the mysterious all-powerful organisation to whose rule the individual had to submit completely] wants you to re-marry.' She knew that she could not refuse outright and answered, 'The time is not yet right. The country is not profitable. It is better to wait.' But they wouldn't listen to her and she was taken in a cart drawn by a water buffalo to a village ten miles away where she met her future husband. He was the camp cook who had seen her and selected her as his bride. He was a 'Pol Potist' but not a 'killer'. They were married – which, under Pol Pot, involved making a vow to Angkar, rather than before one's parents and one's community – two months before the Vietnamese arrived. Somaly said that the nights were the worst and that she could remember nothing about the wedding night. A year later, she gave birth to a second daughter whom she named Seila, meaning 'rock'. Unsurprisingly, the marriage did not last, though Somaly said that he was not a bad man, just coarse. She was so shamed by this union that she had brought Seila up to believe that she had the same father as her sister, the dashing 'puissant' Air Cambodge pilot. Her elder daughter, Pranita, knew the truth.

All this came out one morning a day or two after we first met. We had gone upstairs to the deserted dusty restaurant on the fifth floor of the Hôtel Asie where no-one ever went and no food was ever served. I am not even sure that there was a kitchen. We were sitting there, drinking sweet coffee with tinned milk and talking about Pranita's forthcoming exams. But when I asked about her other daughter, tears began to roll down her face. I thought perhaps the child was ill or something and then she told me the story of Seila's birth.

Somaly's youngest sister, Bhopa, was also forced to marry during Pol Pot time, to a man whom Somaly described as a '*voyou*', a French slang term meaning 'thug' or 'hoodlum'. He disappeared almost as soon as the Vietnamese troops arrived, having, to use an old-fashioned term that seems oddly appropriate in this context, de-flowered the girl. She was therefore left in the invidious position of being neither widow nor maid and, being penniless, stood little chance of finding another husband. Mme Sun Saphoeun had told me that the trauma of a Pol Pot marriage often put women off marriage (and, she implied, sex) for good but Bhopa clearly craved a more conventional way of life than the one that the cruel hand of fate had dealt her. Premarital chastity was – and is – expected of girls but divorce had been permitted in Cambodia since a new law was passed in 1987 (confusingly, Somaly said that, even before the new law, there had been many divorces though a party member would lose his privileges if he divorced). However, it was hard to know what stigma would attach to a doubtful previous marriage to a Khmer Rouge ruffian. She would be further hampered in that she came from what, in pre-war Cambodia, would have been a middle-class background. Somaly herself was clearly desperate to obliterate the memory of her own Pol Pot-arranged marriage, though simultaneously unable to keep her story to herself. It was almost as if by telling it over and over again she would somehow purge herself of the experience. In her sister's case, and given the present economic climate in Cambodia, the absence of personal fortune was probably more of a stumbling block than her lack of virginity.

The shortage of men after the Pol Pot period also meant, according to both Somaly and Mme Sun Saphoeun, that Cambodian men could now take their pick of women, many of whom had to be content with being either concubines or 'second wives' who would be expected to hand over their earnings to the man. And I had heard from a journalist on the Singapore paper, the *Straits Times*, that many Singapore businessmen kept 'second wives' in Phnom Penh. Mme Sun Saphoeun said that men rarely earned enough to provide for their families, only enough for 'cigarettes and break-

fast' so the women had to go out to work and often were able
to bring in much more, working as shopkeepers or importers –
'*commerçantes*'. She added, with an air of irritable disdain, that
men were more often 'a drain' and that the only point of having
a man in the house was as a 'solid support'.

Somaly's sad little story touched me enormously. There was no
shortage in Cambodia of people who had suffered as much or
more but there was something very moving about her situation.
She was a woman of refined and delicate sensibilities and her
descriptions of the horrors of the intimacies of that second marriage were painful to hear. How much more painful to have had
to endure those intimacies. She was delighted by any hint of luxury
– and not in an empty-headed frivolous way. There was something
endearing about the pleasure that she derived from, say, a tiny
pot of Dior anti-wrinkle cream (a free sample that I found in my
sponge-bag and gave her). She liked me to look smart – which I
almost never did – and would comment approvingly on the rare
occasions I made an effort with my appearance. She was endlessly
protective of my resources, anxious that I shouldn't pay too much,
that I shouldn't be cheated, that nothing untoward should happen
that might give me a bad impression of Cambodia.

The evening before Sophy and I left for Kampot, I took Somaly
and her daughters out to dinner at a restaurant built on wooden
platforms on stilts out over Boeng Kak lake a little way out of
the centre of town. We went by *cyclos*: Pranita and I crammed
into one, Somaly and Seila, who always clung to her mother in
an ecstasy of passionate affection, in another. My *cyclo-pousse*
claimed to be called Robespierre.

I asked Somaly to order because I wanted dinner to be a treat
for them. She asked whether I would eat traditional Cambodian
food so I said 'Yes, of course' and we were served some ghastly
dish of smoked fish, cold and very salty and full of tiny sharp
bones, and green papaya. The Tonle Sap produced such a mass of
fish each year that the only way to preserve it was to salt it and,
unfortunately, salt fish formed the basis of many Cambodian
dishes as a result. I remembered Mr Dang, who, in addition to
being a terrific gourmet, shared along with many Vietnamese, a
healthy contempt for the Cambodians, warning me that I would

not eat well in Cambodia and telling me that the Khmer national dish was a dead fish (dead, not just put out of its misery for the occasion) floating in soup. I should have told him that Henri Mouhot in the 1850s reported '. . . his [the Annamite's] food is abominably nasty. Rotten fish and dog's flesh are his favourite food.' Once we were out of Phnom Penh, Sophy and I often had wonderful food – but successful ordering in Phnom Penh, even when accompanied by Cambodians, was a question of luck and I often fell back on something safe like an omelette.

Somaly and the girls ate hugely which was the main thing, and I picked at a prawn or two and some rice. The restaurant was cooler than in the centre of town and it was nice to be outdoors enjoying the night air and what little we could see of the lake in the dark, even if we did have to lard ourselves with insect repellent against the swarms of mosquitoes, breeding in its stagnant waters.

Pranita was a soft, curvy girl in her late teens with a sweet smile and exquisite manners. She had high rounded cheekbones and a waist-length plait of black hair. She was pretty but not exceptional. Her sister, Seila – the rock – was unlike any other ten-year-old girl I had ever met. She was very beautiful with a tawny skin, almond-shaped eyes and a little beauty spot to the right of her full mouth. She was dressed up to the nines and covered in her mother's jewellery, wearing antique sapphire earrings and a collection of fine gold chains set with tiny rubies and sapphires. She had a curious deep voice, like a young tigress growling, and, though she spoke no English or French – unlike Pranita who had a smattering of both – I could sense immediately the strength of her character and that she was intensely wilful.

I gave her a rubber shaped like a dice and Pranita a bright yellow ballpoint pen of cunning Japanese design. When Seila saw the pen which she preferred, she flew into a rage and said that she didn't want the rubber. Somaly became very embarrassed and began apologising but I thought it was funny and found another biro, a red one, for her. Somaly said that Seila was nothing like Pranita nor other children of her age, that she would announce that she wanted to be kept by a rich man and that she would only marry for money – which is not the kind of thing well-brought-up young Cambodian women are meant to say. I thought that

Seila would make an excellent courtesan or the mistress of a powerful and dangerous man. She was clearly going to grow up to be powerful and dangerous herself. Somaly looked at her, with love and a degree of alarm, as if wondering what she had given birth to. It was difficult to be sure but I thought if anyone could handle the secret of her shameful birth, Seila could.

Sophy had also been forced to marry by the Khmer Rouge but his marriage had lasted and he had two small sons. He had taken part in a group marriage ceremony which seemed to have been arranged rather like a table-tennis tournament. You discovered who your partner was – in this case, your spouse – by looking at a list. Apparently in some cases, Angkar arranged marriages without asking the consent of the individuals concerned and without the future spouses having ever before laid eyes on each other. This led to situations such as when the bride, having lowered her eyes throughout the ceremony, would fail to recognise her bridegroom after the rites had been performed.

As we ploughed along the road to Kampot, Sophy told me about his marriage – his wife suffered chronically from undiagnosable illnesses after years of deprivation under Pol Pot – and about his longing for his pre-Pol Pot sweetheart whom he still sometimes saw. She, too, had been forced to marry but her husband had either died or disappeared. Given what Mme Sun Saphoeun had said about men having two wives, I wondered whether Sophy might not feel like indulging in a bit of polygamy. He said that he could only do so if his wife were to agree and if she did agree, he said, 'I would blame her because I do not want to do like that.'

The road was appalling, having been sabotaged or 'cut' by the Khmer Rouge. Along the roadside, against a painterly backdrop of sugar palms, lotus ponds and rice fields, men and women were tottering under the back-breaking weight of baskets piled high with stones to fill the holes in the road. These workers earned 300 *riels* a month, about fifty cents. Small children shouted and threw pebbles at the car. I asked Sophy what they were saying. He said that they were asking for money or sweets.

The drive took three-and-a-half hours and seemed far longer

but we were lucky. Ten years before the same journey would apparently have taken three times as long though it was hard to imagine how the road could have been worse. More than the hospitals, more than the beggars, more than the curfew, more than anything else, the condition of the roads brought home to me the truly parlous situation in which Cambodia presently found itself. You can usually get a fair assessment of a country's economic state from the condition of its roads. In Laos there were no major highways; the roads in Vietnam were poor by most western standards but traversable; in much of Cambodia – the north, north-east and south-west, for instance – there were no roads at all and those that existed in the rest of the country were very poor. More than ten years after the Vietnamese strode into Phnom Penh, the country was still in administrative chaos. To go anywhere was a major enterprise and communications were still very primitive. There were few telephones outside Phnom Penh and no guarantee that telegrams would arrive. The one train that ran from Battambang to Phnom Penh and vice versa was so often blown up by the Khmer Rouge that it could scarcely be regarded as a viable means of transport and often stopped overnight *en route*, thereby making the twelve-hour journey take two or more days.

As I sat for hours in that pick-up truck, every muscle in my body protesting furiously as we dipped into yet another crater, I understood where every spare *riel* had been going for the last eleven years: to finance the civil war.

Kampot was a dusty, one-horse town perched on the banks of a wonderful river, the Prek Thom. Jim Pringle had told me to stay in a hotel looking onto the river but, for reasons – who knows what reasons – that was not to be. I was shown to an enormous and filthy room with four beds on the third floor of a charmless concrete block. I chose the one with a shocking pink nylon mosquito net, ruched and gathered like a petticoat at the Folies Bergère. Outside, Phnom Penh Radio was blaring from loudspeakers at each of the four corners of the square but a sluggish power supply meant that it was only running at half-speed and everything was slurred and distorted. No-one but me seemed to mind or even notice and there were groups of people on bicycles gathered beneath each speaker. After a lunch of fresh prawns with chillies and lime and a special spicy salt imported from Thailand (which I later discovered to be monosodium glutamate), Sophy disappeared to report our arrival to the committee and I took a *cyclo* round town.

The *cyclos* in Kampot, like those in Siem Reap, were little open carts, pulled, rather than pushed, by the *cyclo-pousse*. We crossed the river and set off down a red dirt track, pitted with huge puddles from the monsoon rain. There were a few larger carts, laden with old tyres, wood and stacks of baskets, pulled by small ponies, and a couple of fat pigs wading slowly through the water. The road was bordered by shacks roofed with coconut matting and, as we stopped to turn, a woman waved me to a stop in front of her home. I went in and sat on the floor, a platform made of split bamboo, and everyone came to have a good look at me. My hostess was a fine-looking old woman with short grey hair and a mouth stained with betel. Conversation was difficult. She spoke neither English nor French and my Khmer was as ever limited to a few basic courtesies. But we smiled and bowed to each other in an amicable fashion and she pinched my arms and legs. I gave her a tiny double-sided mirror with a reproduction of Fragonard's 'Girl on a Swing' on its cover. It had regular mirror glass on one side and a magnifying mirror on the other. She peered at her toothless gums and laughed with surprise at the larger reflection.

By dusk, the town was suffused with a soft hazy pink light and the public radio had fallen mercifully silent. Against the darkening sky, a battered 'Shell' sign glowed orange over a derelict petrol station. The river was broad and still and the old colonial houses on the waterfront had a mellow weathered air to them. A sleepy plump man who had been hanging round the building – I don't think that it was really a hotel – where we were to stay, offered to take me for a drive in his car. I got in and settled down on one of the furry front seats, protected by fluffy lime-green nylon covers. He had the radio tuned to a station playing some soft fluting oriental music and we drove slowly and in silence round the town till it was dark. Later, I couldn't face company and, while Sophy went to have dinner with his aunt, I ate alone in a hot little restaurant off a side-street. Seafood was good in Kampot and they brought me a huge plate of small crabs cooked with chilli and ginger. At another table, some young men in uniform were getting drunk on French brandy – Hennessy. They were drinking it by the bottle and I wondered how they could afford it.

I slept surprisingly well in my huge dirty room and dreamt about Princess Michael of Kent. Just before dawn, Phnom Penh Radio and the cocks started up. We collected Sophy's relations and drove out into the countryside to a beautiful wild place surrounded by rolling bluish hills where the river paused in a huge pool and his aunt and her sons and daughters could bathe and wash their hair and do their laundry.

Sophy's aunt, Kim, was a stout jolly Chinese woman in her fifties with a mouthful of gold teeth who made a good living selling prawns and farming. Her father had been brought to Cambodia as a slave by a rich Chinese man and, when his owner died, he was set free and married a Cambodian wife whom he met in the market in Phnom Penh where she had gone to sell fruit. Kim was their daughter. She was not really Sophy's aunt, being the second wife (as in wife number two) of his elder brother from whom she had been separated in Pol Pot time and with whom she had not got back together. The elder brother now lived with wife number one and five children in Kandal province but Sophy remained fond of this lady and called her 'aunt'.

The women modestly draped themselves in cotton sarongs and entered the water thus clad while the men bathed in trousers. I took off my skirt and went in up to my waist. The river was flowing fast, frothing and foaming over the rocks, and cool and very clean. I could feel the current tugging at my ankles. We had to shout to make ourselves heard over the roar of the water. Two men standing on long bundles of bamboo lashed together with rope rushed past us and, steering themselves with poles, effortlessly negotiated the rapids. Further up the river was the Tuk Chhou waterfall but Sophy said that we couldn't go up there because 'our combatants' had laid mines there. Later that day, the doctors from Médecins Sans Frontières told me that four hundred Khmer Rouge had come into a nearby village and stolen everything and that their driver had had to turn back only eight miles out of

Kampot on the road to Phnom Penh. They said Kampot was *the* province of the Khmer Rouge but that they felt safer here than the MSF team did in Siem Reap.

In Kep, more than anywhere else in Cambodia, the past rose up to greet me. I had already realised that neither Phnom Penh nor Angkor were representative of the country as a whole. The quality of life (communications, prospects for employment and so on) was better in the former, and in the latter, the splendour of the ruins overshadowed everything else. Visiting Angkor was like taking a step back in time, but in Kep the past seemed just around the corner.

A handful of Sophy's 'cousins' came along for the ride, crammed into the back of the pick-up. They brought a bag of oranges and a beachball. We were, after all, going to the seaside. As we rolled into the empty town and parked on the esplanade, an old man, his head turbaned in a *krama*, came to greet us. He said that he was fifty-seven and a road-sweeper. He looked eighty and had been a road-sweeper in Kep since 1960 when the town was a chic seaside resort for the French and Sihanouk and his entourage. After Sihanouk was deposed, many high-ranking officials in the Lon Nol Government took over the beautiful villas but from 1973 to 1979, the town was under the control of the Khmer Rouge. They tore out the underground petrol tanks at the old Shell filling station and dumped the bodies of their victims in the pits. Small wonder that Kep had a reputation for being haunted.

Now no-one lived in Kep. It was a 'ghost' town and though the villas could have been re-built and made habitable, the five hundred or so families living around the town, many of them Muslim Chams, preferred to camp in shacks and tents. The nearest school was a mile away. At weekends, people came from Kampot to enjoy the beach and food was sold at stalls along the waterfront but, apart from a few soldiers up the hill at Sihanouk's summer palace, the town was deserted.

It seemed appropriate that Chams should have chosen this lonely spot to settle. Over the centuries, their kingdom, Champa, once a great power, had gradually been ground into the dust by ' the Vietnamese's conquering *Nam Tien* (march to the south), and they themselves had gone from being a great power to just another minority group. A number still lived in southern Vietnam, where I had seen the beautiful remains of their ancient cities and temples, but thousands had fled to Cambodia. In 1975 there were estimated to be at least 250,000 Chams in Cambodia, but of the groups persecuted by Pol Pot, none suffered more than they did. Their language, Bahasa-Cham (a relation of the Bahasa spoken in Indonesia and Malaysia), and dress were banned. Mosques were destroyed or desecrated, used, like pagodas, as granaries or pigsties. They were forced to eat pork while the Khmer population starved. Copies of the Koran were destroyed. Cham dead were buried upside down, that is, not facing Mecca. And they were murdered in purges. Over ninety thousand were massacred – mostly in the Kompong Cham area. The arbitrary Khmer Rouge decree abolishing all minorities had the greatest effect on the Muslim Chams who were twice doomed; for their 'foreign race' and their 'reactionary' faith. Khmer Rouge policy and practice nearly brought about their extinction as a people.

It was all terribly sad. I thought of Vung Tau and Bao Dai's immaculately preserved palace and contrasted the decay of Kep. At one end of an avenue of tamarind trees stood a lovely Italianate villa with a graceful balcony and arched window, which once housed Sihanouk's courtiers. It was now a complete ruin, the roof gone and the rooms open to the sky. The casino was full of rubble and piles of smashed tiles, and cattle were tethered in what had clearly once been the private gaming rooms. A large white ox was slowly depositing a pile of excrement in the main room. Up the hill at the end of a winding drive overgrown with bougainvillaea lay Sihanouk's villa, a single-storey building with pretty verandahs and gazebos and a magnificent view over the bay. It must have been lovely once but the roof had caved in, the walls were stained and the floors crawling with insects. It appeared to be empty but then we found a very young soldier asleep in a hammock round the back. He said that the other nine soldiers who were guarding the villa with him, had gone out fishing.

I floated on my back in the tepid green sea looking up at Sihanouk's house perched on the cliff. I was depressed by Kep: by the decay, the neglect, the ghosts. It made me wonder what chance Cambodia had of recovery. This was the first place I had visited where the evidence of destruction and decay was so strong. Phnom Penh was kept vibrant by its population; Angkor, given its great age, was actually in remarkably good condition and I had expected it to be ruined. It would be disconcerting, not to say, extraordinary, if it wasn't, just as it would be if the Acropolis or the Colosseum were intact. But in Kep it was as if the fine Georgian terraces of Edinburgh's New Town or some of the lovelier bits of Paris had been laid wantonly to waste. It was frightening, too, because it was so recent. Here today, gone tomorrow. It made me feel uncomfortably mortal.

Relations with Sophy were a little tense too. He was, I felt, behaving as if he was on holiday and, while it seemed churlish to grudge him some fun, his behaviour was deeply irritating. Every time I turned to ask him a question, he was off somewhere, throwing a ball or gossiping with one of his relations. I was also annoyed about money. It was impossible to budget because we kept being over-charged or having to pay bribes. As we left Kampot where I had flown into a fury at what we had been made to pay for our nights' sordid accommodation, he had told me that he had given fifteen dollars to the chief of the provincial committee. I said, 'That's far too much and why?'

'It's necessary.'

'So you are telling me that we have to bribe these people?'

He didn't understand the word 'bribe' but, when I began to explain, he nodded and said. 'Yes, corruption.'

On the road to Takeo, we continued the conversation. I knew that virtually everyone in Cambodia was short of money – the average salary of a government worker, including, for instance, a doctor, was around three dollars fifty cents (depending on the rate of exchange) and, as a result, almost every civil servant would either be moonlighting or taking bribes in order to survive. But it wasn't done to talk about it – at least not officially. Jim Pringle had been refused entry to Cambodia for six months after writing an article in which he claimed that the 'corruption (and nepotism) has not yet reached the levels attained during the American-backed Lon Nol regime but is approaching that of the earlier administration headed by Prince Norodom Sihanouk . . . '

But while I was happy to give money or cigarettes to, say, peasants or beggars or to tip for services, I didn't see why we had to give really quite large sums to officials. Sophy reluctantly explained that the telegram he had sent requesting permission to visit Kampot and stay overnight had apparently never arrived. It had certainly never been answered and therefore we didn't really have permission to be in Kampot at all. So when we turned up, as it were unannounced, we had to pay to be allowed to stay. I asked him whether he thought that the telegram had really not arrived or whether this was simply a ploy. He shrugged and didn't reply.

The reason for returning to Phnom Penh via Takeo was to see and possibly spend the night at a house built by the infamous Ta Mok. During the years of terror under the Khmer Rouge, when the country was divided into 'zones', Ta Mok ('Ta' means grandfather), as leader of the South-Western Zone, carried out extermination campaigns against real or imagined enemies of Pol Pot – purges of suspect Khmer Rouge cadres and their families. He was known as 'the Butcher', 'a lanky balding peasant with piercing eyes' whose 'name struck terror in the hearts of people' and whose 'troops were the cruellest of all'. Ta Mok now lived in north-east Thailand just over the border with Cambodia and was Commander-in Chief of the northern provinces of Cambodia, including Siem Reap.

Ta Mok's former home was rather a splendid place on a promontory jutting out into the middle of Lake Takeo and reached by a long causeway. It had been built on the site of a Buddhist pagoda destroyed by the Khmer Rouge and was a large attractive white building set in a garden full of red bougainvillaea. The water level in the pretty, still lake was low and there were a couple of fishermen standing in water up to their waists. The house was now a hotel owned by the province and used mainly by passing dignitaries. The manageress was sitting outside with three young policemen who giggled when I tried to talk to them and said they didn't know what they thought about anything because they were 'shy'. The manageress said that she didn't believe that there would be elections and that, if there were, she didn't know who she would vote for. She thought that the Supreme National Council was 'nonsense' and that Sihanouk was 'not a good politician, not truthful because he changed his position very quickly'. She said that she and her husband didn't earn enough money and that they and their two children didn't have enough to eat.

Sophy was impatient to get back to Phnom Penh and even I couldn't see that much would be gained by staying here. As we drove away from Takeo, passing an old sign that said 'Welcome' in Khmer, French and English, we passed a woman on a bicycle, a *krama* slung between the handlebars as a cradle for her baby. It seemed such a brilliantly economical device. In the West, we have a different tool for everything. Here everything had a hundred different uses.

By the time we got back to Phnom Penh, my shoulder was hurting so much that I could hardly move. Sophy took me to his aunt's house where she had a couple of Vietnamese masseuses as lodgers. Away from the main drag, the roads were almost as bad as the one to Kampot. It was late afternoon when Sophy left me and nearly dark in the large warehouse-like room at the back. The masseuses were very pretty, one plump, one slender, and both wearing pyjamas rather than the *sampot* which most Cambodian women wear. There was no electricity and, as the light faded, one of them lit a lamp made from an old whisky bottle full of petrol with a rag stuffed into the neck of the bottle.

I unbuttoned my blouse and lay down on a hard wooden bed covered with a thin piece of matting. The two girls immediately set to work, pinching and kneading the flesh of my arms and legs. They cracked the bones in my fingers, toes and spine, and – with one swift and rather terrifying movement, when for a moment I thought my head was going to be wrenched off – released my neck from the painful angle into which it had been forced by the car journey. It was very pleasurable, particularly since there were two of them and so at all times some part of me was being attended to. They chattered and giggled throughout like little sparrows and, at the end, when I felt like a piece of rusty machinery whose joints had finally been oiled, they asked for 700 *riels* – just over one dollar.

The next day, I visited one of the orphanages in Phnom Penh. It was a nutritional centre and most of the babies there had been abandoned and were suffering from malnutrition and its side-effects: deformed rib-cages, harelips and cataracts. Some of the children were older: toddlers who wrapped their arms round my legs and said, 'No go away.'

I had gone there on my first visit to Phnom Penh and been horrified. This time I was prepared and the experience was more enchanting than harrowing. The babies, presumably different ones, were still suffering from the same range of conditions but they seemed lively and affectionate, crawling all over me like puppies. One little blind boy was wearing a pair of Mickey Mouse shoes that squeaked like a rubber duck every time he took a step. He was walking round and round, a blissful smile on his face, listening to the sound. In the nursery school, the children were singing songs and playing games. I had bought some packets of sweets in the market and produced them. This caused a near riot but eventually everyone had two sweets and there were some left over for the teachers.

Not all the children were orphans. A few of the babies had been brought to the centre by their families because they were suffering from malnutrition and they would go home in time. Others would be adopted by Cambodian families who, the centre's director told me, wanted girls because they stay at home. Some would go to foreign parents though the Cambodian authorities were becoming more reluctant for foreigners to adopt Cambodian children.

Outside on the verandah, an American woman with a long hairy upper lip was cradling a tiny baby girl whom she had adopted. She was a thirty-five-year-old unmarried chiropractor from Washington who had been trying to adopt a child for some time. 'The biological clock was ticking and I decided that I wanted to have a child but I wasn't with anybody and I didn't want to go through pregnancy alone so I thought, "Why not adopt?" I had dreams about adopting a baby. I *knew* that it was what I was *meant* to do.'

I had often fantasised about doing the same thing – and adopting one of these children might well seem like philanthropy as well as self-indulgence – but I was too cowardly or selfish to pursue it. I thought of the stringent laws in Britain governing the adoption of children and how difficult it would be for someone of thirty-five, let alone someone who was not married, to adopt a British child but she said that, in the United States, it was reasonably easy. She was going to call her Alexa Rasmey, meaning 'sunrise' like my guide at the Royal Palace, and would be taking her to America within a few days. She showed me the baby's passport photos. They were black-and-white and the child looked tiny and very oriental. I wondered what sort of life she would have in Washington with her amiable alternative-culture American mother.

We left for Kompong Cham early the next morning. On the way out of town, we passed by the bank so I could change a hundred-dollar bill into smaller denominations for the necessary bribes. Fertiliser sacks full of *riels* were being unloaded onto the pavement. The mark of an economy in disarray is always the wads of notes needed for even a cup of coffee. While we waited for the bank to open, Sophy said that Mme Sun Saphoeun had told him that we might need to take an armed guard to Ratanakiri and that it would cost 'much money'. I asked, 'How much?' He had no idea. Then he said, 'If we do not go to Ratanakiri, I think maybe you should go home.' I said that was out of the question and he lapsed into silence. Later, on the road to Kompong Cham, he said gloomily, 'I think I make a mistake take you to these places without permission,' and added that the new Foreign Minister, Hor Nam Hong, had said that anyone who made a 'mistake' with a foreigner, would lose his job.

Kompong Cham, where Pol Pot went to school and where Heng Samrin was born, is in the centre of Cambodia, north-east of Phnom Penh and now one of the richer provinces with Hun

Sen's brother, Hun Neng, as the chairman of the provincial committee. To get there, we would have to cross the Tonle Sap river
by ferry at Prek Kdarm. The road was better than the one to
Kampot but the weather was depressing – grey and drizzling. At
one point, the water in a stream we were crossing had risen so
high that it was level with the bridge and, further on, people were
pushing their bicycles and walking in water up to their ankles.
The trees had a curious floating look to them as if they were no
longer rooted. At the ferry crossing, in amongst the usual motley
collection of food vendors and beggars, I saw something
uncomfortably familiar on a large enamel dish. Closer investi-
gation revealed these to be tortoises, grilled still in their lovely
shells, their ripe buttercup-yellow eggs spilling out from under
the shell. I told Sophy that in England we kept tortoises as pets
(when they are available – the last time I tried to buy one, I was
told it would cost £300, if they could get me one). He didn't know
the word 'pet' and even when I had explained, I got the feeling
that he thought the whole idea of keeping pets, particularly tortoises, was rather strange. One man, in a brilliantly-coloured,
multi-tiered hat, had twenty two-month-old piglets in a basket.
He had paid 2,700 *riels* for each one and was hoping to sell them
for 3,000 *riels* each. Another man had fifty-three ducks hanging
upside down on the back of his motorbike. These had been bought
for 250 *riels* each. He was hoping for a thirty-*riel* profit.

We stopped briefly in Kompong Cham to pick up a local guide
and to visit Wat Nokor and some of the other monuments. The
guide, a toothy garlic-smelling individual whom I disliked on
sight, was a mine of dreary information. But, during lunch, he
suddenly said, 'I lose two children! How?' We looked at him in
surprise. It turned out that his two little daughters had never come
home from school the previous afternoon and nobody knew where
they were. He seemed to be taking it pretty calmly. There were
no search parties, no talk of child molestation and no suggestion
that he not accompany us to Wat Nokor.

Wat Nokor, though considerably more modest, was built
around the same time as parts of Angkor by Jayavarman VII who
had seen off the Chams in a naval battle, probably on the Mekong
near Kompong Cham, in 1179 or 1180. Somewhere within its

shadowy portals bats squeaked. The guide said that Pol Pot's soldiers used to sharpen their swords on the right buttock of one of the stone lions and pointed to a worn patch. In contrast, the walls of the pagoda, a more recent building, were covered with charming 1950s frescos of maidens bearing lotus blossoms and celebrating the Buddha's birthday. It was all very pretty but lacked the force – and somehow therefore the beauty – of Angkor. It was as if it had been scaled down, reproduced in miniature.

We pushed on to the rubber plantation at Chup of which Somaly had such happy memories. It had been renamed '7th January' after the date of the Vietnamese invasion. In 1969, the Americans had bombed the plantation and the factory had been destroyed. Under Pol Pot it was re-built and the plantation restored to working life. Seventy people died there then, either of starvation or killed by the Khmer Rouge and, after 1979, the bones of the dead were discovered. The supervisor had been there since the late 1950s and had worked for the French and the Khmer Rouge. He said that during the latter period, everyone was hungry but they had to work days *and* nights. Now their workers came from Takeo where the rice fields were not yielding enough rice for them to feed themselves.

The plantation itself was lovely: eighteen thousand hectares of cool grey-green rubber trees, planted in orderly lines, but the factory was a nightmare. The smell was overpowering and repulsive, and the lumps of grey latex, like soggy suet pudding, floating in dirty water, were pretty disgusting too. We spent the night in a guest bungalow filled with mosquitoes the size of horseflies. To get to the bathroom, a squalid unlit hole with a stone tub full of cold water, I had to go through Sophy's room and, rather than do this, I resorted to peeing into a tin can. All night long I hovered on the edge of wakefulness to the sound of termites eating away at the fabric of the building and in the morning there were neat piles of dust in every corner where they had done their work.

I mentioned the mosquitoes to Sophy who could generally be relied upon to become hysterical at the thought of getting malaria. When I told him that I had killed some of them, he said, 'You are sin,' and I was reminded of Somaly saying, '*On ne peut pas dormir la nuit si on écrase un animal.*' I seemed to remember Mr

Dang's conscience hadn't troubled him overmuch when he had run down the dogs on the road to Dalat but I knew that Cambodians took Buddhism more seriously. I pointed out to Sophy that the manager of the plantation had been spraying against mosquitoes. He said that was different because it was not killing them directly. I said that mosquitoes spread malaria and that if they were less concerned about sin, they might have less malaria.

We left the plantation in a misty dawn. There were snakes slithering along the road. As the sun rose in the sky and chased the ragged puffs of mist away, the snakes vanished. Sophy and I talked about literature and education. He told me that a lot of the books they read came from the Soviet Union. I was re-reading *Anna Karenina* and offered to lend it to him but he said that Tolstoy was 'not good for a progressive country'. I tried to explain, without success, that literature and politics were not necessarily interchangeable and that great literature transcended politics.

Sophy was hoping for a posting as a diplomat so that he could augment his income by doing 'a little business'. If he got such a job, he would be sent either to India or the Soviet Union. He didn't want to go to India at all which he dismissed disparagingly as a 'very poor country' but he thought he could make some extra money in low-level import and export to Moscow.

In Kompong Cham, we went to the hospital. There was a woman lying on the floor in the entrance hall. Her complexion was ashen and she looked desperately ill. I asked the doctor what was wrong with her. 'She was pregnant but the baby had hydrocephalus [a condition causing enlargement of the skull and mental retardation] which meant that it wouldn't be able to pass through the birth canal and it would die immediately. We would have had to do a Caesarean anyhow but then the baby burst the walls of the uterus. She has lost a great deal of blood and urgently needs a blood transfusion but we have no blood.' I had heard that there were seven recorded cases of AIDS in Phnom Penh (which suggested that there would be others – unrecorded) and asked him what screening procedures they had for detecting the virus in blood. 'Oh,' he said, 'we can't test the blood. We don't have the equipment.'

Upstairs there were wards full of amputees. Here the war wounded averaged twelve a month but of course not all of them were soldiers. A young man of twenty-three with a wife and year-old baby had lost both legs working out in the rice field. A woman with four children had stepped on a mine twenty-five miles away and lost a leg. Otherwise, it was business as usual – malaria, dysentery, typhoid and tuberculosis. A little girl of ten lay curled on a bed. Her arms and legs were like kindling, distorted by a young lifetime of TB.

I had arranged to take Somaly, her sister and Seila for a picnic at Tonle Bati, about twenty miles from Phnom Penh. Pranita was studying for exams. Seila was wearing a wonderful sugar-pink ruffled party dress and liberally festooned with jewellery. Her hair was plaited with three ribbons. When I looked at her, dressed like a little butterfly, I thought of a phrase I had read somewhere: 'flower of dangerous love'. We drove out to the banks of the Bati river and settled ourselves upstairs in a wooden pavilion overlooking the water. I can't remember what we had for lunch but I do remember that it was all very pleasant. Somaly's sister, Bhopa, was a pretty woman with a tiny high lisping little-girl voice who worked in the bank in Phnom Penh. She said that she was twenty-four. I was puzzled by this because then she would have been little more than a child during the Khmer Rouge period and said so quietly to Somaly who then told me that her sister was actually thirty but was ashamed for me to know that she was still not married at this age.

After lunch we walked round the temple of Ta Prohm, built, like its namesake in Angkor, by Jayavarman VII. The whole thing was on a much smaller scale and though the Khmer Rouge had caused a predictable amount of damage, nature had mercifully been kept at bay. There was a fortune-teller sitting under an awning in one corner of the temple complex. Bhopa described him as a 'guess-man' and we stopped so that I could have my fortune told. It was hard to follow and involved the 'God-King of the Naga' but the gist of it seemed to be that the future would be good, depending on my work. 'If you do everything, it will be success as you wish,' said the old man.

In another corner, a young man was having his head shaved with a huge blade. There was a mane of black hair lying on the ground and, as we got closer, I realised that it wasn't a man at all but a young woman with a fierce proud expression like a bird of prey. Her husband was the man wielding the knife. He had been conscripted and was leaving in a couple of days for the front in Battambang to fight the Khmer Rouge. She was sacrificing her hair as an offering to the Buddha to bring him home safely.

11

Tiger Balm

One morning, as we were driving to the airport to catch the plane to Stung Treng, Sophy asked me what the symptoms of typhoid were. I asked him why he wanted to know. He said, 'My wife is very sick. I think that she has typhoid.'

'But that's very serious, you must take her to the hospital immediately.'

'No, never mind,' he said.

This was his standard response to most things, whether a complaint on my part or some concern of his own as in this case. I think he resorted to this formula for a variety of reasons: he didn't realise how rude it often sounded, he was reluctant to involve me in his own problems and he frequently found it too difficult to explain things to me, both because of the limitations of his grasp of English and the complexities of the situation. It was easier to say, 'No, never mind.'

Sophy had all along been reluctant to go to Stung Treng, partly because he was convinced that he would get malaria in Ratanakiri, and partly because he said he would have 'trouble in his mind' away from Phnom Penh.

'What kind of trouble?' I asked.

His answer was vague and unsatisfactory and when I pressed him, back came the stock response.

'No, never mind.'

But I got the impression that he meant depression or angst of some kind, brought on by unspecified miseries rather than any particular concern for his wife's health.

The flight was delayed for a couple of hours by the arrival of the inaugural Bangkok Airways flight, the first of a new twice-weekly service between Bangkok and Phnom Penh. Since the fall of Phnom Penh there had been no direct flights from Bangkok. Everything had to be routed through Saigon, Hanoi or Vientiane. There was great excitement as the little plane landed and the disembarking passengers, many of them members of the Cambodian *corps de ballet*, were greeted by television cameras and bouquets of flowers.

Eventually we took off around nine-thirty and flew northeast towards southern Laos and Vietnam. We flew over heavily-wooded land, forests in which – according to my *carte touristique*, a pretty pictorial map – tigers, elephants and bare-breasted women smoking pipes still dwelt. Sophy fell into conversation with the couple sitting behind us: a man in the uniform of a high-ranking officer and his beautiful Lao wife whose slim brown fingers were laden with emerald and ruby rings. Then he turned to me and said, 'I tell them your background. I tell them how you abandon your husband.' I had been expecting to hear that he had told them that I was researching a book and was rather put out. I said sharply, 'Husband and I decide to separate. I not abandon my husband and anyhow personal matter. Why are you telling strangers my personal business?' Sophy just laughed.

The airport at Stung Treng consisted of one small hut. The air seemed cooler, more northerly, less tropical. A party of European aid workers were waiting to leave by the plane on which we had arrived. They had just returned from Ratanakiri and said that there was no need at all for an armed guard. We got into a Toyota Land Cruiser with a red cross on it and sat and waited for forty-five minutes till it filled up. The other passengers, among them a timber merchant, with a limp and a goatee beard like Ho Chi Minh's, and his son and daughter, were going to Ratanakiri too, and we agreed to travel together, once permission had been granted, if possible, in this vehicle which belonged to the hospital and therefore to the province.

The hotel, a long single-storey building painted a washed-out pink, stood across the road from the riverbank, in a big neglected scrubby brown garden. It had a high pointed roof like a pagoda but made of corrugated iron instead of gleaming tiles. An empty hammock hung by the gate and the whole place seemed deserted except for a large black sow with a litter of nine wriggling piglets. We all stood around and eventually a slatternly woman, yawning widely to reveal a mouthful of gold teeth, appeared and reluctantly climbed onto a bicycle to go and find the manageress. When she arrived, she was a nice woman with a pleasant open face who spoke perfect French which she had learnt at a Catholic missionary school. The rooms were cheap, only six hundred *riels* a night, and all opened onto the long covered verandah. There was electricity but it hadn't worked for some days. My room was filthy and she apologised, explaining that the previous occupants had only just left and that she had not yet had time to clean it. It had a dark bathroom with one tiny high window, a hole-in-the-ground lavatory and a deep concrete tub full of dusty river water. You weren't supposed to get into the tub but just to pour a basinful of water over yourself. I stripped and soaped myself all over. The water was shockingly cold despite the heat of the day but invigorating and, for a good ten minutes, I felt fresh and cool.

It was a seven-hour drive to Ban Lung, the principal town of Ratanakiri, and we wouldn't be able to leave till the following morning. We left the manageress to her housework and walked into town to find some lunch, past a dried-up fountain whose centrepiece was a group of stocky *garudas*, their puffed-out chests and feathers bravely picked out in acid green. The once-bright paint was flaking and the fountain bowl was filled with rubbish. We ate near the market in a restaurant that looked tatty and fly-blown but produced a wonderful dish of exquisitely tender beef. The old merchant and his children, who were both in their twenties, came too and he insisted on paying for lunch. I was surprised as I almost always ended up paying for everything.

I was already fretting about the cost of the jeep to Ban Lung. I hadn't yet grasped a basic principle of life in Cambodia: that the rich man always pays. In the absence of anyone wealthier, I was the rich man and, though I didn't realise it at the time, I was going to bear the full cost of hiring the Toyota to get us all to Ratanakiri. At this point, however, I was still busy calculating how the cost should be split between the seven people who would be crammed into the jeep. The only other way for them to get there was by bus or hitching a ride in a lorry, a desperately uncomfortable journey that would take even longer and cost 2,000 *riels* a head. I said to Sophy, 'You must explain to them that they will have to contribute to the car hire. I can't afford it all on my own.' 'No, never mind,' was his answer.

Sophy told me that we needed to take cartons of *Fine* cigarettes with us as presents. I had bought a couple in Phnom Penh but he had already given them away: one, plus twenty dollars, to the committee and the other to an old schoolfriend of his who was a doctor at the local hospital. I wasn't best pleased by this largesse on my behalf and said, 'I'm not made of money, you know.' He looked puzzled and said, 'You mean you do not print money?' After lunch, while Sophy went to report our arrival to the committee and to negotiate for the jeep, I went to the little market. It had just a few rows of stalls selling basic goods but I found the cigarettes cheaper than in Phnom Penh, and little plastic bags of monosodium glutamate, the special salt from Thailand. There was no whisky and no bottled drinking water. I bought a little glass lamp which ran on petrol in case the electricity didn't come back, and a present for Sophy, a green-and-white checked sarong which he had been fingering earlier. It was imported from Thailand and not even made of pure cotton but he evidently thought it superior to the *kramas*. When I gave it to him, he was surprised and seemed uneasy, rather than pleased, but later I saw him wearing it.

Sophy was quite vain about his good looks. He would often look at his own dark skin and say, in tones of satisfaction, 'pure Khmer'. He always looked very clean and tidy and was delighted when I gave him some Bic razors with which I had been planning to shave my legs (these won't have been much use to him – Cambodians are relatively beardless) and offered to lend him my shampoo and soap. Like Somaly's pleasure in the face-cream, it was endearing. But I knew that what he really wanted was something foreign and trade-marked: Japanese preferably, or American. He had a pair of *Nike* trainers that a Japanese television journalist had given him and he was very proud of them. I didn't have anything like that to give him. I had packed as little as possible to save on weight, even to the extent that I had brought only one pair of shoes which were now disintegrating and Sophy would make jokes about displaying them in the National Museum when I left. However, I had a few little things: disposable cigarette lighters, lipsticks, pens, and, when I noticed him about to buy a cheap biro, I presented him with one I had bought at Hong Kong airport, another ingenious Japanese affair, with clever retracting motion. He received it with obvious pleasure, saying admiringly, 'Japan' and immediately arranged it in his breast-pocket where he kept looking down at it, then taking it out of his pocket, trying it out, replacing it and patting it.

Stung Treng was a torpid little place, dozing peacefully on the banks of the beautiful Se Kong river which flows into the Mekong. It was badly bombed by the Americans during the Lon Nol regime and many of the buildings still stood gaping and ruined. The airport, the school, the ferry and all the bridges along the roads to other provinces were bombed. In the forest, you could still see craters made by the B-52s. Many people died then and those who escaped didn't dare go anywhere by day, only at night. Only a month into the Lon Nol regime, after the coup which deposed Sihanouk, the forces of the Khmer Rouge took control of Stung Treng, and then it was even worse because 'some people escape US bombs but nobody escape Pol Pot'. The manageress said that before 1970 Stung Treng had been a 'very happy place' but it had yet to recover from the past. I thought it appeared, amazingly, quite happy now with children playing in the dirt and a kind of dreamy stillness about it. There were no *cyclos* but instead little ponies and traps, and those animals that weren't in harness were hobbled by the roadside or grazing on little patches of open ground.

It was a beautiful golden evening with the light of the setting sun glinting on the river. I wanted to go out on the water but that proved too difficult to arrange so the manageress and I took a ride round town, the little cart dipping and swaying in the pot-holes. There wasn't much to see: a big school built by the Vietnamese, a hospital, a lovely old *wat* and the surprising sight of a Eurasian, a boy in his late teens whose father had been French. Down by the riverbank, men were leading their ponies into the water and bathing them. The people were bathing too: women washing their long black hair with little packets of Tide or Omo. I liked Stung Treng. It had an engaging faded charm, its shabbiness more than compensated for by its beautiful situation.

We dined that night in a private room above a large poorly-lit restaurant overrun with kittens. The current was erratic and the lights flickered on and off, revealing a somewhat Dickensian scene of discarded chicken bones, scrawny animals and scruffy people with their heads down on the tables. The restaurant faced a square where the long-distance lorry-drivers parked their trucks and this was clearly where they came to eat and rest. Upstairs was more refined. A single bare light-bulb dangled above our heads, sur- rounded by a fine gauzy cloud of mosquitoes. The old man was again the host and sat at the head of a long table, clapping his hands to summon the waitresses and patting their bottoms. We ate local pâté with pickled ginger and crisp little bits of chicken. The mood was friendly but, unlike Nguyen, Sophy made no effort to translate the conversation and, on the whole, I didn't press him. I remember that we talked about Sihanouk, and the timber merchant expressed the sort of doubts and mistrust that I had heard before. His children were silent. The boy's face was swollen with fever. He had already had malaria four times. This occasioned a fresh outbreak of anxiety from Sophy. Finally I said, 'If you survived Pol Pot time and reached the age of thirty-five without getting malaria, you're not going to get it in Ratanakiri.'

'If I do, it will be your fault and I will send a telegram to Mrs Thatcher,' he answered.

By the time we left the restaurant, a storm was brewing. The night was very black even though the sky was filled with stars and a new moon had just made its appearance. White fork light- ning streaked the sky and was reflected in the glassy black surface of the river. Back at the hotel, I lent Sophy my radio. I had brought it with me thinking that it might distract him and ease the trouble in his mind. It was the latest in digital short-wave from Sony and he was very pleased. Unfortunately, the noise, as he tuned and re-tuned it, drowned out the cicadas. I cursed my generosity. Despite earlier impressions that it was cooler in Stung

Treng than further south, the night was oppressively hot. I lit the little petrol lamp, opened the shutters in the hope of a breeze, settled myself under the mosquito net and lay, sweaty and naked, watching the lightning sever the sky. I must have dozed off because I woke with a start to the sound of torrential rain drumming on the corrugated iron roof. Suddenly there was a noise at my open window where I had left a bunch of bananas. Two drenched young policemen whose job it was to guard the hotel and who had been sleeping in the hammock by the gate, were peering into the room and making what looked like obscene gestures with open mouths and cupped fists. I let out a shriek and grabbed my sarong to cover myself. They disappeared along the verandah and I got up and closed the shutters. Afterwards I remembered Sophy saying that they were always hungry and realised that they must have been asking for the bananas.

The rain cut into the heat and I woke finally, after a fitful night broken by dreams and the crash of thunder, just before five, curled in a cold, clammy heap. I got up and went out onto the verandah. Dawn was breaking over the Se Kong and Sophy was listening to the BBC World Service on my radio. He said that he had only had four hours' sleep and that he had caught a cold.

We set off along a straight red dirt road with the jungle on either side, the driver hunched over the wheel and driving very fast. I was sat in the front and everyone else, eight people in all, piled into the back. The drive took seven hours to travel less than a hundred miles. The road wasn't all bad and the driver drove like the wind whenever he could but it had never had a proper hard surface laid on it. In parts, the monsoon rain had turned it to mud and we had to get out and walk while the driver churned his way through in four-wheel drive. In other places, it was bone-dry but with huge crevasses gouged out of the middle. During the whole time, we encountered only two other vehicles, very few bicycles and oxcarts, or even people. I counted seven birds, the last of which was about the size of a sparrow and emerald green. There were masses of butterflies, sometimes great clouds together, and a couple of swift brown animals, perhaps mongooses, at the start of the journey but nothing else. It was amazingly still and quiet, the jungle on either side interspersed with patches of clearer land looking like orchards, full of long grass and wild flowers: soft red poppies and tiny yellow and violet orchids. Mr Huy had told me that in Cambodia butterflies signify war and worms peace. It looked like it was going to be a bad year.

The plump squinty daughter of the timber merchant lay in the back, gurgling and retching all the way. When we stopped for a few minutes, I wet my handkerchief in a stream and wiped her face. I also gave her a Lomotil (an anti-spasmodic used for diarrhoea) but it didn't help. The poor girl was so ill that I offered her my seat in the front but it would not have been appropriate for the person who was going to foot the entire bill to endure the discomfort of the back and my offer was refused.

Sophy had taken charge of the cartons of cigarettes and was liberally distributing them among the passengers. I told myself that it was silly and mean-spirited to get annoyed but I did nonetheless and, when we stopped to cross a bridge at the provincial border and Sophy gave the soldier there several packets, I got furious and took the remainder away from him. He said, 'You do not understand my purpose,' and then, 'No, never mind. I give you back.' It was an absurd situation. I did not want to fall out with Sophy – I was stuck with him after all – nor did I want to be mean in this desperately poor country but I had tried repeatedly to make him understand that my resources were limited. He would listen, nod in apparent comprehension, saying, 'No, never mind,' and then ten minutes later, tell me that it was necessary to buy another three cartons of *Fine* to give to the members of the committee.

When we stopped for lunch, an unappetising meal of tinned fish in tomato sauce and boiled rice, Sophy and I were still not speaking. I sat at the table, drinking a warm beer and silently fuming. People had heard of my arrival and come to have a good look at me. I was surrounded by staring faces and it suddenly seemed intolerable. I got up and climbed into the Toyota and began to read my book. I was re-reading Shawcross's *Sideshow*, an account of the bombing of Cambodia, and had come to a description of the evacuation of Phnom Penh after the Khmer

Rouge takeover. I read: 'When the hospitals had been emptied, it was the turn of the ordinary townspeople and the refugees. They were ordered to abandon their houses, their apartments, their shacks, their camps. They were told to take with them only the food they could carry. Those who were separated from their families were not allowed to seek them. No demurring was allowed. As the sun began to sink that afternoon, men, women and children all over Phnom Penh straggled bemused out of the side streets and onto the highways. The roads became clogged; people could shuffle forward only a few yards at a time. In the crush, hundreds of families were split, and as they moved on more and more people fell under the strain. The old and the very young were the first to go; within a few miles of the city centre more and more bodies were seen lying where their relatives had been forced to leave them.'

My eyes filled with tears and I felt bitterly ashamed of my pettiness. I couldn't believe that I had really grudged these people cigarettes.

We arrived in Ban Lung soon after three. As soon as we stopped, the other passengers leapt out of the jeep and scattered like stampeding cattle, and with them my hopes of a contribution towards the cost of the car hire. Ban Lung was barely a town, more of a trading station or frontier post in the style of the American Wild West, and so spread out as to seem almost empty. The houses were dotted on each side of a crossroads with red roads leading off into the hills in all directions. It was as if a space had only been recently cleared for the town and, at any moment, the land might be reclaimed by the countryside pressing in on all sides. The road by the hotel led down to a small lake on which there was a little island. Sophy informed me that the island regularly floated from one side of the lake to the other and that, in 1983, three Vietnamese soldiers had drowned, diving in the lake, trying to find out why the island moved.

At first sight, the hotel, an unkempt concrete block, seemed spectacularly sordid, even by the standards to which I was rapidly becoming accustomed, but a couple of women appeared to make the bed and flick a broom around the room and it began to look quite charming, if not very clean. There was a communal bathroom, again with a vat of cold water, and a couple of hole-in-the-ground lavatories, smeared with excrement. The other rooms were mostly occupied by soldiers, lying on their beds smoking. A wooden balcony ran round the first floor of the building and I was standing there, looking out at the lake and the rolling blue-green hills, when an English voice asked, 'Would you like a gin-and-tonic?'

It belonged to the doctor from Health Unlimited, a woman in her late twenties, who had come to see whether we had brought any mail. She was expecting a letter from her lover in Africa. Later that evening after dinner, I went and drank whisky with her and her co-worker, an intense sandy-coloured man who was also hoping for a letter – from a woman in Austria to whom he had written proposing marriage. No letter had come for him and he was rather dispirited. They had a lovely house with big rooms and a wooden terrace with a hammock, all lit by oil lamps, and a tiny kitten with one of those stumpy South East Asian tails. For all that, they seemed keen for company and we sat and talked for a couple of hours about Asia and England and the problems that they faced here. Loneliness was one. Telegram and military radio provided the only link with the rest of the country and letters had to be carried to Phnom Penh by hand and posted there. Malaria was another. Sophy's fears were not, after all, without foundation. There was some new or different strain of the disease in Ratanakiri which could fell even the hardiest and they had great difficulty persuading the people to take pills. Given the choice, they preferred injections and really had far more faith in an old-fashioned sacrifice to the spirits of a duck or chicken or pig's head.

The doctor gave me a bottle of Paludrine tablets for Sophy whose anxiety about getting malaria was making us both miserable. The doctor said that the pills were virtually useless and caused lethargy and that she took no precautions against malaria, preferring to treat the disease if and when she succumbed. But I thought that, at worst, the tablets would act as a placebo and allay Sophy's fears. He was a great one for taking pills anyway and placed great faith in all western drugs with which he would regularly and indiscriminately dose himself. Clearly believing that it was better to be safe than sorry, in Phnom Penh he would supplement western medicine by frequently visiting the Vietnamese masseuses who lodged at his aunt's for 'cupping'. This was supposed to cure headaches, colds and other minor ailments, as well as induce a general sense of well-being. A lighted rag was placed in a glass to create a vacuum and the glass then applied to the skin which would be sucked up into the glass, making a round red mark like a love bite. Sophy was always covered with these marks and also weals made by having a coin drawn hard along the skin which was supposed to have a similarly beneficial effect. He swore by these remedies (and also by the properties of a monkey corpse fermented in rice wine) and was always trying to persuade me to be cupped or coined but I didn't much want to be covered with livid weals.

Out in the wild countryside, the bare-breasted pipe-smoking women of my map and their loin-cloth-sporting husbands lived and hunted. Driving along the red roads, we would sometimes glimpse them; the men carrying sharp *parangs* and crossbows and bamboo quivers full of arrows, their long hair coiled in neat buns; and the women, naked to the waist, bent double under the weight of gourds filled with water. They were smaller even than most Cambodians and looked, for want of a better word, more primitive. I had heard their legends, how the Brou tribe was founded by a black dog and a woman who were the sole survivors of a gigantic fire, and of their animistic beliefs which led them to perform sacrifices to the animal spirits of the forest. They were as exotic as any wild animal and some, like the Kreung, had been there since the time of Angkor. But now the Khmer authorities were seeking to 'reform' them, to make them 'more like Khmer' and to put an end to their remote and semi-nomadic way of life. I was told that the Khmers laughed at them and tried to make them wear clothes. A number of them had already been forced to leave their traditional circular villages in the mountains and been re-housed in new Khmer-style 'linear' villages close to the roadside. It was these that I was taken to see: 'symbols of progressive villages', in the words of the local guide. It was rare, in Cambodia, to hear that kind of rhetoric and consequently all the more chilling. I thought of Mme Sun Saphoeun's response when I had asked her if Cambodia was suited to Communism. She had answered, 'People in Cambodia like to be free to do what they want.'

Twenty or so small children lounged disconsolately on benches in a bamboo hut. The village was otherwise deserted. Everyone else left soon after dawn to go to the forest and the fields. The children were being taught to read and write Khmer. Of the thirteen different minority groups living in Ratanakiri (which include Lao and Vietnamese whose original homelands border the province and where only thirty per cent of the total population of sixty thousand is Khmer), only four had a written language. The authorities maintained that in order for them to benefit from education, they must learn to speak, read and write the language of the country in which they lived. You could see their point – up to a point – but it was not going to be easy. The minorities often did not want to send their children to school and even if they agreed to, they would rarely send the girls. Each student was offered 420 *riels* a month to persuade him or her to come to school but even that didn't always work. The authorities estimated that it would take them fifty years to educate the minorities. I thought it might take longer and, judging by what I saw of their policies, at the end of it, if they were successful, the minorities would have lost most of their cultural identity. It didn't look good.

The sandy man from Health Unlimited had given me a translation of a Brou prayer to the spirits. It went like this:

> Oh Spirits of the Forest
> I mark the soul,
> I ask to stay here.
> The tobacco waits to harden,
> The rice waits to grow.
> That the dreams will be favourable
> We clear the trees
> That the rice will be as abundant as the grains of sand,
> and hard as the sacred stones, as iron.
> I stay here,

I mark the forest,
Allow me to stay!
That the ginger will grow
That the garlic will be abundant.
I am going to stay!
The tobacco is sown, that it can be gathered.
The rice planted that it can be harvested
I mark the soil
I will cut the trees
Ancestral spirits of the forest.

We visited a Brou village, one of the new 'progressive' ones. It was almost empty and most of the houses were shut up for the day. The houses were attractive – on stilts with walls made of dark and light rushes woven in different intricate geometric patterns. There were some small children, their bellies distended with malnutrition, and a few women, including an ancient crone with a baby tugging fretfully at a withered nipple. There was no way that she could have been his real mother or actually suckling him so I supposed he was at the breast for comfort. When I asked a pretty smiling girl with a flowered sarong and a necklace of white beads dangling between her naked breasts if I could take her photograph, she gestured at her breasts and then went into her house to put on a blouse and a different sarong.

The only village I ever saw that seemed original was one inhabited by lepers, who had perhaps not been encouraged to move for predictable reasons. It was high in the hills and accessible only by a narrow overgrown track. The Toyota pushed its way through with difficulty. Leprosy has a fearsome reputation and, though I was curious, I was also scared. But few realities live up to one's worst expectations and the only leper at home was a little man squatting under his hut whose toes and fingers had been destroyed by the disease. All that remained of his hands were a few stumps protruding from his wrists. He had been ill since the time of Sihanouk but had only been treated over the last few years. The spread of the disease was not yet under control and there had been one new case in the village last year.

One evening, we fled the communal bathroom and bathed in

the beautiful Yak Lom lake, surrounded by mountains formed from ancient volcanic cones. In a Tompoun village nearby there was said to be an elephant. There were supposed to be a number of working elephants all over Ratanakiri but this one was the nearest. The elephant was out somewhere in the forest but its owner was there, sitting on the porch of his house and weaving a basket. He said that he and his father had caught the animal in the forest when it was a baby seventeen years ago and that, if I gave him some money, he would go and find it early the following morning and bring it for me to see. The possession of the elephant meant that he was regarded as a rich man in the community but I had been told that the minorities were uninterested in money and only slightly in barter and asked him what he would do with the money. He said that he would buy a chicken and some rice wine. We agreed on a minute sum and I said that I'd be back early the following day.

A fiery dawn was burning into the morning mist as we arrived in the 'elephant' village. The owner had disappeared into the forest to find his beast and all around the village was slowly coming to life as the early-morning domestic rituals of washing, cooking and eating were enacted. From the little woven houses, women, stretching and yawning, were emerging to light fires and boil water while chickens scratched and pigs snuffled in the dirt below. A couple of water buffalo shrugged languidly to disrupt the murky surface of the village pond. There was still a slight chill in the air after the night and it was very quiet. Only the raucous shriek of a cock's crow shattered the peace. There was an intimacy about the scene and a sense of a rural idyll which the provincial authorities' depressing statistics of death, disease and illiteracy belied. A man smoking a pipe with a brass mouthpiece made from a bullet, came to talk to us. He looked about forty-five, handsome and wiry, with a khaki cap worn at a rakish angle, but claimed to be eighty. Either he had led an utterly blameless life or he was not telling the truth.

Just as the sun was finally breaking free into the sky, it was blotted out by a huge brown shape and, for a moment, the whole village went dark. In this dramatic fashion, the elephant made its appearance, its owner on his back, brandishing a *parang*. High up astride the elephant, eclipsing the sun, the little man acquired a dignity and stature that he had lacked on the ground. It was, of course, just an elephant like any other, but a splendid sight all the same. He made it kneel and bow and it waved its great trunk around, nosing the length of my body, smelling me like a dog would.

On the road out of Ban Lung, we passed two young Khmer women, one of them heavily pregnant, carrying a small deer slung from a pole balanced on their shoulders. They had just come down from the mountain where they had killed and disembowelled the animal. Now they were taking it to sell in Ban Lung for 3,000 *riels*. Its eyes were still open and, even in death, it was beautiful. Sophy got them to hack off the top of the animal's head with its little curved horns. He gave them 300 *riels* and put his gory trophy in the car. I found it difficult to reconcile this mutilation with his view that it was a sin to kill a mosquito. The horns weren't even edible.

In Stung Treng, opposite the hotel, there was a little zoo which both fascinated and repelled me. There were a couple of shivering black-faced little monkeys, clutching each other for comfort, and various snakes and lizards, but the *pièce-de-résistance* on my return was what they called a 'fish tiger' cub (this would have been a *felis viverrina*, a fishing cat whose diet includes crustaceans but I think that it was actually a leopard cat, *felis bengalensis*). It was a tiny thing, the size of a kitten, beautifully marked with spots, rather than stripes, and with the milky blue eyes of babyhood. It can't have been that young because it was eating raw meat, chewing the bloody hunks with relish. Its spirit was completely unbroken and it spat and hissed in its cage, showing its claws. I said that I would buy it for twenty-three dollars. The zoo-keeper clearly thought I was out of my mind but I didn't care. I preferred it to die of starvation in the wild than to live in a cage, poked and prodded by children with sharp sticks. Ideally I would have bought all the animals in the zoo, bar the reptiles, and set them free but I would have lost all face. Anyhow I didn't have the money and I doubted the little monkeys were going to live for much longer. But I felt I could do something about the cub. It was agreed that I would hand over the money on the morning of our departure from Phnom Penh and, in return, get the cub which I could release into the forest. I told Sophy not to tell anyone what I was paying for the cub but I was sure that he wouldn't be able to keep quiet about the behaviour of this mad Englishwoman. Perhaps it was mad but I couldn't, at that moment, care more about human beings than animals. At the same time, I felt a little furtive and ashamed as if indulging in some kind of sexual perversion.

A boy who wanted to practise his English escorted me round town. He said that he wanted to discuss the political situation in the country. He didn't like the Government because 'it suppresses the people' and because he was fed-up with the war. I suggested that, even if the Government were to stop fighting, there was no guarantee that the Khmer Rouge would follow suit, but he couldn't understand this. He also said that there were fifty Vietnamese disguised as Khmer in Stung Treng and, with an effective dramatic gesture, mimed throwing off a disguise and revealing that underneath was a Vietnamese. As we walked on, he asked:

'Are there many widows in your country?'

'Yes, but not as many as in Kampuchea.'

'Oh, why not?'

'Because in England we didn't have Pol Pot time so not so many men were killed, leaving widows.'

We were walking down Stung Treng's main street, a wide dusty red road with a few shops and cafés on either side. Teenagers were spilling out of the town's only video parlour.

'Look', he said, gesturing with his hand, 'widow.'

Later I tried to explain the joke to Sophy but he just nodded and said, 'Yes, widow' (or possibly 'video').

Staying two rooms down from me at the hotel were a man and a woman. Sophy said that the man was involved with the training of cadres and that the woman was his secretary. He walked along the verandah towards me, naked to the waist and wearing only the bottom half of a pair of apricot silk pyjamas. Hanging from a heavy gold chain around his neck was a ruby carving of a *naga* set in gold. He said that he couldn't understand why the Cambodians didn't like the Vietnamese; that Vietnam was Cambodia's friend. I found him rather creepy and the conversation seemed almost too much of a coincidence after my talk earlier with the boy.

It wasn't the first time that I had come across the kind of anti-Vietnamese feeling that he had voiced. It was a staple of Khmer paranoia and even educated people like Somaly believed that the Vietnamese were out to rob and dominate the Cambodians. A common Khmer saying talks of being caught between the tiger and the crocodile: it comes from an ancient Khmer prophecy that the Khmer race would one day have to choose between being eaten by a tiger or being eaten by a crocodile. Traditionally the tiger was Thailand which, in 1794, had annexed the northern and north-west provinces of Battambang, Siem Reap and Stung Treng (these were not returned till 1907 in a Franco-Thai treaty: in 1940 the Thais seized Battambang and Siem Reap again and did not relinquish them till 1946.) The crocodile was Vietnam which had taken for itself that part of the Mekong Delta that was once Kampuchea Krom.

But now the Vietnamese-backed government in Phnom Penh had become the crocodile and the Khmer Rouge-dominated resistance the tiger. It was true that, over the centuries, the Cambodians had been given every reason to fear Vietnamese imperialism but, at the same time, however selfish the Vietnamese motives for the 1979 invasion, they were responsible for delivering Cambodia from the terrible thrall of Pol Pot and had been greeted as liberators when they arrived. But they had stayed too long and were now resented. Even after the withdrawal of most of the Vietnamese troops in September 1989, the Government was perceived as a Vietnamese puppet regime whose unpopularity was often exceeded only by fear of the Khmer Rouge. As one of the *cyclo-pousses* in Phnom Penh explained. 'Hun Sen better than Khmer Rouge. Vietnamese better than Khmer Rouge.' It was a case of the devil and the deep blue sea.

*

The evening before we flew back to Phnom Penh, I finally managed to get out on the river for a couple of hours. It was spectacularly beautiful. Clouds streaked across the clear soft-blue sky in shades of brilliant pink and purple. Along the riverbank, trees stood in delicate graphic outline and the angular silhouette of Sihanouk's ruined villa offered itself up to the elements. There were tiny yellow fires flickering on balconies hanging over the water and people bathing, slipping silently into the satiny water, and washing their ponies and motorbikes. Beneath the still sleek surface, there were fish, otters and crocodiles. The sky had coloured the water purple – like folds of heavy silk. The setting sun was always just out of sight, round a bend in the river. I wanted to round the point and see it sinking into the Mekong but it remained elusive. Then, in a final glorious blaze, the clouds turned gold and, as the light faded, the sky and water merged in a soft dove-grey haze. I thought of the Mekong flowing down from Yunan to wind its way through Laos; I thought of the Tonle Sap, the 'Sprawling Sea of Sweet Water', and of the lattice of canals in the Mekong Delta. It was the loveliest sight I had ever seen.

Sophy was waiting on the shore when we got back. We walked past the little zoo where my cub paced in its cage. A couple of damp animals with webbed feet scrabbled in a basket shaped like a lobster pot. They were otters, fresh from the river. As we sat down for dinner, I noticed that Sophy no longer sported the pen I had given him.

'Where's the pen I gave you?' I asked.

'I don't have it anymore,' he answered, looking down into his bowl of rice.

'What, you can't have lost it?' I said.

'No, the doctor took it.'

My companion – or minder – on the river had been a dapper handsome doctor in a blouson jacket, the vice-president of the hospital and a senior figure on the provincial committee. He had asked Sophy for the pen and, when Sophy told him that I had given it to him, the doctor had shrugged and said, 'So now you give it to me.' Sophy handed it over. He felt that he had no choice.

I was amazed and outraged by this story. Suddenly everything he had been saying made sense and I understood why he kept asking me for cigarettes and five-dollar bills. I felt very sorry for him, caught between me and the bureaucrats whom he dared not offend, trying to keep us all happy. While I had been out on the river, he had gone to see the committee but he wouldn't tell me what had happened, saying only, 'No, never mind. It is my problem.' I had one pen left, a black one which I had been using. I gave it to him and told him to hide it.

I spent a restless night, worrying about the cub and whether I was doing the right thing, and woke at five, feeling sick and shivery. Sophy had locked my door to protect me and I couldn't get it open. I vomited into the hole in the ground and lay down on my damp bed, clutching my stomach. Later we walked through the food market. Sophy wanted to buy some meat to take home. At the meat stall, there was a little pile of matted skins with the webbed feet still attached. So much for the otters. I stopped worrying about the cub and the rightness of my actions and bought a hunk of pork for it to eat.

They had the cub ready for me in a little basket fastened with a piece of thin wire. I handed over the money. It weighed almost nothing but I could hear it spitting and snarling inside the wicker. I undid just enough to slip in the pork and it settled down, gnawing loudly, making a humming noise like a distant engine or a large bumble-bee. I kept the basket on my lap as we drove to the airstrip. Beyond the runway lay a huge field of waist-high grass and beyond that, the forest. As I started to undo the wire, the cub began to struggle furiously and, as soon as there was an opening, it was out, gone in a flash, disappearing into the long grass. We flew high over the forest and I hoped that the cub would survive. From the luggage compartment at the back of the plane came sounds of pitiful whimpering as a couple of puppies whose flesh was especially tasty, made their doomed way to Phnom Penh.

12

The Cheshire Cat

Pakse, the southern Lao town that was the jumping-off point for Wat Phou and Champassak, was only a hundred and forty miles across the border from Stung Treng but it was not possible to go there direct. Nor was it possible to alight at Pakse when the tiny Lao Aviation plane stopped for re-fuelling. Instead, I had to fly from Phnom Penh to Vientiane where, if I was lucky, the appropriate *laisser-passer* would be waiting, and then go back down the country to Pakse. It was tempting to jump ship in Pakse and try to go overland to Champassak. I wondered what would happen if I just slipped away and leapt into one of the little taxis made out of motorbikes that lined the street outside the airport. There were no other westerners on the flight and only eight passengers in all so it seemed unlikely that my disappearance would have gone unnoticed for long.

I didn't much want to go back to Laos. I had nothing against the country and I liked what I had seen of the people – Leuth excepted – but energy and enthusiasm were essential to tackle its bureaucracy and, at this stage, both were in short supply. However, my failure there was a sore point and it had become a point of honour at least to make another attempt to get out of Vientiane so off I went. I had sent a telegram from Saigon to the Honorary Consul before I flew to Cambodia and was hopeful that he would have been able to overcome some of the obstacles that the Laos so loved to place in the way of foreigners.

At Pochentong airport I said a tearful farewell to Somaly and promised to come back to see her. She looked doubtful. It was a promise that foreigners always made and rarely kept. Nguyen, my interpreter in Vietnam, had told me, when I passed through on my way to Phnom Penh, that John Pilger and I were the only two of the dozens of writers, journalists and television crewmen with whom he had worked who had ever contacted him again.

The previous evening Somaly had come to the Asie while I was packing, and everything that I didn't really need, I gave to her. She went away with a carrier bag of half-full bottles of shampoo, extra bars of soap, anti-malaria tablets, anti-diarrhoea tablets, anti-biotics and a box of Tampax. This last puzzled her hugely. I explained how to use them and assured her that they did not hurt, that even girls who were virgins could use tampons, but she remained unconvinced and told me that they used bits of rag that had to be washed, rather like old-fashioned cloth nappies. I also gave her ten dollars which was all I could spare (I had given Sophy a larger sum as a tip). She burst into tears and attempted to refuse. She was only persuaded to accept the money when I insisted that it wasn't a tip – which it wasn't – but a present, that I wanted to give it to her and that I wished it could be more.

Little Wattay airport in Vientiane was its usual torpid abandoned self. After I had cleared customs and immigration and had my *visa de court séjour* stamped by an indifferent official, I emerged to find the British Honorary Consul waiting for me. He invited me to stay at his house. His wife had found life in Laos difficult and was back in England. We drove in his air-conditioned Volvo through Vientiane's empty streets to a pretty villa behind a large wire gate. We left our shoes at the door so as to avoid marking the polished floors. Inside the house was cool and spacious. It was both extraordinary and blissful to be in a comfortable house with hot water and a video player. There was a swimming pool in the garden. Downstairs in the dining room the table was laid with silver and crystal and a boy in a white jacket served tinned soup in pretty flowered china bowls. It all felt rather unreal.

Despite many promises, Mr Bounneme of the Ministry of Foreign Affairs had *not* come up trumps and the Honorary Consul had resorted to negotiations with Lao Air Booking, the little travel agent who had tried – unsuccessfully – to get me a *laisser-passer* for Luang Prabang last time. The upshot was that *laisser-passers* to both Luang Prabang and Pakse were forthcoming but only on a tourist tour and at a steep price. I had only enough money for one of the two expeditions and barely the strength for either. I could have borrowed the money but then I would have had to re-pay it and I had already spent a small fortune. I chose Luang Prabang, ancient capital of the Lao kings, which lay about three hundred miles north of Vientiane, superbly positioned at the confluence of the Mekong and the Nam Khan rivers. It was the cherished dream of every retired French colonial officer to end his days in Luang Prabang, the Shangri-La of the Orient, a beautiful indolent Lao wife at his side, attending to his every need.

The decision made, we went out to dinner. In 1954, Graham Greene wrote: 'Vientiane is a century away from Saigon,' and relished the contrast. Now it was a lifetime away from Phnom Penh. We had dinner in a chic newly-opened little French res-taurant called the Nam Phou after the river (*nam* means river) and it was like being in New York or Paris or even London. A pretty Lao woman in a beige raw silk trouser-suit and a mass of heavy gold jewellery came up to us and started talking, in a vivacious society fashion, about Geneva and Rome. We ate *baguettes* of French bread with a creamy chicken liver pâté and drank red wine. There were no restaurants like this in Phnom Penh and no people like its clientele either. The Honorary Consul had entertained a minor British royal here when he had visited Vientiane and was full of funny stories about the nobleman's camp little valet who had been thrown into confusion by the refusal of his Lao hosts to allow him into the kitchen to prepare special food for his master who could hardly be expected to eat the sticky rice, fermented fish and baked anteater that were among the staples of Lao cuisine. The man, it appeared, was addicted to chocolate and crates of the stuff had to accompany him everywhere, along with some special kind of English mineral water.

But, despite the restaurants and the social life, there were draw-backs to life in Laos and it was these that had upset the Honorary

Consul's wife. Late one night while he had been sleeping peacefully in his bed, the sixty-one-year-old manager of the Vientiane
branch of the Mitsui trading house had been kidnapped. He had
been driven in his own car to the Mekong and taken across the
river to Thailand where he had been held prisoner for nine days
by four men thought to be members of a Lao right-wing resistance
group. His wife and a housemaid had been left gagged and tied
up in the house in Vientiane. Hearing this story, I remembered a
novel called *The Paradise Eater* by a Canadian writer which I had
found in the bookshop of the Shangri-La hotel in Bangkok. It
wasn't very good but the plot turned on a grisly double murder
in Vientiane. Despite the bloody nature of the killings, Vientiane
was described, in the book, as 'an extremely quiet town' in which
the telephones don't work. ' "Someone in search of peace and
quiet," ' said the main character, a dissolute VD-ridden American
called John Field, ' "would have been very happy in this place." '
But perhaps it wasn't as tranquil as it seemed.

After this incident, the Honorary Consul had been advised to
buy a big dog to protect his family and had acquired a beautiful
big grey chow in Bangkok. His wife and little daughter adored
the animal but it had turned rabid and had to be destroyed. Its
head had had to be stored in the deep-freeze till it could be taken
to Bangkok for analysis and the entire family had to be treated
for possible rabies. Then their cat had been knifed, and the servants
would never do anything that his wife asked.

Cambodia had drained me both physically and emotionally. It
was as if I had seen and done too much and I was suddenly
completely exhausted. The change of scene from Phnom Penh's
amiable squalor to the comfort of a beautiful air-conditioned villa
in Vientiane left me confused and ennervated, rather than stimu-
lated. I knew more than I wanted to – about myself as much as
anything else – and I wanted to draw back, to shut off. I lay in
my cool bedroom gazing at the cases of wine which the Honorary
Consul kept there, or sunbathed by the swimming pool, drinking
cold beer, reading trashy novels and playing with the cat, an
ugly but charming beast, who seemed to have recovered from the

stabbing though it had left him blind in one eye. I felt no compulsion to explore Vientiane further or even really to leave the house though, fearful of imposing too much on the Honorary Consul's hospitality, I forced myself to take occasional very slow walks around the town.

On one of these reluctant promenades, I thought I saw Leuth and ducked into beautiful Wat Pha Keo, the museum of religious art, which had been built originally to house the Emerald Buddha which the Siamese had looted in 1778. Along with virtually every *wat* in Vientiane, it was burnt down during the Siamese-Lao war of 1828 and then re-built in the late 1930s. It was a lovely place, reached by a flight of mossy steps, built in brick faded to a dull terracotta, weathered by time and the elements to a patina that suggested a far greater age and, as a museum, mercifully lacked the garish and recently-touched-up murals depicting various episodes in the life of Buddha with which many of the other *wats* were decorated. It contained an impressive selection of Buddhas in a variety of engagingly-named poses, some of which the guide book claimed to be uniquely Lao such as the bronze Buddha 'Admiring – or Contemplating – the Tree of Enlightenment' and the Buddha 'Calling for Rain'. A Buddha 'Calming Quarrels', his palms up in a gesture that said, 'No, this has really gone on long enough' stood next to an enormous stone tortoise.

After that, I kept a weather-eye open for Leuth but there was no sign of him. By now he had probably been committed to the local asylum or made friends with a more accommodating woman. Darachit would, I knew, be back in Moscow and I couldn't remember exactly where his family lived. But the ex-patriate community in Vientiane was full of good works and one day an American woman asked me if I would come and give a talk to her English class. I thought it was time that I did something to earn my keep and agreed.

The class was held on a pleasant open terrace overlooking the Mekong and the students were mainly in their late twenties and early thirties. When I arrived, they were completing a questionnaire which involved asking each other such questions as: 'What is your favourite colour, or flower or food or drink?' Then they had to write, 'So-and-so's favourite colour is blue or red or whatever it might be.' I joined in this and then stood up to make my little speech. The idea was that I should tell them about myself and what I was doing and then they would ask me questions. I spoke for about seven minutes, slowly and clearly, telling them that I was a writer and how old I was and that I was not married, trying to pre-empt all the obvious questions. When I had finished, they wanted to know what I thought about Laos and what I was going to write about it. It was difficult, if not impossible, to know what to say and my answer was clearly less than satisfactory. A young man put up his hand and said, 'But you hardly know Laos. How can you be sure that what you write will be correct?' He had a point but I couldn't do much about it. Secretly, I knew that I was marking time till I could go home and it wasn't really fair on Laos. Also I wasn't going to be able to see as much of the country as I had once hoped, and the nature of Laos itself – or what I dimly perceived it to be – was elusive at best. Unlike Vietnam and Cambodia, Laos's history was not written, as it were, on its face, and its people, though charming and hospitable, seemed oblique and evasive. I wanted to understand but all I ever got were little clues, tantalising and ultimately unhelpful. A British historian once said: 'Laos is like the Cheshire cat. One minute it's there, the next it has disappeared; and sometimes, while you're watching, it begins to fade, until there's nothing left but the smile – the Lao smile.'

There is a Lao phrase, *bo peniang*, which translates roughly as 'no problem' and is used continually, if not to excess. A Frenchman in Phnom Penh had called it *'la phrase fétichiste'* and certainly I found that a little *bo peniang* went a long way. I already knew of another Lao expression which meant 'maybe tomorrow – or someday' and I was all too familiar with the philosophy behind such phrases and its end result – that it was extremely difficult to get anything done. Perhaps Laos was like the Cheshire cat. I thought that it might be more like a hermit crab – you poked it and it disappeared into its shell.

I left for Luang Prabang the morning after the climax of the That Luang festivities. Downtown Vientiane had more or less come to a standstill as hundreds of people thronged towards the 'great shrine' to pay their respects. The normally austere stupa was being given the full treatment: it was decorated with red, orange and yellow fairylights and a full moon beamed behind its gilded spire. Prayers were being broadcast through loudspeakers and monks of all ages from the very old to the very young were accepting congratulations from the general public. Outside the stupa complex, there was a fairground atmosphere with stalls selling snacks and soft drinks and cheap plastic toys. I felt too tired and low to make much of it and anyhow couldn't see that it was so different from a hundred other such events. It certainly lacked the earthy vigour and vulgarity of the village *boun bang fay*.

But Luang Prabang – ah, Luang Prabang – that really was something else. Vientiane, for all its charm, was not beautiful: Luang Prabang, like an exquisite idealised vision of the East, was dazzlingly so. From my balcony, I could see a golden spire shimmering in the heat haze on the roof of a white temple at the top of a hill rising above the centre of town. The hills were bluish-green descending to grey-green fields, and all around were the usual entrancing vignettes of oriental rural life: water buffalo lazing in the fields, young women in brilliantly-coloured *sarongs* chasing small children or chickens, palm trees reflected in pools of water, wisps of smoke from a kitchen fire, and everywhere flashes of gold from the roofs of the *wats* catching the rays of the sun.

Luang Prabang, to which King Fa Ngum first introduced Buddhism in the fourteenth century, was always a major religious centre. In the past, it contained over sixty *wats* and now had thirty-four or thirty-five – depending on your source of information – enough, like pubs in Ireland, for there to be one on every corner. They were all in immaculate condition, gleaming with fresh paint and repeated sweepings and polishings. In the Fifties, Norman Lewis complained that 'A year or two's neglect might greatly improve Luang Prabang' but I found their sparkling appearance immensely cheering. Here, in the Buddhist Arcadia of Luang Prabang, the roads were *not* full of pot-holes; here there was *not* a pile of garbage on every street corner.

Around two, after a lunch which included four or five slices of

Spam, a spotty girl who spoke neither English nor French, appeared from Lao Tourism to take me on a tour of Luang Prabang. I was clearly intended to get my money's worth as this involved visiting nearly every *wat* in town, rushing from one to another at high speed at the height of the afternoon sun. Our itinerary included the hill that I had glimpsed from the hotel – Mount Phousi at whose summit was That Chomsi, a stupa supposed to contain the, or a, footprint of the Buddha. While she leapt ahead like a mountain goat, I trailed resentfully in her wake up the three hundred and twenty-eight steps that led to the pagoda, nearly fainting with heat and exhaustion. When we finally reached the summit, from which there was a spectacular view of the Nam Khan and the Sisavang Vong Bridge (Sisavang Vong was the penultimate Lao king who died in 1959), I tried, with what little breath remained to me, to explain that if she brought an elderly tourist up that hill at three in the afternoon, she would almost certainly kill him.

Back at the hotel, a party of leathery old Americans was complaining how boring Laos was. Their tour had *not* included a sprint up Mount Phousi. My face was puce from the heat and my exertions on the hill. I had forgotten to bring a bathing suit so I wrapped myself in a batik *sarong* and swam slowly up and down the pool thus clad. At the poolside there was a small group of Europeans, sitting drinking whisky and talking and a pair of hip Los Angeles record producers who had come to South East Asia to get in touch with themselves and *determined* to have an adventure. There was also a British journalist from the *Sunday Times* and, though we didn't really take to each other, I found the familiar exchange of names and gossip reassuring. It was easy and I wanted ease. My face slowly subsided as the sun went down and a welcome chill crept into the air. The Europeans were Dutch and Belgian. One of them, the Belgian, was an agronomist, developing different varieties of rice, who had been in Laos for years and, in the time-honoured fashion, had gone a little native. He had a Lao *copine* and had built himself a wooden house on the banks of the Mekong. Of the Dutchmen, one was just visiting while the other had spent much of his working life in Indonesia. They were doctors specialising in leprosy. There was a leper colony thirty-five miles up the Mekong with ninety-four patients.

I spent the following morning in the former Royal Palace. Like all such places, it was full of interest, each footstool telling a little story of its own. The present palace was built in 1904 by King Sisavang Vong in the year that he came to the throne and was a pleasant enough building with quarters for the servants in the basement. I was always agreeably surprised by the modesty of these establishments: only the Royal Palace in Phnom Penh smacked of hubris. Here the king and queen's bedrooms were simply furnished with bulbous 1930s suites though it is true that the king's bed was made of teak and ivory and decorated with the three-elephant-head image that used to appear on the country's flag. Each elephant had inlaid ivory tusks. Their majesties' bathroom was entirely yellow including the bidet and urinal. It had two yellow lavatories and two yellow basins as well as a yellow bath. The walls of the king's reception room were covered with sub-Gauguinesque murals depicting scenes of everyday life in Luang Prabang in the 1930s. These were the work of a French painter, Alix de Fautereau, and portrayed an idyllic way of life in which exquisite maidens with waist-length black hair co-habited cheerfully with white elephants and the king was nothing if not benign. It might not have been so far from the truth. The French certainly loved Laos in the old days and tolerance or *bo peniang* forgave a multitude of sins.

But, in 1977, the last king, Savang Vatthana, the son of Sisavang Vong, and his family were sent into internal exile in Sam Neua province in northern Laos and nothing more was heard of them till 1989 when Kaysone Phomvihane, the then Prime Minister and Party Secretary, reluctantly admitted to journalists in France that the king was dead. 'I can tell you the king died of natural causes. He was very old. It happens to all of us,' he said. Unofficial sources, however, laid the blame for the old boy's demise at the door of an unfortunate combination of physical weakness induced by the harsh conditions of the mountainous jungles and a broken heart caused by separation from his people. Like his father, the late king had devoted himself enthusiastically to the restoration of his beloved Luang Prabang which had been badly damaged both by fire – all the houses were built of wood – and war. Of the fate of Queen Khamphoui and Crown Prince Vong Savang, nothing was known though they were believed also to be dead.

The reasons for the decline – if that is the word – of the Lao monarchy were not clear. The Lao kings seemed to have been a reasonably easy-going bunch who were not unpopular with their subjects. At the time of the Japanese defeat in the 1940s, when the French asked him to muster some troops to fight against the invader, King Sisavang Vong replied, 'My people do not know how to fight, they know only how to sing and to make love.' But, however agreeable, the royal family happened to be in the wrong place at the wrong time. The reasons for the rise of nationalism and, with it, socialism were perfectly understandable. The Laos, like the Vietnamese and the Cambodians, were absolutely fed-up with being the plaything of a foreign power. Since the beginning of the eighteenth century, Laos had fallen prey to its more powerful neighbours: the Vietnamese to the east and the Siamese to the west. Though Laos had never initiated a war, it had scarcely known a moment's peace over the years, menaced by the Burmese, the Siamese (and later the Thais), the Vietnamese, the French and the Americans. According to Eisenhower's 'domino theory', Laos, not South Vietnam, was the key to South-East Asia. The result of such a history seemed to be that most Laos felt that any political system, including the present one, was better than domination by a foreign power. Of course, those who had fled the country in 1975 or been sent to re-education camps might take a different view (though I was surprised to hear from the Belgian agronomist that people laughed when they talked about the re-education camps and referred to them as *'l'université politique'*) but, for many Laos, nationalism rivalled Buddhism as the religion of the country. Unfortunately for the kings of Laos, they were not felt to be appropriate to the new order and on 2 December 1975, the leaders of the Pathet Lao, meeting in the gymnasium of a former American school in Vientiane, formally abolished the monarchy and established the Lao People's Democratic Republic.

The Royal Palace contained a roomful of gifts from foreign heads of state. In amongst the silver from Burma, the sculptures from India and the porcelain from Japan, was a gift from President Nixon, rich in irony if nothing else. This was a model of the Apollo XVII spacecraft and a pebble from the moon acquired on the Apollo's mission in 1972 – a year in which the Americans were busily raining bombs on those parts of Laos through which the Ho Chi Minh Trail passed. The inscription read: 'This fragment is a portion of a rock from the Taurus Littrow Valley of the Moon. It is given as a symbol of the unity of human endeavour and carries with it the hope of the American people for a world at peace.'

Luang Prabang, the last paradise, was astonishingly lovely. It soothed me and the tensions created by Vietnam and Cambodia began to ease. I wanted to stay there for ever, almost as much as I wanted to be at home, in my own bed with my cat and my familiar beloved things.

I liked the half-timbered houses which lined the steep little streets and I liked the monks in their yellow robes – the idea, apparently, was that if one of your parents went to hell, he or she could catch hold of the robe and pull himself or herself out of the pit. That was why all boys or men entered a monastery as a monk for at least a day after the death of a parent – just in case. The wife of the Australian Ambassador in Vientiane (who lived in what used to be the British embassy before the British decided that they couldn't afford to keep on the embassy and in whose garden an old friend of my parents, Sir Fred Warner, had kept a little zoo when he was ambassador) was acting as consultant on a guide to Luang Prabang which she had lent me. The author, Vannothone S. Thongsith, had included this poem to his native city.

> Oh Luang Prabang City
> Remain as thee be
> Your beauty surpasses Utopia
> And you are the land of plumeria.

Emit your fragrant odour to me
When I am away from thee
Chomsi and Xienthong Monasteries
I can never erase from my memories.

So long I've been away
I leave my soul stay
How long, how far I've been
I shall always be seen.

I wasn't entirely convinced by the poem but Wat Xieng Thong was certainly very beautiful. High on a promontory with the Mekong on one side and the Nam Kham on the other, it was the most splendid and perfect of the *wats* of Luang Prabang and was the '*siège du Diocèse*', the cathedral, as it were. I liked to go there shortly before dusk when the light was at its softest and the whole place was suffused with the glow of the setting sun. It was approached by a wide stairway guarded by two large white cats with livid red mouths. Across the road, an identical pair flanked a broad flight of steps leading down to the Mekong. There would often be a group of young monks sitting on these steps, smoking and listening to the radio, but despite this apparent informality, under no circumstances was I to consider approaching them. The rules governing the conduct of women in regard to monks were, as far as I could make out, an absolute minefield. You should never talk to them, touch them or hand them anything and you should even avoid looking them straight in the face. I was terrified of committing a *faux-pas* and causing offence. It seemed better to give them a wide berth.

Wat Xieng Thong, the 'Golden City Temple', was built by King Setthathirat in 1560. The whole *wat* complex contained twenty-five edifices of varying sizes for every imaginable religious purpose, ranging from *l'abri du tambour*, where the drum for summoning the monks to prayer was kept, to a whole array of stupas, to the splendid *sim* (the main chapel) on whose rear wall there was a mosaic of the tree of life and from whose side protruded an elephant head made entirely of little fragments of mirrored glass.

But the loveliest building was the royal funeral chapel whose gilded doors were decorated with carvings of semi-erotic episodes from the Ramayana. In one panel, Rama and Sita stood entwined in an exquisitely tender embrace, their golden forms against a background of scarlet. The term 'semi-erotic' was the one used in my guide book but the scenes depicted were of such a grace and sympathy that 'semi-erotic' seemed a little on the clinical side. With its superb setting, the whole place was as beautiful as any of the great European cathedrals and, though it was difficult to be sure, I thought possibly more beautiful than anything else I had seen in that part of the world. Angkor and the great religious plain of Pagan in Burma where over two thousand pagodas are strewn were, of course, of a different order.

Aside from the *wats*, the palace and the heart-stoppingly beautiful scenery, the charms of Luang Prabang were largely atmospheric. I knew, however, that Henri Mouhot was buried here and was determined to visit the grave of the great French explorer and naturalist, who had breathed his last in Luang Prabang in 1861 after he had spent four years travelling through Siam, Laos and Cambodia, longing for the French to bring their 'civilising influence' to these barbaric countries. The *'mission civilatrice'* was a favourite theme of his: 'European conquest, abolition of slavery, wise and protecting laws, experience, fidelity and scrupulous rectitude in those who administer them, would alone effect the regeneration of this state' was his verdict on Cambodia, after visiting Angkor.

The guide from Lao Tourism had never heard of Mouhot or his grave nor was it on any tourist itinerary but I insisted and eventually someone was found who knew the way. Off the road, down by the banks of the Nam Khan, in a little raised clearing, was a large plain square tomb made of white stone, patched with cement. It bore only the most basic inscription, 'Tomb of Henri Mouhot 1826-1861', followed by the words, 'Doudart de Lagrée fit élever ce Tombeau en 1867, Pavie le Reconstruisit en 1887 [Auguste Pavie, the French vice-consul to Luang Prabang at the time].' There was a further carving to the effect that the tomb had been restored once again in May 1990, six months before, by the French who lay proud claim to Mouhot despite the fact that his expedition was financed by the British Royal Geographical Society, his own country having declined to support him. The undergrowth around the tomb was teeming with tiny black leeches, no bigger than matchsticks, and perfectly easy to dislodge. I had always thought that leeches were great fat things, gorged with blood, that hung on like grim death.

The normally good-natured Mouhot had been in a bad way by the time he died. The final entries in his journal are waspish and ill-tempered. He complains of the 'frightful noise' the Lao priests make, 'chanting from morning to night' and of being 'pillaged by petty mandarins and chiefs of villages'. He says, 'At Bane-Nuien I found the Laotians even more ungrateful and egotistical than elsewhere' and described women with 'often enormous and repulsive' goitres; others at 'five-and-thirty . . . look like old witches'. The penultimate entry reads 'Attacked by fever' and the last simply 'Have pity on me, oh my God . . . !'

Poor old Mouhot! Whatever the obstacles placed in my path, I had not found the Laos ungrateful nor egotistical and the women were among the loveliest in South-East Asia. I had been spared the leeches, the mosquitoes and the malaria. The Laos, of course, were not so fortunate. The country was almost empty with a population of as few as four million spread over an area a little larger than Great Britain; their children were dying with monotonous regularity (the infant mortality rate was twenty-five per cent, far worse than in Cambodia); malnutrition was endemic. The countryside was ravishing as were the *wats* but that wasn't going to be much use. It was hard to imagine change or productivity here in poor, empty, secretive, beautiful Laos where the French had never even bothered to build roads because they could always use the planes. No wonder the colonists had loved it. It was like looking in a mirror. They could make of it whatever they wanted. *Bo peniang* indeed.

One day, a Sunday, accompanied by an astonishing retinue of maid, butler and bottle-washer from the hotel, as well as the guide from Lao Tourism, I took a boat to the Pak Ou caves, where, it was claimed, snakes were once worshipped. As I was on a tourist jaunt, I had to do tourist things. This expedition was no hardship. We chugged up-river towards China passing a few rusting hulls of American military boats left over from the war and some long pirogues, ferrying people from one side of the river to the other, the passengers standing upright in the narrow boats; the women with parasols or umbrellas open over their heads to protect them from the sun. The river was sometimes so flat and still that it might have been a mill-pond; at others, it was suddenly full of swells and currents and little whirlpools. On either side there stretched a wonderful jungly landscape interspersed with little cameos of water buffalo, naked bathing children, women in *sarongs* doing the laundry, fishermen. The further we went, the closer the mountains came, their ancient jagged silhouettes like woodcuts out of an old book on Asia.

In 1974, when Laos still had a reputation as a paradise for wandering hippies, a couple of friends of mine hitched a lift on a rice-barge from Luang Prabang to Vientiane. Laos was not quite the oasis of calm that they had expected and they were told not to sit on the roof of the boat in case they attracted a stray bullet. The barge made periodic stops at little villages along the way and, at one of these, in among the curious villagers was a group of very young soldiers, barely into their teens and armed to the teeth, who marched them at gunpoint uphill to their encampment. My friends, who were barely *compos mentis* having smoked themselves silly in the opium dens of Luang Prabang and had topped up with marijuana on board, thought that their final hour had come. One of them was so scared that he was actually sick – though that might have been the opium. They were taken to see the commanding officer who greeted them with a broad smile and the words, 'Do you know my friend, John Stuart, in Vientiane?' By a curious coincidence, they did know Stuart, an anthropologist, with whom they had visited a brothel. The commanding officer, it transpired, was simply bored and wanted to practise his English.

*

After a couple of hours we stopped for lunch at a pleasant spot where a covered bamboo terrace overlooked the river. We spread a tablecloth on the floor and unpacked the picnic basket. There were little baskets of sticky rice, hard-boiled eggs, pieces of fried chicken and bananas. The Dutch doctors were there too, having invited their Lao colleagues on a Sunday outing. They were already merry with *lao-lao*, and, after I had drunk my share and inspected the buddhas in the dank Pak Ou caves, we went for a swim in the Nam Ou. The previous evening I had thought of swimming in the Mekong at Luang Prabang. The sight of the children leaping in and out of the water made it seem very tempting but the doctors had said that you could pick up some hideous parasite which would destroy your liver. But they approved this clean, cool, brown water. Above us a sheer cliff-face rose hundreds of feet into the sky.

On the way back I lay on the roof of the boat and caught the sun. The Dutch doctors rode alongside in their boat and we tossed the bottle of *lao-lao* back and forth across the water. Back at the hotel, dizzy with sun and *lao-lao*, I fell into a deep sleep and dreamt that I was in a dreary *pension* in Paris struggling to rinse my hair in icy water. When I woke, it was dark and I could hear a band warming up somewhere nearby. I got up and, dressed in a black sleeveless tee-shirt with a low neckline and a red *sarong*, went out onto the terrace by the pool. One of the hotel reception-ists was getting married to a man from Lao Tourism and the reception was being held at the hotel. The visiting Dutch doctor went to bed early but I stayed up late with the other one drinking whisky and dancing the *lam vong*. Luang Prabang had done much to ease the *cafard* that Cambodia had enduced and Vientiane enhanced. I was feeling happy, relaxed and in a mood for fun.

We danced and talked and danced and talked for hours under the stars and one thing led to another and I spent what turned out to be a perfectly agreeable, if rather sleepless, night in my room with the Dutch doctor, a nice balding man who smoked and drank too much. He had been married twice and was lonely and a little gloomy but it was only for one night and it was pleasant enough.

As we lay in the dark, I asked him, perhaps rather crudely, whom he usually slept with. He said, 'No-one.' I wondered why he didn't find a Lao girlfriend like so many foreigners did but he said that he wanted someone he could talk to. He was restless and insomniac and sometime in the early hours, I awoke to find that he had left the bed. He was standing on the balcony smoking and staring out into the night. The full moon which had lit up the spire of That Luang now hung low in the sky like the belly of a pregnant woman whose time was near.

Shortly before dawn he kissed me and left for a couple of days on a field trip up-country. I had been quite keen to go too and he was keen to take me but my guide had become very agitated at the prospect of any deviation from the set programme and the Lao doctor who headed the expedition was reluctant to take responsibility for my presence. It would have been foolish to insist. I turned over and went back to sleep.

Those comforting sensual hours in the dark put the seal on the cure effected by Luang Prabang's healing magic and restored my faith in myself.

I filed the encounter away in my little store of erotic memories of the East. There's something about those places: the strangeness, the dreamy warmth, the scent, the fact that no-one in the real world – or my real world – knows where I am and what I am doing: all these combine to create an atmosphere ripe for adventure. It's not really about sex *per se*. For months when travelling, I would never think about sex or love at all and then suddenly a particular combination of circumstances would indicate that the moment was right. It began – this tendency to associate the Orient with eroticism – when I first went back to China. I had spent the afternoon with a man in the precarious intimacy of a Ferris-wheel cabin looking high over Canton while the wheel revolved very very slowly. Later we found ourselves in adjoining rooms in the White Swan Hotel overlooking the Pearl River. It was impossible to say 'No' even if I had wanted to.

So it was with the Dutch doctor. The moment had seemed right but, when I woke again, I was relieved that I hadn't been able to go with him on the field trip. During the night, my red sarong which I had draped over the balcony, had blown away and now hung like a brilliant signal flag from a bush on the side of the hill. In the dining room, over breakfast, a Swedish woman acting as companion to an elderly American lady in a wheelchair told me that all the people in her group had been wondering whether I was travelling alone. When she told them that I was, they clucked and said that I shouldn't wear such a low-cut top, that I was just asking for trouble.

Perhaps I was. Or perhaps I was just searching for the past and whatever came with it.

Postscript

On 23 October 1991, in Paris, a peace agreement was finally signed by all four Cambodian factions: the Hun Sen government, the Khmer Rouge, the Khmer People's National Liberation Front and the Armée Nationale Sihanoukiste. Sihanouk was appointed head of the Supreme National Council which embodied Cambodian sovereignty and whose role was to offer advice to the United Nations Transitional Authority in Cambodia (UNTAC) which was to organize elections in early 1993 and to implement the Paris Peace Plan.

Sihanouk, after thirteen years of exile and fifty years after his ascension to the Cambodian throne, returned to Phnom Penh on 14 November 1991. He arrived fifty-five minutes late, on a Boeing 707 Air China flight which was supposed to have left Peking at four a.m. Hundreds of Cambodians in traditional dress or uniform including monks, nuns and Chams were waiting at the airport and hundreds more lined the roads. A ten-foot-high hand-tinted photo-portrait of Sihanouk as a young man faced the runway. There were copies of this picture, which made him look like a 1930s matinée idol of dubious sexual tastes, all over Phnom Penh including in the *wats* and one obscured the exterior of the Pavilion of the Shadow of the Moon.

Shortly before eleven, the plane was heard, and at 10.55 it landed. Sihanouk's grey head appeared through the cabin door, closely followed by his hands pressed together in the *sampeah*. After a couple of hours of greeting ceremonies, the Prince, accompanied by Hun Sen, rode triumphantly into Phnom Penh in a white convertible 1963 Chevrolet Impala with red leather upholstery which belonged to a rich Thai who had lent it previously to both Imelda Marcos and

Miss Universe of Thailand. A uniformed chauffeur whose wife and five children had starved to death during the Khmer Rouge reign, sat behind the wheel.

I had wanted to come back to Cambodia both to see Sihanouk in the flesh and to renew my friendship with Somaly and her daughters. I arrived a few days before Sihanouk to be sure of finding somewhere to stay. Somaly met me at the airport and said that now she believed that I had not forgotten her. As we drove into town, she told me that corruption in Phnom Penh was rampant, worse than ever, '*presque comme l'anarchie*' and that she was not optimistic that Sihanouk's return would solve Cambodia's problems. On a brighter note, she told me that her sister, Bhopa, was getting married to an agricultural engineer and that Pranita, her elder daughter, had passed her *baccalauréat* and was working as a tourist guide before going to university. We stopped to drop another passenger off at the Hotel Monorom and Pranita was in the lobby, her around face glowing, her waist-length black hair shiny with health and the shampoo that I had sent her from England.

'Pranita,' I said, extending my hands to greet her.

'You . . . are . . . fat,' she said, completing the unflattering sentence with a radiant smile.

'Thanks a lot.'

At first glance, neither Phnom Penh nor the Asie seemed to have changed much though the latter had been repainted and its prices had almost trebled. A notice on the stairway wall which began 'The Office of Hotel Asie is very pleased to announce . . .' cheerfully advertised the increase but there was still no hot water. A chambermaid wearing a badge saying 'Jesus Loves You' clasped my hand and said, 'You are my friend. I miss you.'

As darkness fell, the changes to the city became more obvious. There were now neon signs on every building and a string of fairy lights decorated even the façade of the Asie. The curfew was no longer in force and halfway down the Boulevard Achar Mean, an unfinished building exploded with disco music. Only the ground floor was complete and that was operating as a nightclub where Vietnamese and Cambodian prostitutes sought custom from the foreigners newly arrived in town. In the old Bayon restaurant, iced claret was now served in thimble-sized glasses and the limbless beggars had disappeared from outside its entrance. Inflation had doubled but the price of caviar had gone down, now that there were fewer Russians in town.

One evening shortly after his return, Sihanouk held a press conference in the lovely open-air pavilion that used to be the King's dancing hall. It was notable for three things: firstly, Sihanouk's much-vaunted charm ('charisma' is the word preferred by most journalists) which I had never before encountered and wanted to experience; secondly, Sihanouk's volubility, which bordered on anecdotal garrulousness (he talked for three hours and answered no more than five questions); and thirdly, the fact that he said nothing new and nothing significant. It was a performance. Nothing more.

In the days that followed, Sihanouk kept busy. He had himself appointed Head of State and the 1970 Lon Nol coup declared illegal. His son and designated heir, Prince Norodom Ranariddh's FUNCINPEC (Front Uni National pour un Cambodge Independent, Neutre, Pacifique et Cooperatif) party formed a coalition with Hun Sen's Government.

A week after I left Cambodia, Khieu Samphan, the 'acceptable face' of the Khmer Rouge and president of Democratic Kampuchea under Pol Pot's gruesome regime, returned to Phnom Penh and was nearly killed in a mob attack. Bleeding and battered, he flew back to Bangkok only hours after his arrival. Son Sen, Pol Pot's security minister, who had been directly responsible for the running of Tuol Sleng and who had returned without incident to Phnom Penh a couple of days after Sihanouk, left with him. In the interval between the arrivals of the two Khmer Rouge representatives to the SNC, Sihanouk had announced publicly that he would support the notion of an international tribunal to judge Pol Pot, Ta Mok and Ieng Sary for the crime of genocide.

On 30 December 1991, Khieu Samphan went back to Phnom Penh. At the time of writing, an uneasy peace prevails in Cambodia though there have been anti-corruption riots in the capital and sporadic outbreaks of fighting in the countryside. The already fraught political situation has been further complicated by Sihanouk's sons, the Princes Ranariddh and Chakrapong, who, having loathed each other for years (with Ranariddh preferred by Sihanouk and Chakra-pong the favourite of Princess Monique), engaged in open warfare in February when armies loyal to the two clashed in northwestern Cambodia, leaving several soldiers dead or wounded. Chakrapong had been appointed deputy premier to Hun Sen and the quarrel flared up when a thousand of his men moved to join the Phnom Penh army. And, in late February, the commander of the Australian contingent of UNAMIC was wounded when Khmer Rouge troops opened fire on a UN helicopter. After the helicopter incident, for which the Khmer Rouge disclaimed responsibility, predictably blam-ing the Vietnamese, Sihanouk who once described Khieu Samphan as 'a killer but a patriot', announced that Khieu Samphan was 'a man who honours his word'. Over fifteen thousand UN troops are to be deployed in what has been described as the 'largest and costliest [peace-keeping] operation in UN history'. Re-patriation of the thou-sands of refugees is due to begin in the spring of 1992. Elections are scheduled for a year later. Everyone hopes for the best. Everyone is wary.

April 1992

Index

Index

Index

Vientiane, Laos 33; airport 9, 241; British Honorary Consul in 12, 14, 31, 34, 37, 241, 242–4; cinema in 29–30; Lane Xang hotel 9–10, 12, 19, 31, 39; Museum of the Revolution 28; nightlife 39–40; restaurants 11, 12, 13, 20, 39, 242; *samlo* driver *see* Leuth; Siamese attacks on 30, 35; Sisattanek (district) 16; and That Luang festivities 23, 245–6; torpor in 36; violence in 243; Wat Phra Keo 51, 244

Vietcong 79, 118, 119, 120, 133

Vietminh 69, 118, 152, 159, 161–2

Vietnam: AIDS cases in 147, ancestor worship in 61; beer 90; 'boat' people 115–17, 150; Buddhism in 64–5, 101, 135–6; Cao Daism in 71; Catholicism in 68–9, 139; Cambodia and 72; Chams in 209; clothes 22, 25, 50–1, 75; coast of 112, 127, 128; cock-fighting in 147–8; communication gap in 109–110; Communist party line 154, 159; Emperors of 105, 106–7; family structure 61–2; food 66–7, 85–6, 94, 96, 111–12, 141; French in 105–6, 107, 148, 152, 161–2; health problems in 72; heroes of 49, 58, 134; history and 134–5; Hoa Hao in 71; language 68–9, 123; Laos and 32, 33; National Liberation Front 79, 146, 166; New Economic Zones 59;

pagodas and temples in 64, 65, 95, 96, 97; population 34; rice production in 80, 86; roads 43, 48; telephones 108; USA and 141, 160; women's position in 76–7; *see also* Hanoi and Saigon

Vietnam War 1, 2, 30–1, 40, 79, 118, 225; Christmas Bombing (1972) 152–3; and Da Nang 124; and missing US soldiers 160; My Lai massacre 118–19, 120–1; Tet Offensive 119–20, 133, 158

Vong Savang, Crown Prince 249

Vung Tau, Vietnam 62–7; Villa Blanche 66

wai 32

Warner, Sir Fred 250

Wat Nokor, Cambodia 216–17

Wat Phou, Laos 14, 240

West, Richard 160; *Rough Ride to Saigon* 140

Westmoreland, General 120

women: Oriental 92–3; position of 76–7

Wood, W.A.R. 30

Xi'an, China: terracotta army 4

Xuan Huong Lake, Vietnam 103

Yak Lom lake, Cambodia 234

Yersin, Alexander 101

Young, Gavin 90, 115, 116

Yung, Mr 90, 91